JESUS TODAY

LIVING LIFE AS JESUS WOULD

MARC ESTES

CITY BIBLE
PUBLISHING

Portland, Oregon, U.S.A.

PUBLISHED BY CITY BIBLE PUBLISHING

(FORMERLY BIBLE TEMPLE PUBLISHING)

9200 NE FREMONT, PORTLAND, OREGON 97220

PRINTED IN U.S.A.

City Bible Publishing is a ministry of City Bible Church (formerly Bible Temple), and is dedicated to serving the local church and its leaders through the production and distribution of quality restoration materials.

It is our prayer that these materials, proven in the context of the local church, will equip leaders in exalting the Lord and extending His kingdom.

For a free catalog of additional resources from City Bible Publishing please call 1-800-777-6057 or visit our web site at www.citybiblepublishing.com.

Jesus Today

ISBN: 1-886849-76-5
Library of Congress Card Number: 00-107879

TABLE OF CONTENTS

FOREWORD

BY LUIS PALAU

Jesus Today is a book that reveals God's heart of compassion for people, especially those who do not know Him yet. That compassion grips the heart of Marc Estes, as it should every follower of Jesus Christ. Marc reminds his readers of the life-changing power of the Gospel. As Christians, we are to be Jesus today to the world around us.

If the people in your world are to find Jesus today, they will find Him in you. That's the premise of this book. And it's biblical. "Christ lives in me," the apostle Paul affirmed (Galatians 2:20). "Christ lives in you" (Colossians 1:27).

If your neighbors are to find Jesus today, if your friends and co-workers are to find Jesus today, they must see the Lord Jesus Christ in your life. Like Dave Finley, the fictional character of the book, never underestimate the importance of living a holy life—a life lived like Jesus lived—pleasing to God in every way. Many Christians, however, stop short of complete obedience to God and seldom, if ever, actually tell people that Jesus desires a home in their heart, too!

Jesus defined His mission clearly: "For the Son of Man came to seek and to save what was lost" (Luke 19:10). And He commands all of us to go and tell everyone. We know His final command to "go and make disciples of all nations" (Matthew 28:19) as the Great Commission, not the great suggestion.

Evangelism is a chosen act of obedience to God's revealed will. It is the highest, most important act of obedience for a Christian, because there is nothing more important to God, "who wants all men to be saved" (1 Timothy 2:4). "The Lord...is patient with you, not wanting anyone to perish, but everyone to come to repentance" (2 Peter 3:9).

Jesus Today portrays the life of one person who solely dedicated himself to advancing the Gospel. Dave Finley is singularly focused on the task at hand and will not turn to the right or to the left. Such focus reminded me of another example of dedication to a mission.

It's been a few years now, but do you remember Captain Scott O'Grady, the Air Force F-16 pilot who evaded capture in Bosnia after being shot down? After his dramatic rescue, my friend Jim Reapsome compared the mission of the church to the Marines' heroism. Jim bemoaned many churches' wasted energy in battles over peripheral matters such as music.

"The devil is having a field day, because every such intramural fight is a gain for his schemes to keep us from doing our primary mission—breaking down the walls of his kingdom of darkness and rescuing people for God's kingdom of light," he wrote in *Pulse*, a missions newsletter. The Marines who rescued Captain O'Grady "did not sit around and argue about which arrangement of the Marine Corps hymn to sing. They pursued a single mission—rescue a downed pilot—and they allowed nothing to sidetrack them."

Jim concluded, "As the old saying goes, we must keep the main thing the main thing, which is to throw life lines of hope and peace to people trampled and overcome by despair."

As Marc points out so well in this book, nothing is more important to God than rescuing what He created. All of us need a constantly renewed tenderness, a continual firing up from God, a revived love for those who suffer and who die without Jesus.

I don't know how long God will give me on this earth, but I am asking Him for a greater and greater passion for the souls of people who still live in selfishness and sinfulness, who are on their way to eternal perdition. This is the example our Lord Jesus Christ has left us and how we should live our lives for Him.

Jesus Today is a book that outlines how one Christian can live his life to the fullest and affect the world around him. As you read it, I pray that you'll rededicate yourself to sharing the Good News at every opportunity the Lord gives you. I hope you can identify with Dave Finley and will come to realize that his life is not that different from yours. We are all Jesus today, may we now live like it.

LUIS PALAU, evangelist and author of
Where Is God When Bad Things Happen? (Doubleday)
and *The Only Hope for America* (Crossway)
www.lpea.org

PREFACE

For the past decade, I have had the wonderful privilege of traveling the globe and ministering to Christians of all denominations and culture. One sad, yet common thread seen in most every church is that 95% of all Christians have never led one person to Christ. Although there is an increasing desire to share the good news with loved ones, many are still plagued with fear and intimidation. I believe this is about to change!

It is through my travels, experiences, personal times of prayer and fasting, and own real-life challenges that this book was written. *Jesus Today* is an attempt to stir anyone that would take the time to read this book and accept the challenge to become more like Jesus to a desperate and dying world.

The desire of our Lord Jesus that we live our lives according the pattern He established while here on earth. I believe that living life as Jesus would is a present day challenge for all Christians. When we do so, we become "Jesus Today" to everyone around us.

In an effort to help you better understand this truth, I want to explain the format of this book. Each chapter begins with a fictional story that will run continuously throughout the book.

The fictional stories are written as a 21st century allegory inspired by the real life stories of Jesus in Scripture. Each chapter is linked together to describe the journey of a young man, who through many challenges and victories in life, strives to become "Jesus Today". I am sure you will find a great deal of yourself in the character of this book, Dave Finely.

The fictional section is followed with the scriptural reference that Dave's story is adapted from. After the Scripture, I have written a practical section that will assist you in living life as Jesus would.

Finally, each chapter ends with a prayer that I encourage you to use in your devotional life. I hope you are encouraged and strengthened by this book as you strive to become "Jesus Today".

MARC ESTES
Summer 2000 ·

INTRODUCTION

It is my pleasure to introduce Marc Estes as one of our new authors. Marc came to City Bible Church in 1996 after several years of traveling as an Equipping Evangelist. His time with us has been spent first in our Publishing Company, then our Evangelism and Assimilation Department. Marc is presently the Director of the Pastoral Department at CBC.

Marc is a gifted leader, a competent administrator/manager, and a mature teacher with a balanced ministry as pastor-teacher-evangelist. He has added to our already great team of leaders using all of his gifts with dedication and passion.

Marc's new book on Jesus in the 21st Century is written in a unique and penetrating style, using Bible facts within today's context. I believe this book will offer a new perspective about Jesus with the possibility of changing our perspective and life focus.

FRANK DAMAZIO
Senior Pastor, City Bible Church

CHAPTER ONE

HIS MISSION:

ALIGNING YOUR LIFE TO THE CALL OF THE GOSPEL

JOHN 3:1-21

T here has got to be more! There has to be more! What is it? Why do I feel this way?"

Dave beat his fists against the shower wall as tears of anguish became lost in the shower stream. His cries of pain floated over the shower door and mixed with the thick steam, creating a sense of despair in the small room. It was the start of another cloudy day for Dave.

He began to realize that his life wasn't turning out like he, or his father, had hoped. He was tired. Tired of the expectations and disappointments. Tired of the homework. Tired of the partying. Tired of the pain. Perhaps more than anything at all, the pain that lived inside of Dave ate at him. He could tolerate the grades, expectations and studying, but the pain was too much.

He slowly stepped from the small shower enclosure and began to prepare himself to face the world one more time. As he stood in front of the mirror with his towel wrapped around him, Dave stared into it. He faced that which he had learned to hate—himself. Just like many other mornings, Dave felt the twinge of disgrace, depression and discontent. The familiar dialogue between the guy in the mirror and the guy imprisoned in his body began to surface.

He quickly became lost in a battle of the mind and got angry with the "other guy" in the mirror.

"Just look at yourself—look deep! You are so together on the outside, buddy, but you're dying on the inside! How much longer are you going to try to build your happiness on being Mr. Fraternity President? Your fake smiles, sarcasm and constant joking don't hide the emptiness and pain. Who do you think you're fooling? How long are you going to hide behind your awards and medals? As if they validate your self-worth. And what about your family name, Finley? Does it really make a difference that your father is a well-known politician? After all, what has it done for you? He has spent his life rescuing the country but has forgotten about you. Some name! Why can't you be like your brother anyway? Michael got the grades, but you didn't. He finished law school, but you can't even fake your way through college. And to top it off, you can't even keep a job, much less build a career. Face up to it, you're nothing!"

Once again, Dave's anger toward his life began to burn. The unresolved pain turned into a silent scream of agony as he recognized the guy in the mirror was himself. The frustration only mounted as he looked into his blue-gray eyes and saw them begin to swell with tears.

"God, you can't be real. If you were, I wouldn't be in the mess I'm in. Where are you now? God, you are a joke. My family is a joke. I'm a joke. It's all a joke!"

The campus was alive with the usual Saturday night buzz. Students filled the University Square coffee tables with books, coffee and talk about the mid-term finals that had mysteriously crept upon them. The faint sound of guitars and singing could be heard over the pounding music that thumped from cars cruising down University Boulevard. The moon was full, the stars were bright and the smell of smoke from wood stoves brought a welcomed scent to the brisk December night.

It had been another long day for Dave. Ten hours of delivering furniture, three hours of sleep the night before and a lingering hangover equated to a pounding headache that could only be cured by some peace and quiet. He knew that if he pulled into the Square parking lot, as was his custom, he would spend the night floating from table to table; talking with all of his friends and wasting another opportunity to think through his problems. He just needed to find a place to be alone and think.

He decided to drive his '67 Mustang down University Boulevard toward the Activity Center. Because it was Saturday night, few people would be at that end of the campus.

In the lot next to the Activity Center, he parked under a tree and climbed up on the hood to keep warm while staring at the stars. He soon found himself immersed in the same inward conversation as this morning's bathroom skirmish. Once the busyness of the day came to a screeching halt and he had time to disengage his mind, he found himself back in the same tailspin of emotions. The anger returned as a light wind touched his face.

Suddenly, something jarred him from his struggle and pulled him back to reality. A scream, followed by the sound of loud music and people laughing revealed that it was another kegger. The sound was quite familiar. The thought of drowning out the pain with beer, buddies and babes seemed like a reasonable solution to his emotional dilemma. But something deep inside told him that the answer to his problems would not be found at that party.

A sound in the nearby Activity Center grabbed his attention. It was the sound of music, but not music that was familiar to Dave. It seemed different. It sounded peaceful. Melodic. Harmonious. Joyful. Heavenly?

The desire to sulk in the atmosphere of another Saturday night party was taken over by this curious, almost adventurous desire to find out what was going on in the Activity Center. His attention was drawn to the sound of hundreds of people singing. It was exuberant, lively, fresh, and victorious. What could it be?

What are they doing? he thought. *Why are they so happy?* Curiosity soon overcame him and pulled him from the hood toward this unfamiliar sound. The closer he went to the Activity Center, the less he could hear the partying from across campus. The desire to get drunk was lost in the feeling of adventure.

I'll walk around the side of the Activity Center to the back where no one can see me, Dave thought. *I can sit up on the hill behind those bushes next to the path and see what's happening through the windows.*

As he walked past the front and along the path to the back, Dave found himself acting as if he were a burglar. *What am I hiding from? Why do I feel like I have to hide?* His curiosity was now mixed with confusion and reservation.

Up on the hill, Dave found the perfect place to monitor this "foreign sound." He sat down on a tree stump and delicately spread the branches in front of him to get a better view. Little did he know that the scene presented to him would be the one that would change his life forever. He believed it was only a fact-finding mission. No commitments. No promises. Just investigation.

What is this? A bunch of those crazy Christians? A church service? Those are the people we make fun of all the time. Dave's mind raced to the many times he sat on the benches next to University Square and laughed at the religious freaks.

As he sat and watched the scene before him, the hardness he had known began to break. At first the cracks were small, but over the next hour, the church service allowed a glimpse into something Dave had only dreamed was possible. The longer he sat, the more his heart began to break. Something was happening to him and he couldn't leave until he found out what.

The war in his mind continued. One minute he thought, *Dave, wake up! They're religious freaks! What about your reputation? What about all your friends?*

The next minute he argued, *Yeah, but what about my emptiness? What about my loneliness and depression? Look at the joy they have!*

Time wore on and the battle within himself raged. After nearly ninety minutes, the sound of laughter flooded out of the building as hundreds of students exited the back doors. Dave sat motionless, not wanting to be seen. Some had remained inside to pray for each other. Dave's eyes were quickly drawn to a man on the platform talking with a group of freshmen.

It's the guy who is always handing out tracts on campus. He must be the leader. I wonder what they're talking about? I sure wish I could ask him a few questions.

As if on cue, the man left the freshmen, walked out the door and began to head up the path to the top of the hill.

"This is too weird," Dave said to himself as he backed away from the path. *He is coming my way! What should I do?*

In his anxiety he rattled some leaves.

"Hey, is someone in there?" The man asked. Standing under the lamp, he couldn't see very well into the bushes. Dave slowly made his way toward the man ashamed of hiding in the bushes. *What if the guy thinks I'm stalking someone?* Upon seeing Dave, the man looked directly into his eyes. "Hey man, you don't look so good. Is everything all right? Can we talk?"

The man introduced himself as Sean, he was the Campus Pastor. Sean quickly became the friend Dave was looking for. He had answers to Dave's difficult questions. In just a few minutes, their hearts bonded and Dave felt as if he could share the feelings that plagued his soul. Sean actually seemed to care.

They talked until well past midnight—just Dave, Sean, and the stars. No music or party noise, just two guys under a lamp talking about life.

With a heavy heart and a big lump in his throat, Dave grabbed Sean's shoulder as he was leaving and said, "Hey Sean, thanks! But, I have just one more question. You mentioned that Jesus wants me to spend eternity with Him. How can I do that?"

Sean's finger was already marking a passage of Scripture before Dave finished the question. "Let me read you the story of a man who is just like you. He asked the exact same question." Sean went on to read the story of Nicodemus, found in John, chapter 8. In that story, Nicodemus, a member of the Jewish Sanhedrin, came to Jesus to talk with him. Jesus conveyed the plan of salvation and explained that He was the "Light" Nicodemus was looking for.

Sean closed his Bible, leaned forward and whispered, "Dave, this is what you need. You need Jesus to be your salvation. You have spent your life running from Him. All He is going to do when He catches you is love you."

The past few hours had softened Dave considerably. As he stood on the path behind the Activity Center, he realized that the answer to that morning's questions was found in Jesus.

Dave put his head down to hide the tears that welled up in his eyes. "You are right, Sean. You are exactly right."

Sean put his hand on Dave's shoulder and said, "Why don't you just stop fighting it and give your life to Jesus Christ?"

"How do I do it? What should I do?"

Sean replied, "Pray this prayer with me." They both bowed their heads and Dave repeated Sean's prayer of salvation:

> "Dear Jesus . . . I want to thank You for this very special moment . . . I recognize for the first time . . . that I am a sinner . . . I realize that I deserve to be punished for my sin . . . but I realize that You paid the price for that sin . . . I don't have to spend eternity in hell . . . because You went to the cross and paid the ultimate price . . . Lord, I ask that You would forgive me for all the bad things I have done . . . every one of them . . . all of my sin . . . and that You would come and live inside of me . . . Please, Jesus, be my Lord and Savior . . . Help me to follow You all the days of my life . . . and to live according to Your Holy Word . . . I thank You for guiding and directing my life to You . . . I confess with my mouth . . . and believe with my heart . . . that I am saved . . . In Jesus' name, amen!"

A great sense of peace surrounded Dave. He suddenly felt as if someone had lifted a great burden from his shoulders. For the first time in his life, he felt the calming presence of his God.

Dave looked at Sean and sighed, "Wow! Thanks, Sean! That was incredible! I don't know what happened, but it feels great! But what's next, what do I do from here? I never want this feeling to leave."

Sean patted Dave on the back and said with a smirk, "Bro', it has just begun. You and I have a great future together. You have a destiny, and God has a purpose and plan for your life. You have no idea how good it's going to get! I'll give you a call and we will do some coffee together."

Dave smiled and asked, "Promise?"

Sean nodded, "Promise!"

As they parted ways from the top of the hill, Dave felt as if a host of angels were carrying him back to his car. "This is awesome! God, You are awesome!"

HIS MISSION

JOHN 3:1-21

After dark one evening, a Jewish religious leader named Nicodemus, a Pharisee, came to speak with Jesus. "Teacher," he said, "we all know that God has sent you to teach us. Your miraculous signs are proof enough that God is with you."

Jesus replied, "I assure you, unless you are born again, you can never see the Kingdom of God."

"What do you mean?" exclaimed Nicodemus. "How can an old man go back into his mother's womb and be born again?"

Jesus replied, "The truth is, no one can enter the Kingdom of God without being born of water and the Spirit. Humans can reproduce only human life, but the Holy Spirit gives new life from heaven. So don't be surprised at my statement that you must be born again. Just as you can hear the wind but can't tell where it comes from or where it is going, so can't explain how people are born of the Spirit."

"What do you mean?" Nicodemus asked.

Jesus replied, "You are a respected Jewish teacher, and yet you don't understand these things? I assure you, I am telling you what we know and have seen, and yet you won't believe us. But if you don't even believe me when I tell you about things that happen here on earth, how can you possibly believe if I tell you what is going on in heaven? For only I, the Son of Man, have come to earth and will return to heaven again. And as Moses lifted up on the bronze snake on a pole in the wilderness, so I, the Son of Man, must be lifted up on a pole, so that everyone who believes in me will have eternal life.

"For God so loved the world that he gave his only Son, so that everyone who believes in him will not perish but have eternal life. God did not send his Son into the world to condemn it, but to save it.

"There is no judgment awaiting those who trust him. But those who do not trust him have already been judged for not believing in the only Son of God. Their judgment is based on this fact: The light from heaven came into the world, but they loved the darkness more than the light, for their actions were evil. They hate the light because they want to sin in the darkness. They stay away from the light for fear their sins will be exposed and they will be punished. But those who do what is right come to the light gladly, so everyone can see that they are doing what God wants."

THE VALUE OF LOST ITEMS

Have you ever found yourself looking for something of value that you misplaced or lost? One of my early morning routines is to locate the car keys that seem to always be misplaced! Everything comes to a halt. I commission everyone to partake in a house-wide search for Dad's keys. Drawers are opened, papers are shuffled, and counters are scoured for these priceless little brass objects that will start my car and allow me into the office. After a few minutes of passionate searching, much to my surprise and embarrassment, my wife politely shouts from the top of the stairs, "Honey, I found your keys in your pants pocket." I thank her very much and remind myself not to put them there again. Can you relate?

Let's increase the value of the lost item to a relational level. Have you ever lost a loved one through a broken relationship? Have you ever lost contact with a close friend who moved away? Has someone you loved and cared for disappeared from your life, never to return? The pain and agony of losing something of this value can cause your entire world to come to a screeching halt. Thoughts of finding that one who is lost can permeate every waking moment.

A few years ago, my wife and I experienced this pain through the tragic kidnapping of a twelve-year-old girl in my daughter's fifth grade class. We immediately came to the aid of this special couple to offer our support, prayers, and friendship. In all of the years of being a parent, I could never have imagined the pain this couple was experiencing. The very thought of one of my precious children being torn from my care by a stranger is incomprehensible.

As the days turned into weeks, and the weeks into months, I saw the lifestyle of this couple radically change. Their every waking moment was consumed with the passionate pursuit of finding their daughter. All of those things that had once seemed to be important now had little value. Their television was turned off, their nights of fun and games were cancelled, social events were no longer important—they were on a mission! Friends came together for prayer vigils and candlelight services, and large work parties gathered to distribute hundreds of thousands of posters. News media, such as *America's Most Wanted* and *Unsolved Mysteries,* covered the story to assist in spreading the news of their kidnapped daughter. Reminder ribbons were tied to trees, cars, and house doors. Every ounce of time, money, and energy was spent hoping to find something that was lost, their precious little daughter.

The months turned into years, and to this day, their daughter has never been found. And so the search continues. Through this tragic event I learned a life lesson concerning lost things. The value one places on that which is lost determines the sacrifice one is willing to make to find it. My missing car keys may require a few minutes of my time to search and another few minutes to adjust my attitude, but the loss of a human life would be worth the sacrifice of anything I had. It is no wonder Jesus said, *"And here is how to measure it—the greatest love is shown when people lay down their lives for their friends"* (John 15:13). For my desperate friends, they would give anything, regardless of the price, to once again be able to hold their precious daughter in their arms.

The opening story of this chapter portrayed a campus pastor named Sean, who understood this vital principle. He realized that the Devil had kidnapped the lives of young people, including Dave Finley. He too, had given his life, his time, his energy to reaching lost people on a college campus. In this particular instance, it was Dave who can now be found in the loving arms of his heavenly Father. Like Jesus with Nicodemus, Sean was willing to sacrifice his time and energy in order that Dave might be saved. He understood that Dave's soul mattered to God.

LOST PEOPLE MATTER TO GOD

If you were to ask Jesus today, "What is on your heart?" I believe one of His first responses would be, "Lost people!" From Genesis to Revelation, the Bible clearly portrays God's passionate love for people. God's desire is for all to have an intimate, eternal relationship with their heavenly Father. However, due to the sin of mankind, lost people have been kidnapped by the Enemy and held captive. God's mission, through the ministry of Christ and His Church, is to release those who are bound and bring them to their eternal home.

In the discourse with Nicodemus, Jesus shares just how much God loves lost people. In the middle of the discussion, Jesus said, *"For God so loved the world that he gave his only Son, so that everyone who believes in him will not perish but have eternal life"* (John 3:16). This powerful Scripture reveals God's love for humanity.

"For God so loved the world . . ."

The actual Greek word for love, *agapao*, in this Scripture implies that God's love for humanity is the highest form of love known to both God and man. God's immeasurable love for us, those who are lost, is illustrated so clearly in the following Scriptures:

> 1 John 3:1: *"See how very much our heavenly Father loves us, for he allows us to be called his children, and we really are! But the people who belong to this world don't know God, so they don't understand that we are his children."*

> Ephesians 2:4-6: *"But God is so rich in mercy, and he loved us so very much that even while we were dead because of our sins, he gave us life when he raised Christ from the dead. (It is only by God's special favor that you have been saved!) For he raised us from the dead along with Christ, and we are seated with him in the heavenly realms - all because we are one with Christ Jesus."*

". . . that he gave his only Son . . ."

Not only does He have a great love for us, but He has also shown His love by giving up that which He treasured most, His Son! God's love for you is measured by the value of what He was willing to sacrifice in order to get you back from the kidnapper, Satan!

> Mark 12:6: *"Until there was only one left—his son whom he loved dearly. The owner finally sent him, thinking, 'Surely they will respect my son.'"*

> Romans 8:32: *"Since God did not spare even his own Son but gave him up for us all, won't God, who gave us Christ, also give us everything else?"*

Jesus loves you and I beyond measure. Furthermore, He has an equal and unwavering measure of love for the lost. His love for Christians, compared to a drug-addicted prostitute, is no different. He is no respecter of persons. God is consumed with a passion for people. All people! His willingness to give up what was most dear to His heart is an outward indicator of His inward love and passion for you and I. Lost people matter to God.

Jesus Came to Seek and Save the Lost

The primary theme of Christ's mission on earth was to "find" lost people. Without a direct intervention from God, the possibility for any one of us to be "found" was hopeless. Scriptures record 199 situations in which Christ ministered to people. Of those 199 situations, 128 were evangelistic.[1] From town to town, sunrise to sunset, whatever His situation or location, He set His eyes on finding those who were lost. It was His passion, His destiny, His mission. Jesus, like His Father, was concerned with lost people.

> Luke 19:10 (emphasis mine): *"And I, the Son of Man, have come to seek and save those like him who are lost."*

Jesus' first recorded ministry situation is found in Luke 2:41-52. In that story, we find Him at the age of twelve, traveling with His parents to Jerusalem for the Feast of Passover. Although only men were required to attend the three annual festivals, His mother, a devout woman, chose to attend as well. Jesus, because he was twelve, was considered "a son of the law" and, according to custom, was put under a course of instruction and training on fasting and attendance in public worship, in addition to learning a trade.[2]

Although Jesus himself was there to listen and learn, His parents found Him three days later talking with the teachers in the temple courts. I believe this to be one of Christ's first evangelistic encounters.

I have always wondered what those teachers in the temple must have thought upon their first introduction, unknowingly, to the King of kings. Although Scripture doesn't reveal His actual words, I can just imagine the crackling voice inflections of this adolescent, sharing inspired revelation from the prophets of old—*"The Lord has appointed me to bring good news"* (Isaiah 61:1), and *"I will gather all nations and peoples"* (Isaiah 66:18), and *"The ends of the earth will see the salvation of our God"* (Isaiah 52:10). Envision the proud cheers, the nodding heads of intellectual agreement as he quoted memorized Scripture from the prophet Isaiah. Little did they know He was speaking of Himself.

From that first account onward, Christ would experience countless opportunities for touching the lost. Even in His very last contact with mankind, as Jesus hung on the cross, His patience, self-control, and love was beyond measure. It has been said, "They didn't need to nail Him, for His love would have held Him there." If I were Jesus, I would have called down a legion of warring angels and struck dead every enemy on the spot! Thank God, for the sake of humanity, that I am not Him!

But Christ had something else on His mind—lost people! He wasn't consumed with thoughts of revenge or even feelings of resentment. I am sure if one of us were to ask Him when we get to Heaven, "Lord, didn't it hurt? Couldn't you have found another way?" He would turn and say with a tear in His eye, "Yes, but there was something that hurt even more—a lost world! A world that I created and loved. For me, the physical pain was nothing if this lost world could be found!"

As the sky darkened over Golgotha, Jesus scanned the crowd, not with eyes of rebuke, but with eyes of compassion. He saw the soldiers who had just crowned Him, spitting on Him. He saw those in the distance who had screamed, "Crucify Him." All he could do was look up and pray, *"Father, forgive them"* (Luke 23:34). Once again, His words were a true sign of His passion for those who were lost.

As His strength waned, as He slipped in and out of consciousness, gasping for oxygen, slowly suffocating, a faint voice was heard. It was a crackling, despondent voice, one filled with desperation, begging to be found. He lifted His head, only to find one of His crucifixion partners begging for mercy. He was lost. He was in desperate need of a Savior. In the last recorded ministry situation of Christ's earthly ministry prior to the resurrection, He said, *"I assure you, today you will be with Me in paradise"* (Luke 23:43). With that closing statement, the thief on the cross was found. His days of pain and agony came to a close. His life had just begun. This evangelistic moment would imprint forever on the annals of history irrefutable evidence that Jesus had a passion to reach lost people.

We are Called to Seek and Save the Lost

It has been said that the last words spoken by someone before leaving this earth are the most important. Jesus, in his final address to His disciples before His ascension, declared to all those who would follow Him the necessity of taking the Good News to every creature.

Mark 16:15-20: *"And then he told them, 'Go into all the world and preach the Good News to everyone, everywhere. Anyone who believes and is baptized will be saved. But anyone who refuses to believe will be condemned. These signs will accompany those who believe: They will cast out demons in my name, and they will speak new languages. They will be able to handle snakes with safety, and if they drink anything poisonous it won't hurt them. They will be able to place their hands on the sick and heal them.' When the Lord Jesus had finished talking with them, he was taken up into heaven and sat down in the place of honor at God's right hand. And the disciples went everywhere and preached, and the Lord worked with them, confirming what they said by many miraculous signs."*

The disciples received their marching orders from their Master. Reach lost people! Once the instruction was understood and communicated, Christ ascended, leaving them everything they needed to accomplish God's purposes. The disciples then dispersed to accomplish this goal, to reach the world for Christ, and they *"went everywhere and preached"* (Mark 16:20). As they did so, they may have remembered the first time Jesus sent them out to minister. There was Jesus, aware of a lost world full of millions of people. And in front of him were twelve men that He would one day commission for the task. In that moment, He told them, *"The harvest is so great, but the workers are so few. Pray to the Lord who is in charge of the harvest, and ask Him to send out more workers for His fields"* (Luke 10:2).

LOOK AT THE HARVEST

In order to become people who love like Jesus did, we must have a place to start. I believe that it should be a simple place, one we can all use to begin our journey. Picture yourself on a hike above a vast wheat field. It's early in the morning and the gentle wind is blowing the wheat in waves. As you stand there, look at the harvest, for it is plentiful and ripe.

The Harvest is Plentiful

Not much has changed since the time of Christ. There are still over three billion people worldwide who have not heard the Gospel of Jesus Christ. In the United States alone, there are approximately 262 million people, of which 187 million have yet to accept Jesus Christ as their Lord and Savior.[3]

How many people do you currently know who do not know Jesus today? Your next door neighbor? Your friend at work? How about your brother or sister? What about your child or your parents? I am sure you can quickly think of many people in your life right now who are lost and need to be found.

The Harvest is Ripe

Not only do we have many people around us every day who need Jesus, but I think you would be amazed to find out just how "open" they really are. Many studies have shown that one out of four people today would go to church if they were just invited. That calculates to 65,500,000 people in our nation who are waiting for an invitation. If Jesus were physically on the earth today, wouldn't He look for ways in which to tell them about the Good News?

All you have to do is turn on your television or open a newspaper to see how ripe the harvest truly is. People are searching for spiritual things. One of the psychic networks report that they receive over 480,000 calls per day, netting twelve million dollars in daily profit. I would call that ripe! The onslaught of New Age seminars, yoga workshops and self-help business plans are evidence that people want to find the truth. What they need is Jesus . . . today.

I am convinced that the problem has much more to do with the laborers than with the harvest. People are willing to receive; however, Christians are unwilling to share. We must once again realize that we are the ones who must tell them! We are called to reap the harvest. We are His mouthpieces. We are "Jesus Today!"

Despite the harvest being ripe, it still remains ignorant to the revelation on the Gospel. George Barna exposes some staggering truths regarding our friends and neighbors: "Nine out of ten American adults cannot accurately define the meaning of 'The Great Commission.' You might laugh at such a preposterous notion, but also seven out of ten American adults have no clue what the term 'John 3:16' means, while only one-third could give an accurate description." The irony is that eighty-eight percent of all Americans label themselves as "Christian."[4]

One morning while praying, I asked the Lord, "Give me Your heart for the lost today." His polite, yet convicting, response was, "You couldn't handle that burden." Pressing on, I put my hand on my heart and sensed the

Lord ask me a question that would have lasting impact. He said, "What does that heartbeat represent to you?"

I confidently responded with a gentle whisper back, "It represents life, Lord."

Another moment passed, and the Lord returned my reply with a convicting thought that, to this day, has never left my mind. "Marc, to Me, that heartbeat represents death!"

I lay on the floor, confused with the response. Suddenly I remembered the painful words of my dear friend, Francis Anfuso, "Every time your heart beats someone dies, most of them unsaved."

I began to consider the ramifications of that statement. My heart beats up to 100 beats per minute, 6,000 per hour, 144,000 per day, 52,560,000 per year! I wonder how big hell will actually be to accommodate that many lost souls? As I began to weep, I realized that the Lord was answering my prayer. . . . In a small measure, He was imparting to me His heart for the lost.

The Laborers are Few

When it comes to accepting your responsibility to share the Good News, how do you score? Are you smiling now, saying, "Yep, upon reaching Heaven, I am confident I will hear from my Master, 'Well done.'" Or are you wiping the sweat from your palms, wishing that this chapter would come to a quick close? If you are like most, you would agree that a Christian is called to share his or her faith daily. But unfortunately, most who agree with this principle have rarely personalized this confession by turning their convictions into actions. Sadly, ninety-five percent of all Christians have never led one person to Christ. It is no wonder Jesus said, "The laborers are few."

Unfortunately, you are not alone! Many studies have shown that four out of ten of those willing to share the Gospel believe they will not do an adequate job of sharing their beliefs. One out of every three say they enter into a Gospel presentation feeling they won't have the right answers. Three out of ten are usually worried that the person they are sharing with will be upset or offended by the nature of the discussion, while one out of seven feel uncomfortable speaking to others about spiritual matters.[5]

The laborers are few, but you can choose today to join their ranks! It can be hard work, but the rewards far outweigh the negative. See the harvest and know that God wants you to help gather it.

BECOMING "JESUS TODAY"

What value do you put on that which is lost? What is a soul worth to you? The degree to which we understand what awaits someone without Christ will determine the level of sacrifice we are willing to put on ourselves, our lifestyles, our finances, our time, and our energy to see that person saved.

Jesus, today, would take the focus off of inadequacies and shortcomings. He would focus on His God-given strength, not His human limitations. He would show compassion to a world in need. He would recognize that His authority is stronger than all the power of the Enemy.

A few years ago, I heard a story about someone who understood the value of a soul. Unfortunately, he didn't do much with his revelation, as he was an atheist. Let his words challenge you to reconsider what value you place on souls and to make some adjustments to become "Jesus Today."

> If I firmly believed as millions say they do, that the knowledge and practice of religion in this life influences destiny in another, then that religion would mean to me everything. I would cast away earthly enjoyment as dross, earthly cares as follies, and earthly thoughts and feelings as vanity. Religion would be my first waking thought and my last image before sleep sank me into unconsciousness. I would labor in its cause alone! I would take thought for the morrow of eternity alone. I would esteem one soul gained for eternity worth a life of suffering. Earthly consequences would never stay at my hand, or seal my lips. Earth, its joys and its grief, would occupy no moments of my thoughts. I would strive to look upon eternity alone and on the immortal soul around me soon to be everlasting happy or everlasting miserable.

The call upon every Christian is to be a partaker in spreading the Good News and to become "Jesus Today" to a dead and dying world. I am thankful that I have been redeemed and given a new life. But God's plan of salvation doesn't stop with you or I. There is a price attached. We are carriers of a "divine, life-giving virus" and must spread it to all with whom we come in contact. The price is to become messengers of reconciliation.

2 Corinthians 5:17-20: *"What this means is that those who become Christians become new persons. They are not the same anymore, for the old life is gone. A new life has begun! All this newness of life is from God, who brought us back to himself through what Christ did. And God has given us the task of reconciling people to him. For God was in Christ, reconciling the world to himself, no longer counting people's sins against them. This is the wonderful message he has given us to tell others. We are Christ's ambassadors, and God is using us to speak to you. We urge you, as though Christ himself were here pleading with you, 'Be reconciled to God!'"*

God has entrusted us with His message, today. He has made us His ambassadors for today. The word "ambassador" literally means "the highest diplomatic representative of one's domain." His kingdom will only be built through His people—you and I. How will they hear unless someone tells them? He is counting on you. Don't let another moment go by. Find a quiet place and spend some time with Him, praying the following prayer.

MY JESUS TODAY PRAYER

Dear Jesus,
I pause for a moment to thank You
For everything You have done for me.
Thank You for loving me while I was yet a sinner.
Thank You for paying the ultimate price on Calvary
For my sins and for my soul.
Lord, I am forever grateful to You.
Lord, Your willingness to give Your all for me
Gives me a glimpse into Your loving heart.
Although I can't comprehend it, and at times don't feel it,
I know that You love me and value me very highly,
Inasmuch as You have called me a child of God,
An heir of God, and a joint-heir with You.
Forgive me for being pre-occupied
With what is important to me,
Not what is important to You.
I ask that You help me to daily
Align myself to the call of the Gospel upon my life.
I ask that You help me to see the value of a soul.
Help me to make the changes necessary
In my time, my energy, and my finances.
Let me show You my heart through my actions
And not through my intentions.
Give me strength to stand
And faith to believe.
Give me opportunities to share
And give me souls for my inheritance.
And most of all, Lord,
Let me become "Jesus Today!"
Amen

CHAPTER TWO

HIS EYES:

RECEIVING

NEW

EYESIGHT

TO SEE

THE HARVEST

JOHN 4:4-43

The phone rang, jarring Dave from a sound sleep. "Hello?"

"Dave, where are you? We're waiting for you."

Sean's wake-up call challenged Dave and his commitment to Sean's discipleship group. Even though he had been getting up every Saturday morning at seven for the last eight weeks to meet with him, it still wasn't an easy task. As he glanced at the red numbers of his alarm clock and saw 7:05, he quickly replied, "Sorry again, Sean. I'll get dressed and be right over."

Dave was having the time of his life. He knew he had been given a second chance. In a matter of weeks his depression, loneliness, and emptiness had seemed to vanish for good. He had new friends and Sean became the loving big brother that Dave always wanted. It was a relationship that he never received from Michael. The desire for partying had turned into a hunger for prayer and Bible reading. He even looked at women differently because of his newfound passion for Jesus. Everything that Sean had promised was taking place now that he had made Jesus the most important thing in his life.

Sean closed the pages of his well-worn Bible, leaned forward with a pointed finger, and with that predictable look of intensity whispered, "It is not enough to be thankful for what Christ did on the cross! The Gospel demands a response from those who have received the message. We just heard clearly from the Word that we are new creatures and our past is gone. All things are new. Praise God! However, Paul continued to tell us what we were to do with our new lives. He gave us a ministry of reconciliation. We are God's messengers! We are ambassadors!

"Listen once again to his exhortation in 2 Corinthians 5:17-20, *'What this means is that those who become Christians become new persons. They are not the same anymore, for the old life is gone. A new life has begun! All this newness of life is from God, who brought us back to himself through what Christ did. And God has given us the task of reconciling people to him. For God was in Christ, reconciling the world to himself, no longer counting people's sins against them. This is the wonderful message he has given us to tell others. We are Christ's ambassadors, and God is using us to speak to you. We urge you, as though Christ himself were here pleading with you, "Be reconciled to God!"'"*

Dave lowered his head to avoid contact with Sean's piercing, blue eyes. He pondered the challenge and debated with himself, "Sean is so right, but I still don't know what to say or how to share with people." The images of friends and family passed through his mind. "What will they think? What will I say?"

Sean ended the meeting then with a final prayer. The invitation to hang around for donuts quickly turned the mood in the living room from sobered silence to festive celebration. Free food was always a highlight for the group of new disciples.

After a few minutes, the group began to disperse. Sean reminded them of the painting party down at the campus ministry office. Free pizza and pop was a sure guarantee to get one hundred percent attendance for this long-overdue project.

———————————— ▬▬▬ ————————————

The campus square was buzzing with the usual Saturday night activity. Five hours of paint fumes sent Dave and the rest of his Christian friends out onto the square for a breath of fresh air in the cold February night. It all seemed so different. The loud music, couples making out in public and beer bottles crashing against the earth no longer drew Dave's attention. As he looked around him at all the people, Dave's mind returned to the discipleship discussion from that morning.

"They're all so empty. I can see it! They are hiding their hurts and pains behind the facade of laughter and partying. They need Jesus."

His heart began to race as the Holy Spirit reminded him about HIS responsibility to share with them. "You are the one. You are My ambassador. You are My messenger." The words were like a two-edged sword that pierced Dave's heart.

Suddenly, the conviction was melted by an overwhelming sense of fear. It was if he were standing with his legs tied together, motionless and helpless, in front of a Mack truck raging toward him at fifty miles per hour. He could feel his countenance change and his courage wane. And he felt all alone.

Dave did not recognize the spiritual war in his mind or understand he was the battlefield. The Holy Spirit was illuminating the lost-ness of his generation and spurning him with urgency to share the message of the Gospel. But the Devil was using his age-old tactic of paralyzing God's people with the smokescreen of fear.

"Hey guys, how about that pizza?" Sean really appreciated the time and effort his disciples had given. The least he could do was buy some pizza to repay them for the hard work. The invitation also served as the perfect distraction to release Dave from his spiritual dilemma.

———————————————

Charlie's pizza joint was filled to capacity. Since it was so close to the university, the dining room was nearly always filled.

After climbing out of Sean's van, Dave walked ahead to grab the door and hold it open for the rest of the guys. Before anyone could walk in, Bill Daniels, one of Dave's fraternity buddies, came rushing out. Dave had spent many nights hanging out with Bill and getting drunk. It was evident that Bill wasn't thinking about partying. His eyes were filled with tears, and he was definitely looking for an escape from some unknown problem.

Dave saw him, but not with his spiritual eyes. He was concerned for Bill's obvious distress, but at that moment, his hunger took priority over his friend's problems, whatever they might be. As he followed the rest of the guys inside, he missed an opportunity to touch the life of someone God had put in his path. Just as Dave was about to follow his friends inside, Sean grabbed his arm and said, "Hey, why don't you guys get a table and order some pizza." He slipped Dave some money and went after Bill.

———————————————

The three large pizzas and four pitchers of Pepsi were devoured quickly, but even after two hours of pinball, and collegiate banter, Sean still had not made it in to eat. With full bellies and the recollection that there was a church service early the next morning, the well-fed "disciples" wrapped up the two pieces of pizza they had saved for their missing leader and tromped out of Charlie's to find Sean.

As they reached the door, his fraternity partner came running in. Bill's countenance had completely changed since their similar doorway encounter just two hours before. No words were exchanged between them, but their eyes were drawn together like two magnets. Dave could see that something had happened. There was a twinkle in his friend's eyes and a huge grin across his face.

"Wow! What happened to him?" Dave thought, looking at the rest of his buddies. They all filed out of Charlie's just as Bill sat down with his group.

As Dave and his friends walked toward Sean's van, they saw him standing under a nearby lamp. He too had a happy face. He seemed to be energized, alert, as if it were the beginning of the day.

One of the guys said to Sean, "Sorry it's cold, but it's your favorite— pepperoni and olive."

Sean shook his head as if to decline the pizza. They all knew something unusual was going on.

"Do you guys know what you just missed? . . . The opportunity of a lifetime! When we were heading into Charlie's earlier tonight, each of you saw Bill come running out, looking distraught. That's what I was talking about this morning. You didn't see the opportunity to share the Gospel. We have been praying for Bill for months now, and the Lord answered your prayers right before your eyes, but you didn't see it!"

————————— ▬▬▬▬ —————————

The music in the background was drowned out by Bill's excitement. As he tried to explain the peace and freedom he felt, more of his fraternity buddies stopped what they were doing to listen. Right before their eyes was a miracle. Bill had changed. He said things they all thought they would never hear. "You have to come meet this dude. He is for real! He will pray for you too—it will change your life."

Everyone was astonished. But something about what Bill said made more sense than anything they had heard in a long time. As if puppet strings were attached to them, many rose from their seats and went with Bill toward the door. The rest were too shocked to move. Bill led his friends to Sean who worked quickly to help these fraternity guys understand the Gospel.

It was a lesson Sean's disciples would never forget. It would forever impress on them the need to look at every person and situation in a new way, to continually focus on what is unseen, not on what is seen.

For them, it was another principle to employ in living life as Jesus would—to see the harvest with His eyes.

JOHN 4:4-43

He had to go through Samaria on the way. Eventually he came to the Samaritan village of Sychar, near the parcel of ground that Jacob gave to his son Joseph. Jacob's well was there; and Jesus, tired from the long walk, sat wearily beside the well about noontime. Soon a Samaritan woman came to draw water, and Jesus said to her, "Please give me a drink." He was alone at the time because his disciples had gone into the village to buy some food. The woman was surprised, for Jews refuse to have anything to do with Samaritans. She said to Jesus, "You are a Jew, and I am a Samaritan woman. Why are you asking me for a drink?"

Jesus replied, "If you only knew the gift God has for you and who I am, you would ask me, and I would give you living water."

"But sir, you don't have a rope or a bucket," she said, "and this is a very deep well. Where would you get this living water? And besides, are you greater that our ancestor Jacob who gave us this well? How can you offer better water than he and his sons and his cattle enjoyed?"

Jesus replied, "People soon become thirsty again after drinking this water. But the water I give them takes away thirst altogether. It becomes a perpetual spring within them, giving them eternal life."

"Please, sir," the woman said, "give me some of that water! Then I'll never be thirsty again, and I won't have to come here to haul water."

"Go and get your husband," Jesus told her.

"I don't have a husband," the woman replied.

Jesus said, "You're right! You don't have a husband—for you have had five husbands, and you aren't even married to the man you're living with now."

"Sir," the woman said, "you must be a prophet. So tell me, why is it that you Jews insist that Jerusalem is the only place of worship, while we Samaritans claim it is here at Mount Gerizim, where out ancestors worshiped?"

Jesus replied, "Believe me, the time is coming when it will no longer matter whether you worship the Father here or in Jerusalem. You Samaritans know so little about him, for salvation comes though the Jews. But the time is coming and is already here when true worshipers will worship the Father in spirit and in truth. The Father is looking for anyone who will worship him that way. For God is Spirit, so those who worship him must worship in spirit and in truth."

The woman said, "I know the Messiah will come—the one who is called Christ. When he comes, he will explain everything to us."

Then Jesus told her, "I am the Messiah!"

Just then his disciples arrived. They were astonished to find him talking to a woman, but none of them asked him why he was doing it or what they had been discussing. The woman left her water jar beside the well and went back to the village and told everyone, "Come and meet a man who told me everything I ever did! Can this be the Messiah?" So the people came streaming from the village to see him. Meanwhile, the disciples were urging Jesus to eat. "No," he said, "I have food you don't know about."

"Who brought it to him?" the disciples asked each other.

Then Jesus explained: "My nourishment comes from doing the will of God, who sent me, and from finishing his work. Do you think the work of harvesting will not begin until the summer ends four months from now? Look around you! Vast fields are ripening all around us and are ready now for the harvest. The harvesters are paid good wages, and the fruit they harvest is people brought to eternal life. What joy awaits both the planter and the harvester alike! You know the saying, 'One person plants and someone else harvests.' And it's true. I sent you to harvest where you didn't plant; others had already done the work, and you will gather the harvest."

Many Samaritans from the village believed in Jesus because the woman had said, "He told me everything I ever did!" When they came out to see him, they begged him to stay at their village. So he stayed for two days, long enough for many of them to hear his message and believe. Then they said to the woman, "Now we believe because we have heard him ourselves, not just because of what you told us. He is indeed the Savior of the world."

At the end of the two days' stay, Jesus went on into Galilee.

SEEING THROUGH THE EYES OF THE DISCIPLES

The story involving Dave Finley, Pastor Sean, and the guys at Charlie's Pizza was written to portray a modern day scriptural allegory. In both the fictional story and the passage above, the message is the same: missed opportunities to share the Gospel due to the inability to *see* that opportunity.

The disciples' problem in this passage exposes a common problem our culture faces today: viewing life through natural and temporal eyes, not through spiritual and eternal eyes. Jesus hoped that His followers would begin to *see* the way He saw the world through this event.

On three different occasions in this story, the disciples missed the opportunity to impact the lives of those around them, twice with the Samaritan woman and once with the entire city! As the multitudes ran out of the city to the well, Jesus sealed His point by saying, *"Look around you! Vast fields are ripening all around us and are ready now for the harvest"* (John 4:35). I am sure Jesus' words to them were driven into their heart when they began to recognize faces at the well. The people who came were the same ones they had seen on their trip into town. The conviction must have run deep.

Let's review two specific phrases Jesus used to teach His disciples this lesson on spiritual eyesight:

> ***Lift up your eyes.*** [NKJV] The word "eyes" in this Scripture is the Greek word, ophthalmo. This word is translated "sight with penetration and sharpness."[6] Another translation reads, "metaphorically, the eyes of the mind, the faculty of knowing."[7]

> ***Look at.*** [NKJV] The phrase look on in this Scripture is the Greek word, theaomai. This powerful word means "to behold, view attentively, contemplate with a wondering regard." It signifies a more earnest contemplation than the ordinary verbs for "to see" and is a careful and deliberate vision, which interprets its object, and is more frequently rendered "behold."[8]

The point Jesus was making is clear. Jesus was saying, "Hey, guys! You blew this one! You cannot expect to live your life focused on the natural realm and be useful for the kingdom of God. You must focus your eyes with penetration and sharpness on every situation and interpret it through the eyes of your spirit."

Let's review this scriptural situation through the eyes of the disciples. This is how *not* to see.

The Disciples Had Preoccupied Eyes

In the account of John 4:8, the disciples decided to make their way into the city to fill their hungry stomachs. Preoccupied with the sound of growling bellies, their attention was focused on their personal lives and the pursuit of their own needs. While on their way to the village, they had to have passed by the Samaritan woman, not realizing that she was a candidate for the Gospel and would eventually be the instrument that would bring the Gospel to an entire city. They saw her, but they didn't see her.

Unfortunately, we can be preoccupied with daily busyness, schedules, deadlines, needs, and desires—directing their focus only on their own needs at any given moment. This preoccupation creates spiritual blindness and hinders our ability to see the hundreds of people surrounding us that are looking for someone to reach out and help them with their pain. The following story clearly illustrates this point.

A crowded plane, bound for New York, was held up at the terminal due to the late arrival of a quadriplegic. To complicate matters the large-framed, 265-pound man had to be transferred from the terminal wheelchair to a special wheelchair to fit down the aisle of the plane. Once aboard the flight, attendants rallied together to move the man from his wheelchair to his assigned seat. The plane was filled with people who watched the whole scene, yet no one offered a hand.

As the plane took off, climbing to its cruising altitude, severe turbulence caused the man's paralyzed upper body to be thrust out into the aisle and slumped over. It made everyone on the plane uncomfortable, including the paralyzed man, but again there was no help offered. It wasn't until later that a flight attendant noticed the man and helped him back up.

Later on in the flight, the time came to serve dinner. The flight attendants hurried down the aisles, providing drinks and a selection of pasta or Chicken Caesar Salad to the hungry passengers.

A meal was set before the helpless man, and the flight attendant continued to serve the remainder of the people on the plane. The man sat there helpless, his hope for assistance disappearing with each passing minute. Surrounded by hundreds of totally capable people, their focus was completely on their own personal needs.

There was a pastor a few rows back who finally *saw* the paralyzed man's dilemma. He pushed his meal aside and walked up to the row where the man was sitting, knelt down, put his hand on his shoulder, and asked, "I know this might sound a little funny, but do you mind if I sit next to you and help you with your meal?"

For the next forty-five minutes the pastor and the man had a great time together, talking, laughing, and, of course, eating. Once the meal was over and the attendants were gathering the leftovers, the pastor excused himself to go back to his seat.

As he sat down, he felt the Lord speak to him. "The man you just fed is like the world . . . in desperate need of someone to help. Paralyzed, discouraged, starving, and incapable."

The Lord continued to speak softly, "Do you see the people? They are like my Church, having all that they need right in front of them, but preoccupied with themselves. Every day they see the need, but they just don't *see* it."

The Disciples Had Temporal Eyes

The second half of John 4:8 says that they went into the city to look for food. We don't have the privilege of knowing exactly what took place during their food-finding adventure in Sychar, as none of the four Gospels give us any details.

During their visit, they must have come in contact with, or at least seen, hundreds of people—many of whom they would soon see again at the well with Jesus. However, their temporal view of this city and its inhabitants paved the way for one of the most embarrassing lessons recorded in Scripture.

They saw that was a Samaritan town; a place they were not supposed to embrace full of people they wanted to avoid. But Jesus saw a town that was ripe for harvest, in spite of it's social standing. Being a Samaritan was a temporary issue because Jesus would soon open the door of Salvation to all races. Often, the condition we see people in now will change dramatically when they meet Jesus.

The apostle Paul admonishes the church in Corinth with the same exhortation in 2 Corinthians 4:18, *"So we don't look at the troubles we can see right now; rather, we look forward to what we have not yet seen. For the troubles we see will soon be over, but the joys to come will last forever."*

The Disciples Had Critical Eyes

The last evidence of their spiritual blindness occurred on their way back to Jesus at the well. I can just imagine the look on their faces as they approached the well with Jesus and the Samaritan woman. It is probable that the disciples knew that this woman had her share of problems. Her solitary journey to the well at noon might have indicated a type of ostracism by the other women of the community. There were wells within the city, and her trip along this lonely path made a nonverbal statement of her condition.

Furthermore, the disciples, having been raised with a Jewish mindset, were trained in an environment that despised the Samaritans because they were a mixed people in blood and religion, though they still possessed the Pentateuch and professed to worship the God of Israel. This, too, must have contributed to the disciples' surprised response.

We must also be careful about how we analyze those whom God puts in our path. Often, the color of one's skin, the type of clothes one wears, the amount of money one has, or the type of house one owns determines our perception of whether that person is worthy of our time and effort.

What do you see when you see the homeless person begging for money? What do you see when that young person drives by with his stereo blaring and his head bouncing to the groove? What do you see when a man walks out of an adult bookstore with a stack of videos in hand? How do you view the businessman in his thousand dollar Italian suit and brand new Porsche Carrera? Behind each of the outward facades lie fields of emptiness and pain, regardless of their appearance. Do you see them as Jesus sees them? Or do you see them through the critical eyes of the disciples?

The story is told of a Christian man who became increasingly disturbed at the constant crying from a young, four-year-old girl three seats in front of him. After an hour of non-stop crying, the irritated Christian bolted forward to confront the father sitting next to the crying girl. "Can't you get her to shut up?" The father turned and looked up with his tear stained cheeks and mumbled, "I wish I could. Only God knows I wish I could! But you see, her mommy was killed in a car accident while we were on vacation, and she is now in a pine box under us in the cargo section of the plane."

If only this Christian man would have *seen* this as an opportunity to minister. Instead, he focused on the temporal—his own selfish needs. Imagine if he would have just gone forward and said, "Sir, I am a Christian, and obviously something is wrong with your daughter. Do you mind if I pray for her? Maybe God would comfort her."

There must be a change in the way we view the people God puts in our path. Our desire should be to become more like Jesus, today, and *see* the way He sees.

SEEING THROUGH THE EYES OF JESUS

It is important to understand that the reason Jesus responded the way He did was that He comprehended the value of the Samaritan woman. She was lost, and she mattered to God. Here was a desperate, hopeless person in need of a Savior.

The way Jesus *saw* this circumstance was quite different from the disciples' view. He was focused through the eyes of His spirit, not the eyes of His flesh. He discovered the situation with sharpness and deliberation.

The account with the woman at the well brings us a clear example of seeing people through His eyes. Let's review this portion of Scripture now.

Jesus Had Envisioning Eyes

John 4:6-7: *"Jacob's well was there; and Jesus, tired from the long walk, sat wearily beside the well about noontime. Soon a Samaritan woman came to draw water, and Jesus said to her, 'Please give me a drink.' "*

In this account the disciples chose to go to town, while Jesus remained. Once settled into a place of rest, He found himself in the company of a Samaritan woman coming to draw water. The reasonable gesture would have been to remain silent; after all, she was a Samaritan, and she was a woman. He was tired and deserved the rest. However, like in every recorded situation involving Christ, He looked at her with intense eyes of opportunity. He envisioned what she could become with his help. He knew that He may never see this woman again on earth. Yet, she seemed ready to receive his love. He chose to redeem the time and the situation.

Like Jesus, we are also faced with hundreds of opportunities every day. Our neighborhoods are filled with people in need. Our workplaces are overflowing with those desperately searching for answers. Our campuses are bulging with young minds desiring to be molded into proper vessels. The supermarkets are crammed with people crying out for a friend. Let us position ourselves in every situation as Jesus did at the well, creating opportunities with all who come into our paths and envision their future.

Jesus Had Selfless Eyes

John 4:9: *"The woman was surprised, for Jews refuse to have anything to do with Samaritans. She said to Jesus, 'You are a Jew, and I am a Samaritan woman. Why are you asking me for a drink?'"*

As the story continues, we see Jesus taking the next step toward touching the life of this woman. He had begun by envisioning what she might become, and He now had to look beyond her circumstance, culture, sin, and outward appearance.

It is difficult to understand the extreme tension and racial challenges between the Samaritans and the Jews that made this encounter with Jesus so unusual. Jesus had to *see* beyond the natural with selfless eyes in order to turn this encounter into a positive situation. In his *Commentary on the Whole Bible*, Matthew Henry states:

> The Samaritans were the adversaries of Judah ([see] Ezra 4:1), were upon all occasions mischievous to them. The Jews were extremely malicious against the Samaritans, looked upon them as having no part in the resurrection, excommunicated and cursed them by the sacred name of God, by the glorious writing of the tables, and by the curse of the upper and lower house of judgment, with this law, That no Israelite eat of any thing that is a Samaritan's, for it is as if he should eat swine's flesh.[9]

As we look at our generation, we are faced with similar challenges,. The racial wars between Blacks, Whites, Hispanics, Asians, and all other races are still raging around the world. To make matters worse, we are continually faced with cultural diversities, alternate lifestyles, and thousands of religious views.

If we are going to be "Jesus Today," we must take the position of our Lord and look beyond the barriers that distance us from the very harvest He is intending us to reach. We must pray for selfless eyes.

Jesus Had Eternal Eyes

John 4:12-14: *"'And besides, are you greater that our ancestor Jacob who gave us this well? How can you offer better
water than he and his sons and his cattle enjoyed?' Jesus
replied, 'People soon become thirsty again after drinking this
water. But the water I give them takes away thirst altogether.
It becomes a perpetual spring within them, giving them
eternal life.'"*

As Jesus continued his discourse with the woman, it is clear that His
decision to look beyond her racial background opened her heart. But Jesus
knew His mission was an eternal one. He wasn't there to help her gather
water or simply share some encouraging word. He saw the situation as eternal. Because of that, Jesus sought to lead her through his eternal eyes.

He did so by turning the conversation from the issue of natural thirst
to spiritual thirst. He had every intention of leading her to face the eternal
purposes of God.

First, she does not think him capable of furnishing her with any water,
at least not at the well. She knew the depth of the well and also recognized
that He had no instrument with which to draw the water. To top it off, she
really didn't comprehend who was standing before her, as evidenced by her
comments of esteem for "father Jacob." What Jesus spoke figuratively, she
took literally. Her lack of understanding demonstrates what confused notions
she had of eternal things.

As we personally turn our daily encounters with people into opportunities for Christ, our focus must not only be on *seeing* beyond the cultural
and racial challenges with selfless eyes, but also on viewing each situation
with an eternal focus. Our efforts to touch people must not only be social in
nature, but also have an eternal goal.

Jesus Had Supernatural Eyes

John 4:15-18: *"'Please, sir,' the woman said, 'give me some of
that water! Then I'll never be thirsty again, and I won't have
to come here to haul water.' 'Go and get your husband,' Jesus
told her. 'I don't have a husband,' the woman replied. Jesus
said, 'You're right! You don't have a husband—for you have*

had five husbands, and you aren't even married to the man you're living with now.'"

The method that Jesus used to draw the woman one step closer to following Him worked effectively. She responded with a desire to drink of this "Living Water." However, Jesus realized that there were some issues that had to be addressed and, with the help of the Holy Spirit, directed the conversation toward dealing with root issues that would paralyze her walk with Christ.

Her life was filled with shame and guilt. Condemned by her own people, and now confronted by her Lord, the time to come clean of her past was before her. Jesus challenged her to face the very issue that had her bound.

In every account, Jesus relied totally on the leading of the Holy Spirit. It was not His own human wisdom, nor was it His natural talents and abilities that impacted the lives He touched. It was a complete trust in the person of the Holy Spirit operating in and through His life.

It is evident that Jesus received specific words of knowledge and words of wisdom regarding this woman's life from the Holy Spirit. The information He shared was known only to the woman. Jesus looked upon this woman through supernatural eyes.

Jesus Had Prophetic Eyes

John 4:19-24: *"'Sir,' the woman said, 'you must be a prophet. So tell me, why is it that you Jews insist that Jerusalem is the only place of worship, while we Samaritans claim it is here at Mount Gerizim, where out ancestors worshiped?' Jesus replied, 'Believe me, the time is coming when it will no longer matter whether you worship the Father here or in Jerusalem. You Samaritans know so little about him, for salvation comes though the Jews. But the time is coming and is already here when true worshipers will worship the Father in spirit and in truth. The Father is looking for anyone who will worship him that way. For God is Spirit, so those who worship him must worship in spirit and in truth.'"*

Jesus' anointing became a magnetic attraction to this woman's empty soul. Her encounter with Jesus quickly changed her mindset from desperation

(*Oh, what a wicked woman I am*) to hope (*Oh, what an opportunity to be in the presence of such a great Prophet!*). Her perception of who Jesus was transitioned quickly, as she first thought of Him as a Jew, then as a nice man, and finally as a prophet. Jesus began to speak prophetically about the condition of her destiny, as well as the destiny of many others in her community.

Seeing with prophetic eyes allows us to lead the lost toward their savior. By looking at them with insight for their destiny, we can speak to their present condition as if it were in the past, thus softening their defenses and creating an opportunity for God to touch them.

When we sense that same openness, the time to speak life into their dead soul has come. By offering hope through Jesus, we can assist the lost meeting Jesus and provide a glimpse into the results if living a Christian life.

Jesus *saw* she was ready to meet the Messiah. Through much patience and wisdom, He knew that her heart was ready to receive the message of the Gospel.

Jesus Had Gospel Eyes

John 4:25-26: *"The woman said, 'I know the Messiah will come—the one who is called Christ. When he comes, he will explain everything to us.' Then Jesus told her, 'I am the Messiah!'"*

The goal of every Christian should be to share the Gospel with those that are lost. Jesus gave this woman good news—the Messiah that she knew would come was talking to her at that very moment!

At that point her curtain was pulled back, her chains of shame were broken, the guilt and sadness that clouded her life turned into an explosion of excitement and revelation regarding her newfound love. She would begin to experience real life. This woman, in turn, would be the vehicle Jesus would use in bringing an entire city to the well. His impact on their lives would give Him the open invitation to remain in the city for days.

Our goal must always be to set our sight on bringing those who are lost to Jesus. The message of the cross is the power of God unto salvation (see Romans 1:16).

WHAT DO YOU SEE?

The principles outlined here can be applied to just about any circumstance:

- Position yourself with an attitude to see each contact with someone as an opportunity.
- Disengage every preconceived opinion regarding their condition and look at them through selfless eyes.
- Engage your mind to see the situation with an eternal goal.
- See how they will be with Jesus as their Lord and Savior.
- Then rely on the leading of the Holy Spirit to guide and direct your entire conversation toward the next point, the Gospel message.

Jesus, today, is in desperate need of followers who will change the way they view the harvest. He wants Christians who will see their world through the eyes of the Spirit and not the passions of the flesh; followers who will see people's inward lostness and not their outward façade; disciples who will see the needs of others and not just the needs of themselves. What do you desire to see? How many will you pray to see every day? Pray the following prayer and take the next step towards becoming "Jesus Today."

MY JESUS TODAY PRAYER

Dear Jesus,
I begin by thanking You today
For allowing me to drink of Your living water.
I also thank You that You have given me
The privilege of worshipping You in spirit and in truth.
It is difficult to understand that anyone
Who has tasted of Your water would thirst for anything but You.
However, I too have sipped from the other wells of
Pleasure, success, and fleshly desires.
I realize that any refreshment from another well
Causes me to lose sight of Your ultimate plan for my life.
Furthermore, it clouds my vision for seeing people
The way that You see them.
I confess to You today
That I feel inadequate sometimes.
There are so many needs
That surround me every moment of every day.
This overwhelming feeling causes me
To ignore most needs that come my way.
I want You to remove my eyes of preoccupation
And let me be occupied with seeing as You do.
Change my temporal eyes
That I might receive Your eternal eyes.
Strip away my critical eyes,
And replace them with selfless eyes.
Let me exchange my natural eyes
For Your supernatural eyes.
Give me prophetic eyes,
That I might speak destiny into the lives of others.
Most of all, Jesus,
Give me Gospel eyes!
Help me to see people
Just the way You see them.
Amen

CHAPTER THREE

HIS EARS:

RECEIVING

AND

RESPONDING

TO HIS VOICE

MARK 10:46-52

Dave knew that time was short. Only a few more days were left to share the Gospel with his old friends before school was over. The list of those people scrolled through his mind like a very long web page—there seemed to be no end! Unfortunately, he was finally realizing that while he saw them daily, he had only started to see them with God's eyes.

This new revelation had changed the way Dave lived the last few weeks of school. He sensed an urgency to spread the Good News while there was still time. The pressure of this talk began to weigh on him as he drove to Sean's house. If he could see their need and reach out to them in that need, but then only experienced negative responses, what was he doing wrong?

Sean's precious wife, Frieda, was known for her famous Fire Fajitas. It was a recipe that had earned her the reputation as the best cook on campus. Only on rare occasions would Sean and Frieda allow twenty-four starving, single college guys to invade their home, but this was a special night—a time to celebrate what the Lord had done with their campus ministry during the school year. Many people had been added to their ministry, making it the most successful year since Sean had taken over the group six years earlier.

As the night drew to a close, everyone was sprawled on the couches in the living room, unable to move from their over indulgence. At that point Sean brought a final charge to the group.

"The Lord has used us to make an impact on this campus. But, it doesn't end here, guys. There are still more people who need Jesus." The sense of accomplishment everyone had felt began to erode.

"People need Jesus! All around you are multitudes of people silently screaming for help. We have to see our world as Jesus sees it. The powerful outpouring at Charlie's Pizza hopefully showed each of you how easy it was to see the world, yet miss their desperate eternal state."

Each guy nodded his head in agreement, including the new ones from the fraternity. They were living proof that Sean's words were right on the mark.

"As you leave this campus to go home next week, I commission you to become a disease to the devil." This radical challenge brought cheers from the group.

"We must become a life-virus for the Kingdom of God, spreading the Good News to everyone."

It was a prophetic statement that would forever be rooted in Dave's fertile mind. It would bring victory and challenges in the days that lay ahead. He did not know how much this profound declaration would change the course of his destiny.

As he left Sean's house, Dave felt that he had what he needed to reach his friends for Christ. His fear had been dispelled.

"Shut up, you freak!" Norman angrily answered Dave. Turning his head, Norman looked out the window of the truck, tired of Dave's endless preaching.

"But you need Jesus!" Dave fired back, hoping to get the last lick in for Jesus.

Within moments Norman's tea pot had reached the boiling point. He exploded, "I don't need your Jesus, and I definitely don't need you telling me about him. Enough is enough!"

Norman and Dave had worked together for over eight months, marking the first time that Dave was able to hold a job for any length of time. They had initially become the best of friends, spending many hours in the moving truck making deliveries for Neilson's Furniture. However, since Dave's experience at Charlie's Pizza their relationship had taken a different twist. Dave seemed to view Norman differently. Their times of laughter had given way to tense debate. They were friends indeed, but now David looked at Norman as a friend in need.

The remainder of the drive back to the warehouse was spent in silence.

Dave was distracted, despite the books that desperately needed his attention. When he tried to study he kept reading the same paragraph over and over, just meaningless words that seemed like a foreign language. He was too caught up in the memory of his conversation with Norman.

On one hand, he felt comforted by the fact that he had stood up for his faith and boldly proclaimed Norman's need for a Savior.

"My commission to you tonight is to become a disease to the devil." Sean's words rang in Dave's ears as if he were hearing them for the very first time.

However, he was grieved by his strained relationship with Norman. Dave was confused by the situation. While he could see Norman's need, he could not seem to reach Norman. How could he be a disease to the devil if people wouldn't respond?

"I don't need Jesus, and I definitely don't need you telling me about him. Enough is enough!" Eight months down the drain. One of his best friends had now become an enemy.

"Was that the right thing to do? Should I have approached Norman differently?" These questions tormented him like the annoying drip-drip-drip of a leaky faucet. The anger and disappointment overcame him as he finally drifted off to sleep with his books still open on his lap.

———————————————————————————

A sense of excitement filled the air of the Activity Center. The time of worship brought a thick presence of the Holy Spirit upon the entire Sunday-morning crowd. It was a refreshing wind, much needed after the last week of sleepless nights, cram sessions, and professorial torment. Finals were over! College was over, summer was around the corner, and the pressure was finally gone.

Sean introduced the guest speaker for that final Sunday. Dale McMurry was a favorite of the campus group. He always seemed to bring the right word at the right time. This Sunday was no different.

"Open your Bibles with me to Matthew 13:16-17 and let's read, *'But blessed are your eyes, because they see; and your ears, because they hear. I assure you, many prophets and Godly people have longed to see and hear what you have seen and heard, but they could not.'"*

Before Dale could even share his revelation concerning this passage, Dave knew that this message was for him.

Dale leaned over the worn, wooden pulpit, looking into the zealous eyes of each listener. "One of the most important ingredients needed for successfully sharing your faith is being led by the Holy Spirit.

"It is one thing to see the needs that bombard you every day, but it is another thing to know which ones you are to respond to. You must also learn to hear what the Spirit is saying."

It all began to make sense; seeing the harvest was only a part of the equation. For the next forty-five minutes Dave did not hear another word Dale said. Lodged in his memory bank was the riveting statement made by Jesus, "Blessed are your eyes because they see, *and* your ears because they hear . . . *and* your ears because they hear . . . *and* your ears because they hear . . . "

Dave's Mustang was backed up to the front door of the fraternity house. After throwing the last box into the trunk, he walked around to the front of his car with Sean following closely behind. His glance caught the reflection of himself and Sean on the shining, red hood. As he paused and looked down, he thought of the night he gave his life to Christ.

Pointing to the center of his hood, Dave said, "That's where I was sitting when I decided to investigate the noise from the Activity Center that night we met." Dave hugged Sean and looked into his tear-filled eyes.

"Thanks, man. Thanks for everything you have done. I will be forever grateful for what you have deposited into my life."

Without any more words, Dave jumped into the front seat of his car, and tried to swallow the huge lump in his throat. As he drove off, tears poured down his face. He painfully reflected on the memories he was leaving behind and the uncertainties that lay ahead. He was headed toward a new life, a new start, a new chapter in life.

As he drove down Main Street, Dave passed the place where his new life in Christ began. Beyond that was the vacant Activity Center, the place filled with so many encounters with God. Further down the street, he saw the campus office. Once filled with zealous interns, it was now dormant until next Fall.

Dave's vintage Mustang literally came to a crawl as he turned his head to see Charlie's Pizza, another landmark from his Christian experience. It was there that he learned to see like Jesus.

As he passed through the final signal and thought of his six-hour drive home, his growling stomach demanded sustenance before the long journey. With all the packing and reminiscing, he had neglected his daily routine of a muffin and coffee. Fortunately, Wayman's Supermarket was still in sight. The very thought of a warm blueberry muffin from the bakery sent Dave racing into the parking lot.

As the automatic doors swung open, Dave's mind also seemed to be opened by the Holy Spirit. As if guided by some divine force, he found himself tuning out the usual grocery store commotion and honing in on the increasingly loud voice of the Holy Spirit.

"Go over to the medicine isle." The Holy Spirit spurned Dave.

I don't have a cold. Why should I go there? Dave debated, a little confused.

"Blessed are your ears because they *hear*." The Holy Spirit reminded Dave of his Sunday morning visitation. "Your obedience today will bring you great joy. Just obey and allow me to do the rest."

Dave knew it had to be the Holy Spirit because he would never have had thought these things on his own.

As Dave rounded the corner, past the towering display of Diet Coke, he froze in his tracks. He could see a familiar face, a friend from his recent past.

"Oh, Lord! It's Norman!" Dave's heart began to pound. An uneasy feeling swept over him, and a queasiness in his stomach made him want to run right out of the store. But in that brief moment as he was deciding what to do next, he remembered a verse he had read that morning—Colossians 3, where it says, *"Let the peace of God rule your heart."*

"Dave? I thought you were gone. Isn't school out?" Much to Dave's surprise, Norman actually sounded excited to see him.

Attempting to salvage their lost friendship, Dave responded, "I'm so sorry I offended you, Norman. Please forgive me. I never meant to make you mad."

"Hey, don't worry about it. We just had a bad day. Besides, I have been thinking about you and what you said."

Dave could feel the lump in his throat growing, but as he swallowed, a sense of faith and peace permeated Dave's heart, followed by further direction from the Holy Spirit. And as if someone else were saying the words, Dave blurted out, "Norman, what do you want me to do for you?"

"I have been blind to God and I want to understand. I have watched the change in your life, and I want what you have. Dave, explain to me this Jesus."

As Dave merged onto the freeway, the discomfort of the long drive home and the uncertainties that awaited him were overshadowed by the joy of being used by God. Just when he least expected, God was faithful to answer the cry of his heart.

The Holy Spirit would set him on a new journey of hearing the voice of God. Dave had learned to hear like Jesus heard, to receive and respond to Him. It was another step toward living life as Jesus would.

MARK 10:46-52

And so they reached Jericho. Later, as Jesus and his disciples left town, a great crowd was following. A blind beggar named Bartimaeus (son of Timaeus) was sitting beside the road as Jesus was going by. When Bartimaeus heard that Jesus from Nazareth was nearby, he began to shout out, "Jesus, Son of David, have mercy on me!"

"Be quiet!" some of the people yelled at him.

But he only shouted louder, "Son of David, have mercy on me!"

When Jesus heard him, he stopped and said, "Tell him to come here."

So they called the blind man. "Cheer up," they said. "Come on, he's calling you!" Bartimaeus threw aside his coat, jumped up, and came to Jesus.

"What do you want me to do for you?" Jesus asked.

"Teacher," the blind man said, "I want to see!"

And Jesus said to him, "Go your way. Your faith has healed you." And instantly the blind man could see! Then he followed Jesus down the road.

HEARING, YET NOT "HEARING"

As we progress through each chapter of this book, it should be evident that we are building, layer by layer, those vital attributes that are needed to become "Jesus Today." First, we must embrace the value of lost people as the foundation. Second, we need the ability to see the harvest through the eyes of Christ. Third, we each desperately need ears to hear what the Spirit is saying.

It is clear that Dave Finley *saw* his working buddy, Norman, as a man who was valued by God and in desperate need of a Savior. Unfortunately, Dave learned the hard lesson of acting without the leading of the Holy Spirit. He *saw*, but he didn't *hear*. In the Scripture above, the crowd, leaving with Jesus from Jericho, made the same mistake. They saw the man shout, *"Jesus, Son of David, have mercy on me!"* yet their response revealed that they did not *hear* the plan of God for that divine moment. Seeing and hearing go hand in hand, as the Scripture says, *"But blessed are your eyes, because they see; and your ears, because they hear"* (Matthew 13:16).

Defining the "Ear"

The ear, as we know it from a natural perspective, is simply a physical organ, the chief instrument by which man receives sound from external sources. However, the Bible is clear in defining the ear metaphorically as the organ of spiritual perception.

Vine's Expository Dictionary refers to the ear as "the faculty of perceiving with the mind, understanding and knowing; being slow to understand and obey."[10]

The Bible is clear to point out the importance of our "spiritual ears":

– The ear of the priest had to be specially sanctified, the tip of the right ear being touched with sacrificial blood at the consecration (see Leviticus 8:23).
– The ear of the cleansed leper had to be rededicated to the service of God by blood and oil (see Leviticus 14:14, 17, 25, 28).
– The earlobe of a servant who preferred to remain with the family of his master rather than become free in the seventh year was to be publicly bored or pierced with an awl in token of perpetual servitude (see Exodus 21:6).
– The cutting off of the ears and noses of captives was an atrocious custom of war frequently alluded to in oriental literature (see Ezekiel 23:25).
– The phrase "to open the ear," which originally means the uncovering of the ear by partially removing the turban, so as to permit a clearer hearing, is used in the sense of revealing a secret or of giving important (private) information (see 1 Samuel 9:15; 20:2, 12-13; 2 Samuel 7:27; 1 Chronicles 17:25; also Psalm 40:6).

As the *International Standard Bible Encyclopedia* states concerning the ear:

> The New Testament promises similarly that "things which eye saw not, and ear heard not" [ASV] are to be revealed by the reconciled God to the heart that in gladsome surrender has come to Him to be taught by His Spirit ([see] 1 Corinthians 2:9).[11]

It was with these things in mind that Jesus referred to the importance of spiritual perception. Eight times in the Gospels and eight times in the book of Revelation, He says, *"anyone who is willing to hear should listen."* In the scriptural account of blind Bartimaeus Jesus chose to demonstrate this important principle through real-life application.

Hearing Through the Ears of the Crowd

Following Jesus around must have been an incredible opportunity. We would assume that hearing the divine teaching straight from the Master Himself and seeing miracles performed by the King of kings would radically transform our life instantaneously. However, even the disciples and followers, who were with Jesus during His ministry, were often unable to grasp the deeper meaning of His eternal truths.

Such is the case in Mark 10, as Jesus is leaving Jericho after a time of powerful ministry in the region of Judea. The crowd and Jesus' disciples had been involved in some serious meetings in which Jesus repeatedly attempted to awaken their spiritual perception. They were able to witness the debate with the deafened Pharisees regarding divorce (see Mark 10:1-12). Jesus had to rebuke His disciples for withholding the children from Him (see Mark 10:13-16). He confronted the rich young ruler for not giving up his riches to follow Him, and then had to explain His words later to His disciples (see Mark 10:17-31). To top it off, He confronted His very own disciples for their immaturity in arguing about who would sit next to Him in glory (see Mark 10:32-45).

Unfortunately, He had to give further instruction in each situation so that His followers would *hear* Him and comprehend the point. He was trying to remove the dullness from their spiritual hearing. But with Bartimaeus, they missed another opportunity to be used by God simply because they were not *hearing* the deep, inward cries of a desperate blind man.

Max Lucado describes this hearing challenge for Christians in his book, *Just Like Jesus:*

> In one of his parables Jesus compared our ears to soil. He told about a farmer who scattered seed (symbolic of the Word) in four different types of ground (symbolic of our ears). Some of our ears are like a hard road—unreceptive to the seed. Others have ears like rocky soil—we hear the Word but don't allow it to take root. Still others have ears akin to a weed patch—too overgrown, too thorny, with too much competition for the seed to have a chance. And then there are some who

have ears that hear, well tilled, discriminate, and ready to hear God's voice.

Please note that in all four cases the seed is the same seed. The sower is the same sower. What's different is not the message or the messenger—*it's the listener*. And if the ratio in the story is significant, three-fourths of the world isn't listening to God's voice. Whether the cause by hard hearts, shallow lives, or anxious minds, seventy-five percent of us are missing the message.[12]

HEARING THROUGH THE EARS OF JESUS

Jesus never intended that it be difficult to hear His voice. His desire is that we all would hear His voice and respond accordingly. Although we are barraged daily with literally hundreds of distractions from the Devil, the world, and the flesh, thank God we are also inundated with the combative voice of the Holy Spirit speaking to us.

A few years ago my family and I were involved in our annual "March for Jesus" event. Thousands of Christians gathered to march through the gambling streets of Reno, Nevada, while multitudes of bystanders edged the streets.

While passing through the main casino area, I saw a Native American man standing in the midst of a large crowd, holding his drink from the casino. Keep in mind, we had already passed thousands of people and had another few thousand to go. Immediately upon eye contact, I sensed the Holy Spirit say, "Go tell him that *I am trying to get his attention*."

My anxiety was instantly apparent as I wiped the sweat from the palms of my hands. I thought, "What a ridiculous thing to say," and I tried to help God understand the twenty reasons why I shouldn't stop marching. Isn't it funny how we try to reason with God? We are called to the ridiculous, and He will do the miraculous.[13]

I ran up to the man and politely said, "Sir, I am a Christian, and I just felt that God wanted me to tell you He is trying to get your attention."

His arrogant response just about knocked me backwards, "You don't understand! I have my own god! Leave me alone!"

Something rose within me as I said louder and bolder, *"You don't understand*! There is only *one* God, and *He* is trying to get your attention!"

He raised his voice and shouted, "*Get out of my face!*"

I took that as my hint to quickly exit the scene.

Twenty minutes later, while gathering at a large park with all the parade members, we watched the last marchers round the corner. Much to my amazement (although I shouldn't have been surprised), the Native American man was walking fifty feet behind them with his hands in the air, crying and singing along with the crowd.

Once he noticed me, he ran up to me and my family, fell at my feet, and started crying out, "Lord Jesus, forgive me for I have sinned and forgotten you. Come back into my life now."

Now that was a real shock. No *Four Spiritual Laws*[14] booklet, no *Two Question Test*[15], no *Eternity, The Ultimate Choice*[16] presentation—just a man crying out the sinner's prayer at my feet.

I spent some time talking with this Shoshone Indian, and it turned out that he had served in Vietnam during the war. While in Vietnam, he stepped on a land mine and was blown to pieces (he had the scars to prove it). He wasn't expected to live.

As he was taken from the helicopter and put on a gurney, a young, female nurse leaned over his dying body and said, "Sir, God is trying to get your attention. You may not make it. Ask Jesus to forgive you of your sins, now."

He cried out, "Lord, forgive me! If you let me live, I will serve you forever."

The amazing part of this story is that after his confession, he slipped into a coma, never again remembering that conversation with the nurse—until he heard me say, "God is trying to get your attention." The very same words, which God had spoken to him years earlier in Vietnam during another critical time in his life, came from the mouth of a stranger on a street in Reno thirty years later!

You never know what will happen when you simply respond to His leading. I believe that these types of opportunities are available every day for every Christian, including you! We must learn to receive, discern, and respond to His voice.

In the story that opens this chapter, we see that Dave Finley had learned to be led by the voice of God. His reward was the conversion of a lost friend. Jesus modeled this type of responsive Christianity with Bartimaeus. Let's look at three simple truths that will help us to hear the way Jesus hears.

Receive His Leading

Jesus was ready to move on to the next town. His work was complete in Jericho. The Scripture reveals that He came in with only His disciples, but was leaving with multitudes (see Mark 10:46). I can just see Him leading the pack of hungry followers, as they anxiously awaited the next miracle. The sound of many sandals scuffling along the dirt path, the dialogues of those discussing Jesus' teachings, coupled with the prayers and praises of many probably made this "March for Jesus" one to remember.

While exiting the city, they all passed by this crumpled man who had edged himself to the road in hope of being touched by this "Jesus of Nazareth." Each person that walked by had an opportunity to touch this man's life. However, he was ignored; left alone to his despair and darkness.

Knowing that he may never get an opportunity to be unshackled from his impaired condition, he attempted to get Jesus' attention. He shouted, only to be rebuked by the crowd. I can only assume that the reply of the hardened crowd launched deep discouragement into his soul.

As the sound of the crowd grew more distant, Bartimaeus screamed in a final attempt to gain the attention of Jesus. Every person must have heard his plea, yet each continued to ignore him and march toward Jesus. But the Scripture tells us, *"Jesus stopped and said, 'Call him'"* (Mark 10:49). The crowd heard the cry of the beggar's voice but didn't *hear* it. However, Jesus *heard* the plea and responded. In this Scripture, Jesus modeled some important principles that we all must follow in order to receive His leading:

1. He had an insatiable desire to be used by His Father.
2. He was willing to adjust His agenda to meet the needs of others.
3. He didn't care what others thought about His radical acts or statements.
4. He expected to be used at anytime, anywhere, with anyone.
5. He was not preoccupied with temporal things that could cloud his ability to hear.
6. He showed prompt, implicit obedience to the voice of God.

Discern His Voice

Once He had received the direction of the Holy Spirit, the Scripture says that He stood still. One can only imagine what took place at that moment. The multitudes were marching forward and their Captain suddenly stopped dead in His tracks. With His head turned slightly and his lips closed, He heard something. It wasn't the cry of a man, but the voice of the Spirit.

As he paused, He discerned the voice. "Should I spit in the eyes this time? What about some mud? How about a good ole' Lazarus shout?" None would do this time. It would be a gentle, calm voice, "Bring Him to me." Jesus knew exactly what this man needed and exactly how to respond.

A few years ago, while walking through downtown Portland, I saw out of the corner of my eye a large group of "street kids" sitting along a brick wall (Portland, Oregon has the largest population of homeless teenagers per capita in the nation). In a hurry to reach my destination, I continued to take a few more steps until I was arrested by the voice of the Holy Spirit.

I stopped for a moment and just listened. I felt as though the Lord wanted me to share the Gospel with these hardened teens. Knowing that I would rather offend man than God, I turned and proceeded over to the wall.

Lined up along the wall were four young people with the most incredible outfits and hairdos I had ever seen. None of them would have ever made it through an airport security check due to the large quantity of metal objects protruding from various parts of their bodies. Mohawks, black makeup, wild facial expressions, and vulgar language made me feel a little out of place.

As we began our conversation every one of them quickly proclaimed to be a devout atheist. (My personal opinion is that God doesn't believe in atheists, so neither should I.)

One of the girls, Sadie, asked me with a mocking tone, "So how do you know there is a God?"

For some unknown reason, I quickly responded, "Because He speaks to me."

The entire group chuckled. Sadie continued her assault, "And how does He speak to you?"

I countered back, "I hear little voices."

At this point they all started laughing, and Sadie started screaming and pointing me out to all the passing people, "He hears little voices! This freak hears little voices!"

Just then the Holy Spirit spoke very clearly to me and said, "She is just putting up a front. She is lonely, hurting, and tried to commit suicide a few nights ago."

Instead of using this as ammunition to win the battle, I felt it necessary to hold off in order to win the war for her soul. I was trying to discern the situation and be led by the Holy Spirit. For a few more minutes I was mocked and ridiculed. Finally, the group disbanded.

As the rest of the group was taking off, I said to Sadie, "Hey, do you have just one more minute?"

Surprised and confused, she said, "Yeah. What's up?"

I leaned toward her and whispered, "I just heard another one of 'those little voices,' and that voice said that you are putting up a front. You are lonely, hurting, and, in fact, tried to commit suicide a few nights ago."

She went whiter than her friends' makeup, tears welled up in her eyes, and she began to sob, "How do you know? Who told you?"

I responded, "Jesus told me."

I proceeded to pray with this young lady right there in front of the wall. This experience is another example of receiving the leading and then discerning the voice of the Holy Spirit.

Many of you are probably saying, "How do I know His voice?" Others might be thinking, "He never speaks to me like that." Some may even be saying, "I have a million thoughts daily. How do I know which is God and which is my pizza?" Please be assured that there is a way to discern His voice.

For many years I traveled with a ministry called Christian Equippers International, and we taught seminars all over the world, including one entitled *Complete Evangelism*. In one of the lessons entitled, "How to be Led by the Spirit," we talked about the eight gentle leadings of the Spirit. Here is the list for your review:

1. Hearing An Inner Voice or Urging
2. Having An Exceptionally Clear Thought
3. Having Thoughts Surface that You Don't Initiate
4. Having A Distinct Intuition
5. Having A Mental Picture
6. Focusing on One Person in a Crowd
7. Drawing People to You for No Apparent Reason
8. Meeting Someone's Eyes and Feeling a Leading

Discerning his voice is not difficult, but it does take some practice. Responding to what we discern is the next step in the process.

Respond to His Request

It is one thing to be able to hear His voice and discern what the Lord is saying. It is entirely different to respond!

I have found that many Christians are great *hearers*, but few are faithful *doers*. It is no wonder that people perceive that God speaks so little. Very few are listening and responding.

The very word, "hear," means to understand and obey. *Vine's Expository Dictionary* gives us this great definition: "being slow to understand *and obey*; put the words into your ears, take into your mind and keep them there; associated with conviction, so *hearing is with obedience*."[17]

Another definition states, "If the ear listens, *the heart willingly submits*, but often the spiritual ear is hardened to respond ([see] Isaiah 6:10; Zechariah 7:11; Matthew 13:15; Acts 28:27). Such unwilling hearers are compared to the 'deaf adder . . . which harkened not to the voice of charmers, charming never so wisely' ([see]Psalm 58:4-5; also Proverbs 21:13; 28:9; Acts 5:57)."[18]

> Luke 11:28: *"He replied, 'But even more blessed are all who hear the word of God and put it into practice.'"*
>
> John 8:47: *"Anyone whose Father is God listens gladly to the words of God."*

Jesus received the leading, discerned, *and responded*. The end result was a breakthrough. The blind beggar was healed.

Psalm 72:18 says, *"the God of Israel, who alone does such wonderful things."* If we are to only focus on our own inadequacies and the fear of the unknown, we will always fall short of being used mightily by God. Most often, I have found that God takes me to the end of my human reasoning and personal limits. It is at that point when He usually steps in with His miraculous power. We must learn to trust Him and respond to whatever He asks us to do. We never know when it might be a life or death issue.

Early one morning, while walking up the steps to a prayer meeting inside the church, an unusual presence of the Holy Spirit hit me. It was still dark and cold. Freezing sleet and snow was falling. At that moment, the most awkward request came from the Holy Spirit, "Run across the street and pray for a man who will walk into your path."

I knew it was God because I would never have thought that one up on my own! I ran down the stairs, jumped the rail, and ran across the highway, only to run into a man, soaking from head to foot.

With no other direction other than to pray for him, I fumbled for a few words, "Uh . . . I was across the street, and I believe that God told me to come over here to pray for you."

I waited for some confirmation. Either a punch or a smile would have done the trick, but he just stared at me. The few moments seemed to last an hour. Suddenly, I noticed the reflection of the street light in the tears building up in his eyes.

He cleared his throat and muttered, "I have been walking around all night long, contemplating suicide. I was just getting ready to kill myself and I made one last plea, 'God, if you are real, put someone in my path.'"

Obviously this was a "God moment." I did not know the outcome before I crossed the street out of obedience. I often wonder what would have happened if I didn't respond. Would he have ended his life? Fortunately, I was willing to receive, discern, *and* respond.

How about you? How many times have you heard the Lord asking you to make a phone call to a long lost friend but failed to respond? How many times have you felt a tug to visit that neighbor who lives next door, but you bowed to the spirit of fear? When was the last time you actually heard the Lord ask you to step out beyond your comfort zone? Did you hear and discern only? Or did you respond?

I will never forget the time when I didn't respond. It was a lesson that haunted me for many months and is one of the main reasons I am quick to respond now.

While living in Lake Tahoe, I was heading into the local post office on a very brisk winter afternoon. I ran into a man whom I had worked with at Caesar's Tahoe before I was a Christian. Immediately, I sensed the Lord asking me to share my faith, as this man was open to receive. Unfortunately, I let the opinion of a peer influence my decision not to respond.

Our small talk lasted only a few moments. I will never forget that last look on his face. He was almost begging with his eyes for me to share with him. I hopped into the car, not even feeling convicted for deliberately disobeying the Holy Spirit. After all, there would be another time, right?

The following morning I went out into my driveway to get the morning paper. While walking back up the steps I unrolled the paper and was stunned by what I saw. The headline read, "Local Man Drowns in Lake." It was my buddy. He had left the post office to work on an underground pipe out on the lake. The boat capsized, and he drowned in the freezing water.

What the world needs is "Jesus Today," not "Jesus Tomorrow." There is a cry in God's heart for us to re-evaluate how we perceive lost people. They are of value, and they matter to God. We must ask Him to place His passion in us, to give us new eyes to see, new ears to hear, and the desire to respond.

Your friends are waiting for you. Your family needs you to respond. Your city is in need of "Jesus Today." Won't you respond now?

MY JESUS TODAY PRAYER

Dear Jesus,
I want to thank You today
For Your grace and love.
Thank You for listening to my prayers
And teaching me that I need to listen to Your voice.
Forgive me, Lord for the times
I have heard Your voice and not responded.
My ears are open, Lord,
Teach me how to listen.
I realize that sometimes You will
Ask me to do something ridiculous.
But that the end result of my obedience
Is that You will do the miraculous.
Help me to receive Your leading
And discern Your voice.
May I always be a responder
And not miss the opportunities You bring my way.
I again put my trust in You
And ask You to guide my every step.
You are a good God
And You speak good things.
Thank You for allowing me
To be a part of your team.
I pause now to listen to You
Speak, for Your servant is listening.
Amen

CHAPTER FOUR

HIS HEART:

LEARNING

TO LOVE

AND CARE

FOR THE LOST

LUKE 10:25-37

The bright orange and purple sky punctuated by a few distant stars brought hope that the heat pelting the East Coast would come to an end, at least for the evening. Temperatures had soared that day to a blistering 104 degrees along with an unbearable 98 percent humidity; a typical sticky, summer day. To make matters worse, a citywide smog warning had been posted, and a visible layer of smog hung over the city like a heavy lid, preventing any respite from the heat and humidity.

The entire city was lethargic. News stations encouraged people to stay indoors to prevent another wave of tragic deaths like those brought on by the previous year's heat wave. Stores and businesses closed early. Children flocked to neighboring pools and fountains to find relief from the heat, and many played long into the evening. Most neighborhoods looked like urban ghost towns. Window shades were pulled down to shield the occupants from the heat, while a strange silence replaced the usual evening chitchat among neighbors on row house porches.

Dave drove home through The City on Interstate 95 still reflecting on his long, yet life-changing, senior year. He needed a place to take a break after four hours in the car. He decided to pull off the freeway to buy a cup of coffee in an effort to stay awake for the final two hours of his drive.

He studied the road signs for a good place to pull off and noticed that the next exit was Downtown Boulevard. This street was home to some of his favorite childhood memories, and he immediately thought of the many times his father had taken him to see the local baseball team play. He had not seen the new stadium and chose to turn off here for coffee and a quick drive by the new home field of his childhood heroes.

As he pulled off the freeway, he noticed the traffic light at the bottom of the off-ramp was flickering. He slowed, looked both ways, and realized that most of the city lights to the right were very faint and that other areas to the left seemed to be completely dark. He wondered if it was an East Coast "brownout" caused by the overuse of air conditioners.

In the distance was a convenience store. The increasing darkness was interrupted by the flickering lights of the neon sign. He turned into the parking lot to make his quick coffee stop.

As he stepped out of the car, he heard a scuffle from the dark shadows to his left, and an icy chill crept up his spine. He quickly reached for his keys still hanging from the ignition, an instinctive precaution that left him vulnerable. His back was turned for just a moment, but it was all they needed. Six young gang members stepped from the shadows and surrounded him. Intent to pass their gang initiation ceremony with flying colors, each one of them glared at Dave with the same hatred. They each held baseball bats, chains, or knives. Dave felt his mouth go dry, and he swallowed hard. He knew that things were going to get worse before they got better.

Quickly, he turned to the oldest of the group and pleaded, "Hey, you guys, I don't want any trouble. I will give you anything you want. Take my wallet, take my car, take anything."

The gang laughed in unison with a mocking. Suddenly, the gang leader lunged forward as two others grabbed Dave from behind and held him firmly. The leader held Dave by the chin, put his whisker-ridden face only inches from Dave's nose, and whispered harshly, "We ain't just after your money, fool. We are wanting you too!"

Dave was shoved back into his car and joined by three of the rage-ridden gang members. As they pulled away, the intense moments in the darkened parking lot were followed by an eerie silence, like nothing had ever happened. There were no witnesses, and Dave was helplessly at the mercy of his captors.

The remaining gang members followed Dave and his carload in their lowered 1962 Chevy Impala. They drove to a remote area just south of Druid Park Pond. Although the area seemed unusually quiet, there were still the faint sounds of late night joggers taking advantage of the cooling evening. Dave prayed that someone would realize what was happening and intervene before it was too late.

The two cars pulled to the end of a dark road. Dave was dragged from his car, and all six gang members surrounded him again. As they began to taunt him, one gang member suggested stripping him naked, beating him and taking his wallet. This appealed to the mob, especially since Dave was wearing some nice basketball shoes that the gang leader wanted for himself.

Dave closed his eyes and braced himself for the first blow. Pow! From behind, Dave was hit on the back of his leg with a baseball bat. The pain was instant and severe, and Dave crumpled to his knees. Covering his head with his arms, Dave tried to deflect the blows as best he could. The beating seemed like it lasted an hour, but in reality the deed was done in only a few seconds. The gang members stripped him and left him there in the dirt.

"Nice watch, buddy. With the blood on it this ought to be proof enough of our initiation." With that, they climbed into the Impala and drove away before anyone even noticed the disturbance.

"Help! Somebody help me! Jesus, help me!" Dave's feeble cry, hardly more than moan, was met by an eerie silence.

There he lay, brutally beaten and left to die, naked and bleeding from his mouth and nose. Pounded beyond recognition, he was sure he was going to die. He tried desperately to crawl for help, but his bruised limbs just wouldn't cooperate. After a few moments of struggle, he finally collapsed. Seconds later he blacked out.

Dave was awakened by the sound of whistling. As he opened his swollen left eye, he could see what appeared to be a flashlight. Immediately he began to moan, which got the attention of the man with the flashlight. It was Bill Davidson, some called him Reverend Bill, a retired eighty-two-year-old minister who walked his dog next to the pond every night between eleven and eleven thirty.

Bill shined the flashlight down to locate the source of the moaning. As the bright light hit Dave's face, the reverend jumped back, startled by what he saw.

Fearing that the muggers were still in the area, Bill whispered, "I don't know who you are, or what happened, but I don't want any part of it!" Immediately, Bill and his cocker spaniel, Dusty, rushed away, leaving Dave alone again.

Just as Bill's hurried footsteps were gone, Dave was startled from the other direction. A car was coming down the road with its high beams shining directly in his eyes. The car seemed to slow down rather quickly. Although Dave could not see who was in the car, a voice came from the driver's side.

"What happened to you, man?"

With the little energy he had left, Dave begged for help, "You have to help me, please! I'm gonna die!"

Kyle Andrews, a social worker on his way home from another late night, looked over the man on the ground with pity. But his wife was already upset enough and he needed to get home! Besides, the guy could talk. It must look a lot worse than it really was.

Without any response, the car shifted into reverse and left quickly. Dave's hopes for survival began to slip away into the night.

Randy Stevenson strolled through the park, fulfilling his commitment to the Lord of prayer-walking his neighborhood daily. Randy was a graveyard factory worker who was praying during what was for him, the morning hour. As he turned off the main road onto the dirt path next to Druid Park, he noticed someone lying on the side of the road. His first thought was that it was another naked, homeless bum sleeping off the evening bottle of booze. But as he came closer to the motionless body, the signs of foul play were quickly evident by the fresh blood, bruises, and cuts all over the naked body.

Randy ran over and tried to wake Dave from his stupor, "Are you alright? Hey you, are you still alive?"

There was a faint nod of the head followed by a short moan, feeble signs of life. Randy assured him, "I will be back in one minute. I will run to my car to get some old workout clothes and a first aid kit."

Within a matter of moments, the stranger was back, assisting Dave in his wounded state. His first priority was to assess the situation carefully. Having been a medic in the army, Randy knew what to look for. Once he realized that no bones were broken, he felt the urge to help this hurting man find a hospital.

Suddenly, aware of the time, Randy looked at his watch, knowing that his compassion and care for this beaten stranger would make him late for work and could even cost him his job. However, this man's situation seemed to be what was most important at the time. After all, Randy believed his boss would understand. He hoped his boss truly believed the comment he had made at lunch last week, "People don't care how much you know until they know how much you care."

Randy quickly helped Dave as best as he could. He carefully put his jogging pants and sweatshirt over him and, despite the pained moans of protest, picked him up and carried him in his arms to his car. They rushed to the local emergency room, where Dave would spend the next several hours.

Randy called his boss and received permission to stay.

At seven a.m., the doctor came into the emergency room, pushed the curtain aside, smiled at Dave and said, "You are a lucky man. It could have been much worse. There was definitely someone looking out for you today! You don't have any major internal injuries, just bruising. I am going to release you now and suggest you take it easy for a few days to give your body a rest."

Dave was relieved to hear these words from the doctor, but his real questions remained unanswered. As the doctor left the room, Dave asked, "Randy, why would God allow this to happen to me? Why do bad things happen to good people?"

Randy looked down at him and said, "I don't know why this happened. I am not God. But I can tell you that God can and will use this for his glory."

Just then, Dave's parents arrived from Newcastle and rushed into the room with gasps at the sight of the bruises and swelling. Randy quickly excused himself, allowing Dave to deal with his panicked parents.

As Dave's mom turned out of the parking lot of the hospital, she barely missed a man slowly pushing a shopping cart along the sidewalk. Dave was immediately irritated that the man had not moved an inch. "Doesn't he realize that being run over by a car, no matter how slow it is moving, does not feel very good?" Dave thought. "What a bum." In that moment, Dave was unable to see the man with God's eyes. "Why doesn't he get a job?"

Just then, Dave had a major revelation. The Holy Spirit interrupted his judgmental thoughts with a convicting realization that he was just like that man with the shopping cart.

"Don't you know that I died for him too?" God's gentle voice prompted a sense of compassion in Dave.

"Can't you see why I allowed you to face such a tragedy? I want you not only to see their condition and hear My voice concerning hurting people, but I want you to love them as I do."

Dave's hardened heart was quickly melted by the sweet presence of the Lord. He began to feel the weight of the homeless man's burden, as if he himself were pushing that cart down the sidewalk.

"I was just like him! Lost and in desperate need of someone to help me." Tears began to flow.

"Lord, You sent someone and heard my cry. Oh, forgive me."

He put his swollen head into his hands and started weeping uncontrollably.

"Forgive me, Lord, for my hardened heart! Jesus, teach me to love people like You do. Change me right now, Lord. Give me Your heart to love the lost like You do. Jesus, I want to see, hear, and love people just like You."

As Dave wiped the tears from his eyes and looked up, the homeless man had disappeared. Vanished! Was it an angel? Was it the medication? Did he even really exist?

Dave knew that wasn't the point. The point was that, just like earlier that day, the Lord was using this unfortunate circumstance to change him. Dave would go home beaten and wounded on the outside, but healed on the inside.

His mom just let him cry, assuming that he was still reeling from the shock of his ordeal. She felt it was not the time to ask all the questions that had built up in her mind. Dave was different, she could tell. His father had noticed too but did not want to discuss it. As far as he was concerned, driving the Mustang back to Newcastle was his duty as a father. After that, there was no need to worry about Dave any more.

God would use the coffee stop in The City as a pivotal moment to make Dave more like Him. With all the opposition he would receive, Dave needed it. Loving with the heart of Jesus was another component that would allow Dave to live life as Jesus would.

HIS HEART

LUKE 10:25-37

One day an expert in religious law stood up to test Jesus by asking him this question: "Teacher, what must I do to receive eternal life?"

Jesus replied, "What does the law of Moses say? How do you read it?"

The man answered, "'You must love the Lord your God with all your heart, all your soul, all your strength, and all your mind.' And, 'Love your neighbor as yourself.'"

"Right!" Jesus told him. "Do this and you will live!"

The man wanted to justify his actions, so he asked Jesus, "And who is my neighbor?"

Jesus replied with an illustration: "A Jewish man was traveling on a trip from Jerusalem to Jericho, and he was attacked by bandits. They stripped him of his clothes and money, beat him up, and left him half dead beside the road.

"By chance, a Jewish priest came along; but when he saw the man lying there, he crossed to the other side of the road and passed him by. A Temple assistant walked over and looked at him lying there, but he also passed by on the other side.

"Then a despised Samaritan came along, and when he saw the man, he felt deep pity. Kneeling beside him, the Samaritan soothed his wounds with medicine and bandaged them. Then he put the man on his own donkey and took him to an inn, where he took care of him. The next day he handed the innkeeper two pieces of silver and told him to take care of the man. 'If his bill runs higher that that,' he said, 'I'll pay the difference the next time I am here.'

"Now which of these three would you say was a neighbor to the man who was attacked by bandits?" Jesus asked.

The man replied, "The one who showed him mercy."

Then Jesus said, "Yes, now go and do the same."

The story of Dave Finley's tragedy is, unfortunately, all too common. Our world is filled with people that have all types of unpleasant circumstances and are desperately looking for someone who would come along side and love them. Yet, just as the story described, there aren't many modern day heroes who are willing to slow down their schedules, shelf their own agendas, open their hearts, and lend a hand to a person in need.

This problem is not just a twenty-first century problem. Hardened hearts and selfish minds have plagued humanity since the fall of mankind. Jesus Himself knew that this problem was rampant and spent much of His ministry touching the hearts of those in need and addressing the hardened hearts of others.

He wanted His followers to realize the importance of loving the lost with their hearts, not just their minds. He taught by example that every person matters to God. The picture Jesus painted with His life was of one hand clasped in the hand of almighty God while the other was reaching out to serve the needs of others. From the woman at the well and the feeding of the multitudes to the healing of the blind man and the woman caught in adultery, Jesus showed that He had an unconditional love for people.

TEMPERAMENT OF THE TIMES

If Jesus were physically alive on earth in the twenty-first century, how do you think He would live? Where would you find Him on a typical day? Who would be His friends? Where would He take His disciples? I believe He would spend a great deal of His time out in the city, conversing with prostitutes, helping single mothers, visiting the terminally ill, and feeding the hungry, to name a few.

In most of the 128 evangelistic encounters of Jesus in the Gospels, He ministered to the needs of people before actually bringing forth the message of salvation. He was concerned for the whole person. He actually cared for the welfare of every individual.

His love drew people to His message. They clearly saw that He cared for them. I am sure that if you were to ask Jesus, "Who is the most important person in your life?" He would quickly respond, "The person I am talking to at this moment."

When it comes to analyzing your own heart concerning the lost that surround you every day, how do you rate? Do you feel their pain? Have you thought lately about helping someone in need? Have you ever considered that simply loving someone and meeting him at his point of need could be the easiest and most successful way to bring someone to Christ? What about the neighbor next door? The person at work? The people you pass by at the store?

There must be a shift in our lives from hardened hearts to hardened hands. 1 John 3:18 admonishes us (emphasis mine), *"Dear children, let us*

stop just saying we love each other; let us really show it by our <u>actions</u>."
The lost of this world are not looking for some polished presentation of religious facts; they are looking for someone who is real, who can meet them at their level, feel their pain, and help bring resolve to their situations. Dave Finley was ministered to through *deed and truth* by a spirit-led, twenty-first century Good Samaritan who understood the heart of Christ toward hurting people.

Recently, while getting gasoline at a local station near my home, a young gas attendant approached me. I will call her "Sally." As she approached the car (Oregon law does not allow the public to pump their own gas), I was taken aback by her extreme statement of fashion. She had shaved her head, had numerous pierced objects in her ears, eyebrows, nose, lips, tongue, and cheeks, and had tattoos on both arms. As I began to pray for her, I sensed the Holy Spirit say to me, "She is a lesbian. Show her My unconditional love."

As she returned my credit card, I said, "Sally, I would sure love to invite you to our church this Sunday."

She paused and responded politely, "Thank you. What church do you attend?"

I pulled out a "Touch Card," held it out, and replied, "City Bible Church."

Her countenance immediately changed, and her polite smile turned quickly into wrathful anger. "I will *never* attend your church! You people don't accept me for the way I am!"

I felt somewhat embarrassed by the immediate attention I was receiving by all the other gas station patrons, but I also felt the gentle touch of the Holy Spirit quickening me with the message of unconditional love. I whispered back to her, looking directly into her eyes, "Sally, I love you unconditionally. I may not approve of your lifestyle, but I accept you as a person." My words had penetrated her heart and caught her off guard, leaving her speechless. As the tears began to well up in her eyes, she turned and ran off.

Early Friday morning, while in prayer, the Holy Spirit instructed me to buy some flowers for Sally and take them to her. Imagine explaining to my precious wife that Jesus wanted me to buy flowers for a new girl I had just met! After hearing the whole story, she approved.

I drove into the gas station and there was Sally, pumping gas across the way. She turned, saw me and immediately lit up with a big smile. Her eyes seemed to twinkle from a distance. I thought for sure she had mistaken me for some other guy. She came running over to the car and said, "Hi. How are you, today?"

I was thinking, *Don't you remember verbally attacking me in front of half of Oregon several days ago?* But instead, looking into her eyes, I said, "Sally, I don't need gas today, but what I do need is to tell you that I really meant what I said to you earlier this week. I love you unconditionally."

To my surprise, she responded, "I know that! The moment you said that you loved me, I felt love come all over me, like I have never felt before. I was so shocked that I went and told all my friends about you. You are not like any Christian I have ever met before."

With that unexpected response, I reached down, grabbed the roses, and handed them to her. "These are for you. They are to just let you know that I really care about you and meant what I said."

As I pulled away, she waved, and the love of God filled both of our hearts. We both learned something through this encounter. Showing people the true heart of Christ will melt the hardest of hearts and open the door for His love to flood in.

Having the heart of Christ toward lost people is a twenty-first century necessity. Without this one ingredient we will fall short of touching the harvest that is ripe and right before our eyes. Here are a few indicators of why love must be our primary tool in touching those around us with the Gospel message.

People Are Weary of Words

Words alone have little impact. Our society is filled with daily newspapers, magazines, television programs, Internet chat rooms, telemarketers, and other advertisements—all promising us something they can't deliver. We are becoming wise and resistant to the "get rich, lose weight, look good, feel great" campaigns that, in reality, bring little or no results. We live in a generation that has been burned repeatedly and has adopted the philosophy of "show me, don't tell me."

Broken Promises Have Become Normal

Promises are no longer sealed with a gentlemen's handshake. Our society is driven by contracts, collateral agreements, and stiff penalties to persuade the selfish motives of an individual's heart to hold true to his or her word.

While on vacation in Southern California, my wife, our friend Maureen, and I decided to get a feel for the Hollywood glamour. We chose to attend a talk show. The topic for that day was "Amazing Children Touching the Nation." Throughout the taping of the show, I was very impressed with the extraordinary exploits accomplished by such ordinary children.

One twelve-year-old girl caught my attention. She was one of the national spokespersons for the AIDS Foundation. She had contracted AIDS at a young age through a blood transfusion. What impressed me so much was her optimistic view toward life, while faced with such an unpromising future.

After the show the featured children and their parents were mingling in the crowd. As I watched this young girl filled with charisma, the thought crossed my mind to pray for her healing. I knew this was probably God speaking to me because, once again, I found myself trying to reason with Him, saying to myself, "Not here. Please, Lord, do I have to?"

Proper ministry ethics caused me to approach her mother for permission first. I introduced myself and shared my desire to pray for her daughter, knowing that she would be overwhelmed by my kind and considerate request. Boy, was I wrong! She began to shout, "You won't go near her! I will never have any of you Christians ever pray for her! Get away from me!"

Once again I found myself in an embarrassing situation, yet I felt the Holy Spirit say, "Just show her My heart."

After calming her down, I asked her the question, "Why do you feel this way toward Christians?"

With tears of pain in her eyes, she said, "When my little girl was younger, we attended church. I was hit with the most tragic situation a parent could face. My daughter contracted AIDS. I ran to my pastor to talk with him and get some help. I knew he would help me since he always said he would be there for us. When I presented my situation, he replied coldly, 'You will have to leave the church. You are no longer welcome here.'"

Broken promises permeate our society, causing people to be reluctant to accept our message without first experiencing our love and acceptance. We must see that love is the doorway to their hearts before actually sharing the Gospel message.

Lack of Trust

The increase of violence, crime, and broken promises has replaced the honor system we used to rely on. Pay-first gas stations, homes with barred windows, and car alarms are all signs of a lack of trust for one another. The fibers of trust have even been dissolved in many churches with the frequent exposure of fallen leaders in the areas of sexual immorality and financial embezzlement. Trust must now be earned over time—it is never just given.

Distorted Perception of God

As we enter the twenty-first century, the mindset of the previous generation is rapidly disappearing, and we are on the verge of a whole new standard for societal thinking. Although Christianity still has its place in our society, biblical principles are no longer the standard by which society functions, and this shift away from Judeo-Christianity has paved the way for a new philosophy that has become the predominate force of our nation. If we think it has been difficult to reach people in a post-Christian, neo-pagan, modern mindset, watch out for the change into the post-modern, destructionist mindset, which is approaching rapidly. Listen to what some of the nation's leaders are saying:

> Princeton Theologian, Diogenes Allen, says, "This change is perhaps as great as that which marked off the modern world from the Middle Ages."[19]

> Leith Anderson, author of *A Church for the Twenty-First Century*, says, "We are experiencing enormous structural changes in our country and in our world . . . changes that promise to be greater than the invention of the printing press, greater than the Industrial Revolution."[20]

> Gene Edward Veith Jr., author of *PostModern Times: A Christian Guide to Contemporary Thought and Culture*, says, "Many people today are sensing that the modern era is over. In nearly every sphere, from academic fields to new social phenomena, the assumptions that shaped twentieth-century thought and culture are being exploded. As we enter the twenty-first century, it seems clear that Western culture is entering a new phase, which scholars are calling post-modern."[21]

This is best summarized by Walter Truett Anderson, who says, "We are presently in the midst of a transition from one way of thinking to another." He cites three processes shaping this transition:

The Breakdown of Belief: Today there is no universal consensus about what is true. We are in a kind of unregulated marketplace of realities in which all manner of belief systems are offered for public consumption. All appears to be relative with no foundation of truth. Truth is different to each person, as it is what you want it to be to you.

The Birth of a Global Culture: All belief-systems become aware of all other belief systems. As a result, it is difficult to accept any of them as absolutely true. The end result has produced a melting pot of religious beliefs with the conclusion that all pathways lead to God.

A New Polarization: Conflicts over the nature of social truth tear at our society. We have "culture wars", particularly battles over the critical issues of education and moral instruction. These wars include abortion, humanism, euthanasia, same sex marriages, gay rights, etc.[22]

With these societal changes facing twenty-first century Christians, our message must be preached through the filter of genuine love and care for the individual. The lost must see the heart of Christ in us! Christ's love will be the element that separates us from the many other forms of self-made religions and will destroy the vain philosophies of the twenty-first century.

A classic example of overcoming these obstacles by showing the heart of Christ is the case of Rob Charnoff. He was a Jehovah's Witness, White Magic, Satanist Jew. When I met Rob he had over sixty necklaces, each one having some cultic trinket hanging on it. There were skulls, animal bones, pentagrams, and a myriad of Indian ceremonial objects.

Over a period of four weeks, I simply loved him, fed him, became his friend, spent time with him, and offered to pray for him. Approximately four weeks into our friendship, Rob said, "So . . . when are you going to do it to me?" I was confused, so he continued, "You know, pray that prayer you've been talkin' about? You know, lead me to Christ?" I didn't have to be a rocket scientist to figure out that it was time to pray with Rob to receive Christ.

After he became a Christian, I made a deal to trade one of his necklaces for one of mine. We went into our bookstore and ordered over sixty necklaces with Christian symbols, trading straight across, one for one. What a joy it was to see him walk out with over sixty new necklaces and a grin from ear to ear.

Recently, Rob came into my office to thank me for showing him genuine love and unconditional acceptance. He told me that he was committing himself to loving others just as I had loved him. He told me that he had spent the last few months giving away his necklaces to people all over Portland, just to let them know that He loved them and cared for them. To be honest, he looks much better without the five pounds of metal around his neck!

A person's perception of God's love and forgiveness directly reflects the way in which he or she will receive our Christian message. Most people fear that God will judge them and make their life miserable. Therefore, love becomes a key ingredient in defusing the misconceptions of those whom God puts in our path.

Actions Speak Louder than Words

The message of the Cross is more than sharing some facts about a historical event. In the past, apologetic arguments left to themselves have done little to compel people to turn their entire lives over to Jesus Christ. Without showing significant care (coupled with strategic intercession) words alone will only result in conversations that yield no lasting fruit.

Donald Posterski comments, "When people were more interested in resolving the meaning of life, offering reasons for faith in Christ often prompted people to reflect and to respond. But the demotion of word has led to a loss of confidence in ideas and reason." [23] Because we are attempting to impact a generation that is no longer motivated by intellect and reason, we must communicate the Gospel to them in a way that goes beyond mere presentation of fact.

SEVEN PRACTICAL INGREDIENTS IN CARING FOR THE LOST

The eternal truths found in this parable are important principles for unlocking the hearts of our friends and neighbors who do not know Christ. His desire is that we would have His heart for the lost and that we would treat people the way He would if he were physically on earth today. If we are going to be successful in reaching the lost as twenty-first century Christians, we need to apply these seven ingredients to our lives.

Caring Goes Where the Lost Are

Luke 10:33: *"Then a despised Samaritan came along, and when he saw the man he felt deep pity."*

There is a significant difference between the Samaritan and the other religious men mentioned in this parable. While telling this story to the lawyer, Jesus mentioned that the Levite and the Priest *did see* the man and his condition, but they *"went to the other side."* The Samaritan, of course, went to where the man was. Scholars have debated the reasons for their lack of concern or involvement. Some have said it could have been that they did not want to defile themselves by touching a bloody man. They could have been on their way to a feast or even the temple. Others have speculated that they may have been preoccupied with 'more important' priorities. This man could have cost them a great deal of time and energy. Others have even stated that to stop and help someone in this area of the country, on this highway filled with robbers and thieves, opened oneself up for the same risk of being beaten and robbed. Whatever their reasons may have been, they missed an opportunity to touch a life and be written about in the Bible in a more positive way.

Stop for a moment and ask yourself these questions:

1. How do I respond when I see someone in need or even in gross sin?
2. Do I see the need but continue on my way, not doing anything about the situation?
3. Do I look at meeting the needs of others as a pleasure or a pain?
4. How often am I put into the path of someone but go to the 'other side' to avoid having to get involved?

If you are like the rest of us, these questions should bring some conviction. At the crossroads of every opportunity is the choice to either be used mightily by God, or simply miss the opportunity to touch a life.

It is only in the case of the Samaritan that he *"came along."* This literally means that he met the wounded man on his level. He got down where the man was, humbled himself, and made the first step toward unlocking his heart. He crossed over the road and crawled down into the ditch. He had to notice where the wounded man was, make the effort to stop his current course, and cross the road. Yes, it required a risk, but one well worth taking for the sake of another human life.

The only way we will ever get the city into our church is to first get our church out into the city.

Recent surveys have shown that many people are reluctant to even walk through the doors of a church building. For many years we have preached a message of "come," not a message of "go." Jesus rarely witnessed inside the temple, and the apostles, for the most part, ministered the Gospel in the marketplace. One simple reason they were so successful is because that is where the lost people were!

The place where you will best be used by God to touch people is where they live. Make it a priority to begin looking for opportunities to show Christ's love in their homes, in businesses, in schools, in offices, wherever there are lost people.

Caring Shows Value over Words

Luke 10:33: *". . . he felt deep pity."*

This Samaritan man wasn't involved in some Saturday service project, nor was he performing a mere religious duty. He truly cared for this wounded man. The Greek word used to describe compassion in this Scripture is the word *splagchnizomai* which literally means "to have your bowels yearning." It gives the impression of "feeling another's pain as if you were experiencing it yourself." [24]

In this parable, Jesus carefully used the best word to describe His heart toward hurting, lost people. Jesus probably knew the condition of the lawyer's heart and was trying to crack the hardness.

Jesus' whole earthly ministry is laced with this one concept, even to the point of bearing our sins on Calvary; Jesus cares about every need we have.

There are forty-six examples in the Gospels in which Christ showed his genuine care for someone in a witnessing situation. Here are a just a few scriptural references (emphasis mine):

> Matthew 9:36: *"He felt great pity for the crowds that came, because their problems were so great and they didn't know where to go for help. They were like sheep without a shepherd."*

> Matthew 14:14: *"A vast crowd was there as he stepped from the boat, and he had compassion on them and healed their sick."*

> Matthew 15:32: *"Then Jesus called his disciples to him and said, 'I feel sorry for these people. They have been here with me for three days, and they have nothing left to eat. I don't want to send them away hungry, or they will faint along the road.'"*

> Matthew 20:34: *"Jesus felt sorry for them and touched their eyes. Instantly they could see! Then they followed him."*

> Luke 7:13: *"When the Lord saw her, his heart overflowed with compassion. 'Don't cry!' he said."*

These scriptures show that Christ cared for those he ministered to. His compassion cracked their hardness and opened the door for real change. In order for our words to matter, we need to make sure we truly love them first.

Caring is not Condemning

> Luke 10:34: *"Kneeling beside him, the Samaritan soothed his wounds with medicine and bandaged them."*

It is important to point out the racial tension and hatred between the Jews and Samaritans. For the Samaritan, it would have been popular and even socially acceptable to leave this man to die. Instead he chose to stop and help.

Note that it says, *"the Samaritan soothed his wounds with medicine and bandaged them."* It does not say that he poured salt on the wounds. He did not say, "It serves you right! You deserve to be punished." Through his genuine compassion, the Samaritan treated the man the way that he would have wanted to be treated. Here is a humorous, yet sad, account of some people's perception of those in the pit:

Subjective Man – "I think I know how you feel."

Objective Man – "It stands to reason that eventually someone would fall in that pit."

Optimist – "Cheer up, things could be worse."

Pessimist – "Things will get worse."

Religious Man – "You need to pray through this season in the pit."

Self-Righteous Man – "I'm glad I am not like that man in the pit."

Judgmental Man – "Serves you right, you deserve that pit."

Self-Made Man – "If you had your act together, you wouldn't be in that pit."

Intellectual Man – "If he were smarter, he wouldn't be in that pit."

Selfish Man – "Better you than me in that pit."

Cynical Man – "Hey, life is the pits."

Fatalist – "Pits happen."

Self-Pity Man – "You haven't seen anything until you have seen my pit."

Humanist – "I feel your pain as you lie in the pit."

Preacher – "Hey, you make a great sermon illustration lying there in that pit."

Hyper-Faith Man – "Just confess it-a, you're not in-a pit-a."

Philosopher – "We need to consider the deeper meaning of this pit."

Theologian – "We need to look at the higher meaning of this pit."

Cruel Man – He walks by and drops a rock in the pit.

Self-Centered Man – "It's not my problem, it's your pit."

Busy Person – "I don't have time for this pit."

Indifferent Man – "Who cares about this pit."

Jesus – Walks by, kneels down, and takes the time to lift the man out of the pit.

Unfortunately, most of us are quick to condemn and judge those who are involved in ungodly habits or sins! We may have never looked closely at the way Jesus led people to Himself through His kindness and mercy. Seeing people through Jesus' eyes does not mean that we approve of their sins; it merely means that we accept them as individuals. We must learn to separate the sins of the person from the person who sins. We are all sinners, and we all fall short of God's glory. If it weren't for the grace of God each of us would burn in the same eternal fire as the prostitute, the murderer, or the thief.

Think back to your life before Christ. How much sin did you allow in your life? How thankful were you for the person who came and loved you for who you were going to be, not for who you were at the time? I will always be indebted to a man named Mike Shreve, who simply loved me, despite my gross sin. He understood that it was the conviction of the Holy Spirit, not the condemnation of man that caused people to become more like Christ.

Caring is a Sacrifice

> Luke 10:34: *"Then he put the man on his own donkey and took him to an inn . . ."*

The Samaritan man was on a journey, just like the Levite and the priest. However, he not only stopped for a moment to help the wounded man, but he also completely altered his plans—much like Dave Finley's Good Samaritan, Randy Stevenson. The Good Samaritan put the wounded man on his animal and walked to an inn.

In this portion of the parable Christ wants us to grasp that genuine sacrifice shows the true condition of one's heart. Knowing that sacrifice is transmitted as unusual love, He made this message of sacrifice frequent throughout the Gospels:

> Matthew 10:39: *"If you cling to your life, you will lose it; but if you give it up for me, you will find it."*

> Luke 9:23: *"Then He said to the crowd, 'If any of you wants to be my follower, you must put aside your selfish ambition, shoulder your cross daily, and follow me."*

> John 15:13: *"And here is how to measure it—the greatest love is shown when people lay down their lives for their friends."*

Sacrifice is not a popular idea in Western Christianity. Sacrifice of time, energy, and finances for the sake of someone else always confronts personal desires and affluence.

The truth of the matter is that you really haven't lived the way Christ intended until you are willing to serve others—expecting nothing in return. The true heart of Christ is helping people out of the goodness of one's heart, not out of expectation of repayment or personal gain.

Caring Produces Life

Luke 10:34: *". . . where he took care of him."*

Without the nurturing care of the Samaritan, the wounded man would have died. His caring produced life. It wasn't his words but his selfless actions that made all the difference in this man's rehabilitation.

A story that illustrates this principle well is the ministry of Catherine Lawes, wife to the warden of Sing Sing prison:

In 1921, Lewis Lawes became the warden at Sing Sing Prison. No prison was tougher than Sing Sing during that time. But when Warden Lawes retired some twenty years later, that prison had become a humanitarian institution. Those who studied the system said credit for the change belonged to Lawes. But when he was asked about the transformation, here's what he said: "I owe it all to my wonderful wife, Catherine, who is buried outside the prison walls."

Catherine Lawes was a young mother, with three small children, when her husband became the warden. Everybody warned her from the beginning that she should never set foot inside the prison walls, but that didn't stop Catherine! When the first prison basketball game was held, she went, walking into the gym with her three little kids and sitting in the stands with the inmates.

Her attitude was, "My husband and I are going to take care of these men, and I believe they will take care of us! I don't have to worry."

She insisted on getting acquainted with them and their records. She discovered that one convicted murderer was blind, so she paid him a visit. Holding his hand in hers, she said, "Do you read Braille?"

"What's Braille?" he asked.

Then she taught him how to read. Years later he would weep in love for her.

Later, Catherine found a deaf-mute inmate in the prison. She went to school to learn how to use sign language. Many said that Catherine Lawes was the body of Jesus that came alive again in Sing Sing from 1921 to 1937.

Then she was killed in a car accident. The next morning, Warden Lawes didn't come to work, so the acting warden took his place. It seemed that almost instantly the prison knew something was wrong.

The following day, Catherine's body was resting in a casket in her home, three quarters of a mile from the prison. As the acting warden took his early morning walk, he was shocked to see a large crowd of the toughest, hardest looking criminals gathered like a herd of animals at the main gate. He came closer and noted tears of grief and sadness. He knew how much they loved Catherine. He turned and faced the men. "All right, men, you can go. Just be sure and check in tonight!" Then he opened the gate and a parade of criminals walked, without a guard, the three-quarters of a mile to stand in line and pay their final respects to Catherine Lawes. And every one of them checked back in that night. Every one![25]

Caring produces life. If we will be faithful to care for everyone we reach out to, we will have the joy of one day seeing the effects of our sacrifice.

Caring Empowers Your Words

Luke 10:35 (emphasis mine): *"The next day he handed the innkeeper two pieces of silver and told him to take care of the man. 'If his bill runs higher that that,' he said, 'I'll pay the difference the next time I am here.'"*

This portion of the parable settles any concern about wrong motive and empowers the words of the Good Samaritan. I am sure that the lawyer was squirming at this point in Jesus' narrative.

There are three significant statements that should challenge each of us concerning how far we are really willing to go in meeting the needs of others:

"The next day . . ." This statement clearly shows that the Samaritan stayed there with the wounded man until the following morning. He didn't just drop him off and leave him in the care of another. His priority was to make sure that this man was going to be all right.

". . . he handed the innkeeper two pieces of silver . . ." A denarii was equivalent to a day's wages. Without anyone asking, and knowing that he would never be repaid, he gave up two days worth of hard work to ensure that the recovering man would not be burdened with his own debt.

" . . . 'If his bill runs higher that that,' he said, 'I'll pay the difference the next time I am here.'" If taking time out of his life and giving the innkeeper two days of wages was not enough, he added the final touch by offering an open-ended ticket for the man. He had genuinely felt his pain as if it were his own and was willing to pay the whole cost for this man's recovery.

An Indonesian missionary applied these Good Samaritan principles literally when launching his ministry:

After moving his family into a slum area in Surabaya and building his home out of crates like everyone else, he figured out that deed had to precede words. Surrounded by devout Muslims, the businessman began asking his well of friends for donations, and then he called the men of the community together. "My Christian friends want you to have this money to build your mosque" was his surprise offer. He then spent the next six months helping them to build the mosque. He began a Bible study for the people with whom he worked, and eventually thirty adult Muslims became believers and were baptized, while thirty teenagers came to afternoon classes.[26]

He knew that his actions would empower his words. The fruit of his labor had an astonishing effect. Doing the will of God showed the Muslims he was attempting to reach that the God of the Bible actually existed in a way that really mattered. Love for people creates love for God!

Caring Draws the Lost to God

It is through the previous six principles that the seventh principle will be implemented. Each ingredient is a stepping stone to bringing a person to Christ. It is at this point that we can share the message of the Gospel with the assurance that our motives are pure and that we genuinely care for the individual we have been trying to reach.

Telling God's truth and doing God's truth are meant to be two parts of a whole. When they stand together, the Church of Christ is not only built up, but it is also given credibility in the eyes of the world, and people are drawn closer to God.

Caring by going to where the lost are; giving credence to our caring though compassion; refraining from condemning the lost; sacrificing our lives for the lost; and caring long enough to see life produced will empower our words and draw the lost toward God. We need all seven components to work together for our caring to work. Choose today to care for the lost—no matter the cost!

MY JESUS TODAY PRAYER

Dear Jesus,
I want to be a Good Samaritan,
A person who loves others the way You do.
You have given me the eyes to see and the ears to hear,
May my heart now beat for the lost.
I pray that You would forgive me
For the times I have been judgmental.
Help me to love others unconditionally
And thus live life like You would.
Help me to remember
That actions speak louder than words.
Help me to care by going to where the lost are
And giving value to lost people.
Help me to love sacrificially
And produce life in others through my caring.
May my caring empower my words
And draw the lost toward You.
I want to be a person
That can love people into the Kingdom.
Make me a person who cares for others
Because they need to be cared for.
Thank You again for the opportunity
To reach lost people on Your behalf.
I put my heart in your hands
And pray for Your will to be done with it.
Amen

CHAPTER FIVE

HIS GRACE:

LOVING

THE UNLOVELY

AND UNJUST

JOHN 8:1-11

The colorful autumn trees were a visual reminder that winter was just around the corner. Childhood memories of raking leaves in the yard were fresh in Dave's mind as he drove past his parent's home. For the past five months he had made it a point to drive the "long way" to work, hoping that he would see his mom and get the chance to speak with her while his dad was gone.

Since arriving back in Newcastle, Dave's father had made it clear that he was no longer welcome in the family home. He had been told that as long as he was one of those "radical religious fanatics" he would have to find another place to live. Dave found an inexpensive one-room apartment across town; however, that didn't make his desire to be with his family any easier. All he could do at this point was pray for his dad and trust God to reunite them in his time.

To make matters worse, he was also having a problem finding a local church where he could fit in. He had prayed continually for direction, but every Sunday left him more confused.

Dave landed a job as a clerk at his older brother's law firm, Browski, Finley and Clark. This was the perfect job for Dave. He had asked the Lord to give him the opportunity to have constant contact with the world so that he could share the Gospel. His daily stops at the courthouse, district attorney's office, and other lawyers' offices gave him the ability to build relationships with all of the clerical staff at each place. Dave could see that these people needed Jesus in their lives.

However, his newfound heart for people seemed to get him in trouble with Mr. Browski. Over the past few weeks, Dave had been reprimanded a few times for spending more time on an errand than he should have. In Dave's mind, he couldn't help it. If someone was in trouble and in need of some love and attention, he felt he had the answer to their problem. But Mr. Browski felt that Dave was to mind his own business and do what he was paid to do—which didn't include meeting the needs of every person in the town. Dave just couldn't help it. After his tragedy in The City, he looked at people's problems a little differently—the way Jesus would.

Amy Jefferson was no exception. Since she was hired on as the office receptionist, Dave knew that something wasn't right. Every time he would talk to her, her head would look down, as if she were ashamed of something. She would never look directly into his eyes. She seemed shy and distant, but Dave sensed this was more from a wounded past than from her personality.

Mr. Browski didn't seem to help her out either. His rudeness and unreasonable work demands seemed to put additional strain on her. It seemed he went out of his way to make her life miserable. He had been out-voted two to one on hiring her and turned all his resentment on her.

————————————— ▬ —————————————

Dave's brother Michael waited for him to show up for their weekly breakfast time. Ever since Dave had come to work at the firm, Michael had made it a point to spend some time with his brother in order to shape him into the worker he should be. Dave arrived a few minutes late and apologized to his brother.

After a few minutes of small talk, Dave shifted gears and blurted out an assault on Mr. Browski.

"I don't mean to be disrespectful or anything like that, but what is up with Mr. Browski?"

Michael looked a little puzzled, trying to figure out where Dave was going with this. Dave could have been referring to any number of Browski-related incidents. "What do you mean?"

"He seems to have it out for Amy. Every time I am in the building, I see him in the reception area giving her a hard time. And he's not trying to be funny."

Although Michael didn't want to expose her past, he felt that it would be necessary to give Dave a proper perspective of the situation. With great reservation and caution, Michael began to unfold the circumstances that led to hiring Amy at the firm.

As Michael shared her heart-wrenching story, Dave was gripped with newfound compassion. Compassion for Amy and her entire situation. Compassion for Michael as he stepped out on a limb and hired her, regardless of her past. Compassion for Mr. Browski that he would tolerate such a situation in his reputable law firm.

It was another usual gloomy Monday morning. The cold, drizzly rain and layer of fog over the city made it a day that would be better spent in front of a warm fire, nestled on the couch with a good novel. The thought of driving documents all over town made Dave as irritable as the rest of the staff.

It seemed that everyone was on edge. Amy was her usual shy self. Michael seemed to be unusually quiet as he got his cup of coffee and headed into his office, closing the door behind him. And Mr. Browski rolled through the door complaining once again about having to park a block from the office and walk in the rain.

"I am sick and tired of dealing with incompetent people!" Mr. Browski shouted. "Can't they just put more parking spots along the side of our building?"

Everyone remained silent.

"And what about this pile of magazines sitting out here all messy. Didn't I tell you on Friday to straighten up around here?" Amy knew those comments were specially directed at her.

"What is with that outfit? Are we running a law firm or a dance club? Can't you get something a little more professional to wear?" Mr. Browski threw up his hands and stormed into his office.

Dave looked at Amy, and he could see tears welling up in her eyes. "That's not the way to start the day," he said to her as he headed out the door for his daily deliveries. "I'll be praying for you . . . and for him!"

Dave left feeling the heaviness of Amy's pain. He could *see* she needed Jesus. He could *hear* the Holy Spirit drawing Him to minister to her. He could *feel* her hopelessness, just as if she were the man left half dead in the ditch, crying out for someone to help. Although he knew her situation from his conversation with Michael, there seemed to be a new *grace* to love her anyway. To love the unlovely just like Jesus did.

Out in the rain he went, his mind preoccupied with Amy's situation, wondering what would happen next.

The office was decorated with all of the Christmas trimmings. Blinking lights surrounded the windows, Christmas cards were strung along the back wall, and bowls of candy canes and fudge covered the counter. Each person had also added his or her own personal touch with decorations on their desks. It was part of the yearly contest. Since the winner would earn a half-day off the afternoon of the last workday before Christmas, every desk seemed to portray the personality of its owner. Including Amy's . . . her desk was empty.

It was the Friday before Christmas, and the staff Christmas party was winding down. Mrs. Applewaite had won the desk contest for the third year in a row and was preparing to leave for the remainder of the day. Suddenly, there was a commotion from the front of the office. Mr. Browski could be heard over the background holiday music. Amy's pity-party rubbed Mr. Browski the wrong way, and he finally decided it was the last straw.

"Why don't you just get out!" he yelled. "You're not wanted around here anyway!" His face grew increasingly red with anger. "If it were my choice, you would never have been here in the first place! You make *me* out to be the bad guy, Miss Jefferson! Haven't you told everyone *your* story?!" His anger only grew until he crossed the line of acceptable behavior.

"Why don't you tell everyone, 'Miss Convicted-Prostitute-Felon!' Tell them how you worked the streets, did drugs, shoplifted; tell them about your three years in the state pen. Tell them how you changed your name and moved here to try to cover up who you *really* are!"

The sweet Christmas spirit was sucked out of the room like a vacuum. Everyone stood stunned. Michael looked on in disbelief. Someone turned and walked into the kitchen area to escape the tension. Others just stared in astonishment.

Something began to stir in Dave. The Holy Spirit brought a righteous indignation. He saw Amy's tears of utter humiliation streaming down her cheeks. On the other side of the desk was Mr. Browski; small beads of sweat had formed on his forehead. At the risk of losing his job, Dave stepped in front of Amy and stared directly at Mr. Browski. It took all the courage he could muster to speak into the situation, but he felt he had come to another incident in which he had no choice.

"How can you stand here and say these things during this very special season?! A season of joy! A season of peace! Where is your good will towards men?"

Mr. Browski just stared, surprised at Dave's challenge to his authority.

"Haven't you ever made a mistake? What does *your* past look like, Julian Browski? Should we dig up all of your bad decisions? I wonder what we would find to broadcast?" Dave's cajoling added tension to the already tight situation.

His attention then focused on people in the room, and his voice of confrontation turned to a soft-spoken compassion. "Look, we have all made bad choices. We all have been given another chance. It shouldn't be any different for Amy."

Mr. Browski took a step backward with a blank look on his face. He realized that he was in the wrong, but his pride kept him silent.

"Can't we all, in the spirit of Christmas, be forgiving as we have been forgiven? Don't you think she already feels bad? Can't we just leave the past alone, and give her a chance for her future." Dave's boldness began to neutralize the tension and allow a glimmer of hope to enter the room.

"We should realize that we all make mistakes, and we have no business accusing her—unless we point the finger at ourselves as well. Let's just leave it alone!"

One by one, each person made their way back to their cubicles. The party was over, at least for this year. All that remained were the plates of half-eaten cake, cups filled with sparkling cider and, after a few minutes, Amy and Dave.

"Hey, I am really sorry about that," Dave said softly.

She looked up into Dave's eyes and sobbed, "I feel so humiliated. I thought this could be my second chance, but now there is no way!"

"Listen, Amy, I actually can relate. I have made some real dumb choices in my past as well. I am pretty ashamed of my mistakes. But I no longer carry the pain and sorrow of those mistakes. It is like I told you before—Jesus Christ has forgiven me and set me free." Amy's curiosity was finally piqued.

"Can it really be that easy? Can He really forgive me and remove all my pain?"

"Yes, He can," Dave said with confidence. "Amy, Jesus says in the Bible that for those who confess their sins, He is faithful and just to forgive them of their sin and will cleanse them of all unrighteousness. Amy, today you can ask Jesus into your heart and no longer be condemned. You too can be set free once and for all. Just go and sin no more."

The conversation had a lasting impact on the lives of both Dave and Amy. For Dave, he was able to lead another lost person to the foot of the cross; for Amy, it was the beginning of a new life in Christ.

As Dave shut the car door, he looked around to make sure no one was around. He put the keys in the ignition and let out a loud shout, "Hallelujah! God, You are awesome! Thank You, Jesus, for answering my prayers and touching Amy's life!"

As he drove by his parent's house, he noticed the silhouette of his family through the living room curtains. He longed to be at home with his family and made yet another plea, "God, if You can save Amy, You can save my dad! Please, Lord, touch him."

It was with that closing prayer that Dave would end another day. A day filled with great tension, yet great excitement. A day which he saw the way Jesus saw. A day in which he heard the voice of the Holy Spirit directing him to divine appointments. A day in which he felt the heart of compassion for the lost. A day marked with the grace to love the unlovely, just as Jesus did. But something was still missing. In order to live life more like Jesus would, Dave needed faith for the impossible.

HIS GRACE

JOHN 8:1-11

Jesus returned to the Mount of Olives, but early the next morning he was back again at the Temple. A crowd soon gathered, and he sat down and taught them. As he was speaking, the teachers of religious law and Pharisees brought a woman they had caught in the act of adultery. They put her in front of the crowd.

"Teacher," they said to Jesus, "this woman was caught in the very act of adultery. The law of Moses says to stone her. What do you say?"

They were trying to trap him into saying something they could use against him, but Jesus stooped down and wrote in the dust with his finger. They kept demanding an answer, so he stood up again and said," All right, stone her. But let those who have never sinned throw the first stones!" Then he stooped down again and wrote in the dust.

When the accusers heard this, they slipped away one by one, beginning with the oldest, until only Jesus was left in the middle of the crowd with the woman. Then Jesus stood up again and said to her, "Where are your accusers? Didn't even one of them condemn you?"

"No, Lord," she said.

And Jesus said, "Neither do I. Go and sin no more."

REMEMBERING HIS GRACE

Can you envision the intensity of the scene? Jesus had just been surrounded by a crowd of spiritually hungry people, when they were interrupted by an angry mob that brought a woman caught in the act of adultery. I can just imagine her being pulled into the crowd, half-dressed, clothes torn, dirt clinging to her sweat-stained face, shaking in terror as she realized her life would soon end.

The words of the Law were clear about her fate, *"Both the man and the woman must be put to death"* (Leviticus 20:10). She had been caught, torn from the secrecy of her hidden sin, and catapulted into eyes of the world to face the consequences of her horrible acts.

However, in a matter of moments—and much to everyone's surprise—the words of Jesus eliminated the certainty of her death sentence. The death penalty was replaced with an unexpected and undeserved display of love, compassion, and grace!

I am sure that she was flooded with an overwhelming sense of gratefulness to the very deepest part of her soul. Receiving an unconditional pardon that she didn't deserve (grace) must have left her grateful for the rest of her life! You can bet that she left a changed woman. Although the Bible doesn't reveal what happened to her after this encounter with Jesus, I am sure that she changed the way she lived because of God's grace.

Can you remember the first time you were introduced to His grace? Do you remember feeling condemned and knowing that your sins had earned you a one-way ticket straight to hell? Do you recall the thoughts that raced through your mind as you realized that Jesus had paid the price for you already and that the ticket's destination had now changed?

That was almost twenty years ago for me. I can still remember the waves of grateful emotion that consumed every waking moment for many months after my conversion. I was just thankful to be alive! I was excited to have another chance at life. If it wasn't for His unfailing love and grace for me, a wretched sinner, I would be either dead or in prison by now.

However, twenty years later, I must admit that there are times when I can forget just how far God has brought me. If I'm not careful, my human nature (my Pharisee nature) kicks in, and I quickly assume that I actually deserve all of God's blessings that come my way. After all, I am a pretty good guy, right?

To add to the equation, the more I work to become like Him, the less I think I look or act like the people living without Him. My attitude has changed, my character is being transformed—I even dress differently since I have become a Christian. This causes me to notice just how different I am . . . and how "sinful" they are!

I am sure that you occasionally struggle with the same challenges. If we are not careful, we can become, to the lost, just like the Pharisees were to the prostitute—a "Mr. Browski" to those who need us most. How soon we can forget His amazing grace!

THE NEED FOR GRACE

Grace is a very difficult concept to understand. All our natural inclinations run contrary to this great truth. Paul Tournier, the Swiss psychiatrist and author, observed that our tendency is to be lenient or indulgent toward our own weaknesses (i.e., "I'm overweight because it runs in my family") while bringing others to account (i.e., "Why doesn't he discipline his eating?"). There needs to be a reversal in our attitudes here.[27] We are quick to judge others by their actions while judging ourselves based upon our intentions.

The truth of the matter is that we all make mistakes, we all fall short of God's glory (see Romans 3:23), and we all deserve to be punished (see Romans 6:23). The revelation of this truth makes the concept of grace worth pursuing. This pursuit must not be just for the fulfillment of one's own self-gratification, but also to dispense, to all those who surround us daily, this divine solution. We must come to the conclusion that *all* humanity is in desperate need of His grace, and we are His vessels, which contain this eternal blessing.

E. Stanley Jones has said, "Grace binds you with far stronger cords than the cords of duty or obligation can bind you. Grace is free, but when once you take it you are bound forever to the Giver, and bound to catch the spirit of the Giver. Like produces like. Grace makes you gracious."[28]

Grace, by nature, is what a person least deserves. It is how God relates to us, and it is how He wants us, in turn, to respond to others. The truth of God's grace, as we receive it and as we exercise it, could be called the starting point of all spiritual progress. As the apostle Paul wrote, *"This same Good News that came to you is going out all over the world. It is changing lives everywhere, just as it changed yours that very first day you heard and understood the truth about God's great kindness to sinners"* (Colossians 1:6).[29]

The need for grace is ongoing. As Christians, we need to give the same grace we have received and in turn help the many people around us who need that second chance, no matter what they might look like.

THE HARVEST IS UNLOVELY

It doesn't take much searching to find people in need of God's unending grace. Our world is filled with people who could be classified as the "unlovely" of society.

Take a moment to reflect back on the last time you came in contact with someone similar to those described in each of the following scenarios. Don't read the descriptions quickly, but stop and ponder each situation:

The Homeless Person: He pushes a shopping cart out in the rain and holds a sign that says, "Please help me. I am hungry and homeless. Will work for food." This person is dressed in five layers of ragged clothing and appears to be quite filthy.

The Single Mom: With four children, she is living on welfare and food stamps (your hard-earned tax dollars). Her children are blatantly disobedient and unruly. They are dressed in worn-out clothing with shaggy hairdos and dirty faces. It appears that she has given up on her children, as well as her own future. The thought of getting ahead seems beyond her reach.

The Runaway Teen: He lives on the street with a pack of rebellious friends. He is dressed in black leather and pierced his nose. White makeup covers his face, and his lips are smeared with black lipstick. His wild outfit is completed with a Marilyn Manson T-shirt.

The Homosexual with AIDS: He lived a life of immorality. He flaunted his alternate lifestyle, hung out at gay bars, and spoke strongly against "judgmental Christians." He contracted AIDS and is in the final stages of this dreadful disease. He is lonely, depressed, and looking for answers.

The Felon: He was recently released from prison after serving three years for child molestation. His arms are covered with prison tattoos. He is now looking for employment and a place to live in your neighborhood. He says that he is interested in getting his life right and is looking for someone to help guide him toward success.

If you were to come in contact with any of these individuals today, how would you perceive them? Would you give them a second look? Would your thoughts be of compassion or condemnation? How would they affect your emotions? Would you be quick to judge them, or would you pray for them? What measures could be taken to show them the grace that was freely given to you?

Whether we are willing to accept it or not, the truth *is* that the harvest is made up of people—like those mentioned above! Jesus came to reach these kinds of people. He touched the poor, the sick, the lost, the abused, the accused, and the accursed. He hung out with sinners, ate with them, and even went to their homes. He died for all sinners (see John 3:16), including you and me!

Jesus' conduct toward the unlovely repelled the Pharisees, who were "more holy" than this group of hurting, lost people. With their noses pointed skyward, they constantly challenged Jesus about His behavior toward sinners. One example is found in Matthew 9:11-13, *"The Pharisees were indignant. 'Why does your teacher eat with such scum?' they asked his disciples. When he heard this, Jesus replied, 'Healthy people don't need a doctor—sick people do.' Then he added. 'Now go and learn the meaning of this Scripture: "I want you to be merciful; I don't want your sacrifices." For I have come to call sinners, not those who think they are already good enough.'"*

Never before has the harvest been so ripe! If we would just look at the world that surrounds us, we would see countless opportunities to love the unlovely. We must assume the responsibility of sharing the gospel with the unlovely. We must see with His eyes, hear with His ears, love with a heart of compassion, and then extend the loving hand of grace.

Pharisaic Response to the Unlovely

This transformation doesn't come easy for any Christian. I have seen this in my own life as well as in lives of many in the well-established church I currently attend.

At City Bible Church, we have made strong headway toward reaching the lost in our city. God has blessed us by bringing hundreds of "unlovely" people into our "lovely" church. The ability to accept the harvest is easier for some than for others. It seems that, in many cases, newer Christians who remember what it was like to live without Christ have greater compassion for the unlovely. While mature Christians, who have worked hard to establish themselves and their families in the church, work hard to protect that which took many years to build. Unfortunately, they see "unlovely" as a threat instead of a blessed inheritance.

I remember standing in the back of our sanctuary with our Senior Pastor, Frank Damazio, during a drama outreach called *Eternity: The*

Ultimate Experience. As we looked out at the packed crowd of over three thousand people, he took a long, deep breath, exhaled, smiled, and said, "I love the smell of sinners!"

I am sure to some that night, the smell of alcohol and tobacco was repulsive, the sound of cussing in the sanctuary absurd, and the style of dress unacceptable. But to Pastor Frank, it was an answer to prayer. God was bringing sinners to get saved. He understood that the best place for these hell-bound, lost people was in the presence of the Almighty, hearing a Gospel message.

Recently, during a Sunday morning service, I had the privilege of meeting a young, homeless man named, Duckman. Through the eyes of a Pharisee, he definitely didn't fit in with our polished church crowd. His last ten visits to other churches validated this fact as he was politely asked to leave and never to return.

During our opening service prayer time, I felt compelled to go over and pray for him and get to know him a little more. My experience with this fine young man reminded me again that "you can't judge a book by its cover." He was a very polite and respectful man. At the end of our time of prayer, he looked at me with a big smile and said, "You know, this is the first church that hasn't told me to leave!" With that comment, I knew that I had properly represented the heart of Christ toward this young man as he was searching for God. He knew, when he left the church that day, that God loved Him unconditionally and accepted him just as he was.

In his book, *The Jesus I Never Knew*, Phillip Yancey draws this conclusion regarding the condition of the modern day Church. He states, "As I read the stories of Jesus and study the history of the early church, I feel both inspired and troubled . . . In view of Jesus' clear example, how is it that the church has now become a community of respectability, where the down-and-out no longer feel welcome?" [30]

We must analyze our heart toward society and make whatever changes are necessary to keep from closing ourselves off from the unlovely. I think we all would agree that there is a certain degree of "Pharisaism" alive and well in almost any church today. Let's look at what role a Pharisee played during Jesus' time on earth:

> Pharisaism, as portrayed during the time of Jesus, was to represent the pure community and the true people of God and

prepare them for the coming of the Messiah by complete adherence to every minute detail of the Law. Jesus met Israel as it strove for true faith in obedience to God but had become totally hardened in formalism, thus barring itself from precisely what it was searching to do, to please God and to prepare itself to receive the coming Messiah.[31]

The society was, in effect, a religious caste system based on steps toward holiness, and the Pharisees' scrupulosity reinforced the system daily. All their rules on washing hands and avoiding defilement were an attempt to make themselves acceptable to God. Had not God set forth a list of desirable (spotless) and undesirable (flawed, unclean) animals for use in sacrifice? Had not God banned sinners, menstruating women, the physically deformed, and the other 'undesirables' from the temple? The Qumran community of the Essenes made a firm rule, "No madman, or lunatic, or simpleton, or fool, no blind man, or maimed, or lame, or deaf man, and no minor shall enter into the Community."[32]

It is our responsibility, as His followers, not to allow this attitude to surface in our own hearts. On one hand, we must continue to pursue the process of sanctification. On the other hand, this process of becoming more like Him cannot be the reason we no longer reach out to those in need of Christ. Allowing this subtle, yet deadly, disease into our hearts causes us to be consumed with our own traditions and robs us of our desire to be "light to the world" and "salt to earth."

The story of the Pharisees with the woman caught in adultery shows us some alarming heart conditions that we must avoid if we are to remain useful in reaching people.

- They elevated themselves above the others (see John 8:3).
- They were outwardly focused (see John 8:3).
- They were quick to point out others' weaknesses (see John 8:4).
- They focused on punishment, not on mercy (see John 8:5).
- They resisted the plan of grace (see John 8:5).
- They elevated approval over acceptance (see John 8:5).

– They viewed circumstance through the mind, not through the heart (see John 8:5).
– They had low tolerance for errors (see John 8:7).
– They were blind to their own spiritual condition (see John 8:7).
– They were unwilling to admit their own sin (see John 8:9).
– They promoted exclusion, not inclusion (see John 8:9).

Let us make it our aim to remove these ungodly traits and habits from our lives and focus on how we can respond to the unlovely the way Christ did.

Jesus' Response to the Unlovely

When I read the Gospels, there is one prevailing theme that demands my attention. It seems that lost people loved to hang around Jesus. I am often amazed at how He attracted multitudes of lost people, yet repelled the religious. He loved to hang out with sinners! He dined with lepers, fellow-shipped with tax collectors, honored women, touched the diseased, laughed with publicans, and defied customs by entering into the homes of pagans—all of which were forbidden by the "religious right."

Jesus was paving an entirely different road to freedom. It was a message of grace. It wasn't a lifestyle of daily sacrifices, empty rituals in empty temples, purification treatments, or association with the elite. His message was simply to follow Him.

Phillip Yancey summed it up by saying:

> In short, Jesus moved the emphasis from God's holiness (exclusive) to God's mercy (inclusive). Instead of the message, "No undesirables allowed," He proclaimed, "In God's kingdom there are no undesirables." By going out of his way to meet with the Gentiles, eat with sinners, and touch the sick, He extended the real hand of God's mercy. To Jewish leaders, Jesus' actions jeopardized the very existence of their religious caste system. No wonder the Gospels mention more than twenty occasions when they conspired against Jesus.
>
> Jesus was putting into practice "the great reversal" heralded in the Beatitudes. Normally in this world we look up to the rich, the beautiful, the successful. Grace, however, introduces a world of new logic. Because God loves the poor, the suffering,

the persecuted, so should we. Because God sees no undesirables, neither should we. By His own example, Jesus challenged us to look at the world through what Irenaeus would
call "grace-healed eyes."[33]

Time and time again, we see Jesus going out of his way to reach out to
the ones everyone else ignored. He brought healing to those others avoided.
Those whom the world saw as useless, He saw as useful. He showed all of
mankind that every person matters to God!

The story of John 8:1-11, as portrayed by Dave Finley and Amy
Jefferson, the receptionist ridiculed by Mr. Browski, is a classic example of
how these principles can be applied in a modern day context. Dave Finley
represents Jesus, Mr. Browski represents the pharisaic mindset, while Amy
represents the "unlovely" adulterous woman in need of a Savior. We need to
respond to similar situations like Dave did and remember it is better to offend
man than it is to offend God.

THE ROLE OF GRACE IN LOVING THE UNLOVELY

The most powerful tool that God uses in reaching past our sin to meet
needs is grace. But how can we dispense of grace? What can we learn from
John, chapter eight? Here are nine principles we can apply immediately that
will help us become "Jesus Today."

Grace Assumes the Same Level as the Sinner

John 8:6: ". . .But Jesus stooped down . . ."

We notice that Jesus chose to first position Himself with the woman,
and not with the Pharisees. He bent down to physically put her on His level.
This very act should remind us that we too were once on the same level as
this prostitute. What she deserved, we deserved. Her punishment was our
punishment. We too are mere sinners saved by grace.

When we communicate on the level of the sinner, the message we
bring has a better chance of acceptance. The perception of inequality (i.e.,
teacher/student, parent/child, holy/unholy) is eliminated. This is not to say
that we must compromise our standards or convictions, but that we do not
elevate ourselves as if we deserve, or have earned, His grace more than the
individual with whom we are communicating.

Many years ago, during the Jesus Movement, a Hippie wandered into a church service already in progress. While the preacher was still speaking, the Hippie marched down the center aisle and sat down cross-legged right in the middle of the floor in front of the pulpit. The congregation became restless at this disrespectful and distracting behavior by their barefooted, longhaired visitor.

Suddenly, an elderly deacon in his eighties stood up, grabbed his cane, and proceeded down the aisle. Many in the crowd smiled, waiting for the elderly man to put this young man in his place.

To their amazement, the elderly man sat down and crossed his legs on the floor right next to the Hippie. The pastor, with tears in his eyes, leaned over the pulpit and said, "What I am about to say, you will never remember, but what you just saw, you will never forget!"

So it is when we get on the sinner's level. Our acts of love, kindness, and compassion will never be forgotten by the individual to whom we are ministering. His power is found in His love.

Grace is Slow to Speak

John 8:6: *". . . and wrote in the dust with his finger."*

Grace is slow to speak, while judgment is quick to respond. One must pause and consider all things before replying.

I have found that it takes a few moments to transition out of my "temporal thinking" and into an "eternal mindset." Slowing down to observe, ponder, pray, and consider the example of Christ is key in showing grace to the "unlovely."

It is also important to remember that most sinners already know they are doing things that are wrong. They already feel terrible about their actions, condemned about their thoughts, and hopeless about their feelings. The last thing they desire is someone to come along and say, "You are a sinner," or, "I told you so." Sometimes the best posture is one of silence. Allow the Holy Spirit room to operate as you flood the sinner with His grace and love.

Grace Ignores the Critical Opinions of Others

John 8:7: *"They kept demanding an answer . . ."*

The Pharisees continued demanding a response from Jesus, and His decision to ignore them made them all the more vehement. For sure, they thought they had cornered Him once and for all, as He could not avoid the imputation of contradicting either the Law of Moses or His own message of grace. However, His silence did not represent one who was cornered without any options, but one who was purposefully ignoring the critical mindset that heaped condemnation upon this lonely, terrified woman.

If we are not careful, we can easily be persuaded by the mindset, comments, and actions of others. To further complicate matters, we are persuaded daily with cultural perspectives that dictate worth and value by the "toys" one owns and the outward appearance of one's body and dress. Society is merciless in stereotyping different sectors of the population and attaching levels of worth upon each group. For example, to some the rich are more important than the poor; the beautiful should be more esteemed than the unattractive; the intelligent deserve more recognition than the mentally impaired; the unborn are of less value than the parents' right to choose; men have more rights and deserve better pay than their female co-workers; and Caucasians are more elite than African-Americans, Hispanics, or other minority groups.

Our mindset must be the mind of Christ, not the mind of the world that surrounds us (see Romans 12:1-2). To properly show grace to the unlovely of the world, we must be ready to face alienation for our decision to side with those who are considered "non-productive" members of society.

Mr. Alter's fifth-grade class at Lake Elementary School in Oceanside, California, did just that. One morning fourteen boys came to school with no hair! Only one, however, had no choice in the matter. Ian O'Gorman, undergoing chemotherapy for lymphoma, faced the prospect of having his hair fall out in clumps. So he had his head shaved to get it over with all at once. Thirteen of his classmates responded by shaving their heads also, so Ian wouldn't feel out of place. Ten-year-old Kyle Hanslik started it all. He talked to some other boys, and before long, they all trekked to the barbershop. When asked why, Kyle said, "The last thing he would want is to not fit in. We just wanted to make him feel better."[34]

Grace Stands Up for the Truth

John 8:7: *". . . he stood up again . . ."*

At this point, the tension in the crowd was growing. The Pharisees had reached a boiling point, the accused woman had reached a melting point, and Jesus had reached a decision point. He would stand for what was right, not what was popular.

It would have been easier to agree with the Pharisees, stone the woman, and gain the approval of His contemporaries. It would have been easier to quote the Law and use it as a platform for another great message. But He straightened up, with the woman behind Him, the crowd beside Him, and the Pharisees in front of Him.

Luke 4:18 says, " . . . *for he has appointed me to preach the Good News to the poor.*" The world says, "They deserve the consequences of their lack of initiative." Truth says, *"He has sent me to proclaim that captives will be released,"* while the world says, "Too bad for them. Better luck next time." Truth says, *"He has sent me to proclaim that the blind will see,"* while the world says, "Leave them alone and don't force your religion on us or anyone! They can find it on their own." Truth says, *"He has sent me to proclaim that the downtrodden will be freed from their oppressors,"* while the world says, "Medicate them, institutionalize them, and get them out of our way. They are a hindrance to the forward progress of man." Stand up and speak the truth. The world needs truth!

Grace Confronts Judgmentalism while Still Remaining Humble

John 8:7: " . . . *and said, 'All right, stone her. But let those who have never sinned throw the first stones!'"*

At last He put them all to shame with this one poignant statement. He avoided the snare they had laid for Him and saved His own reputation. He neither reflected upon the Law, nor excused the sinner's guilt. In confronting the judgmental attitude of the Pharisees, He once again showed the crowd why He came into the world—to bring sinners to repentance. Not to destroy, but to save!

His goal was to bring the young woman to repentance and reveal the hardness of the accusers. In doing that, he hoped they would humble themselves and seek salvation. They sought to ensnare Him; He sought to convert them. Jesus masterfully confronted their attitude and perception of the situation while remaining humble.

Grace Supports the Desperate during Hopeless Times

John 8:9: *"When the accusers heard this, they slipped away one by one, beginning with the oldest, until only Jesus was left in the middle of the crowd with the woman."*

Dave Finley portrayed this point by standing up for Amy at one of the most humiliating moments in her life. Just as Jesus did in the Scripture above, he stayed with her until the crowd had dissolved and all threats were removed.

Grace supports, while Pharisaism tears down. It is at these critical points in our lives that we are most open to the Gospel or, for that matter, closed to it. A desperate person's receptivity to the Gospel is directly proportionate to how he or she is treated during a moment of crisis and who reaches out to him or her during a time of need.

Grace Offers Encouragement and Hope

John 8:10: *"Then Jesus stood up again and said to her, 'Where are your accusers? Didn't even one of them condemn you?'"*

Jesus knew exactly where her accusers were. They were running from conviction. His question was meant to shame them and release the woman from the pain and guilt of their accusations against her. Jesus, being without sin, was the only one who had the right to throw the stone, yet He stood there with empty hands. I can just imagine Him holding out His hands, palms facing up, staring into her dark eyes, and asking, "Has anyone condemned you?"

Grace in its purest form offers hope when punishment is deserved. Grace lifts up, while condemnation pulls down. If there is ever a time when people need hope, it is now. We have the only true message of hope that our hopeless world needs.

Grace Releases from Condemnation and Guilt

John 8:11: *"And Jesus said, 'Neither do I. Go and sin no more.'"*

Christ did not come to disarm the sword of justice so adequately defined in the Law, but to literally become the payment for sin so that justice might be served. In doing so, unmerited favor was released to anyone willing to receive it.

Back in the days of the Wild West, prisoners who had served their time, were given a copy of their "Wanted" poster. The word, *Telesti*, which means "the punishment has been served," was written across their picture along with an official seal from the jail where the sentence was carried out. This important document allowed the released prisoner to travel freely without fear of having to serve time in another city where his poster might still hang. He was released and no longer guilty.

We must look into our workplaces, into our neighborhoods, into our schools, and even into our families at the scores who live under the canopy of judgment, and bring to them the message, *"Telesti."* The message of grace stamps the seal of freedom on their "Wanted" posters and sets them free from the guilt and condemnation they endure. *"God did not send his Son into the world to condemn it, but to save it"* (John 3:17).

Grace Directs the Harvest Toward the Possibility of a Victorious Future

John 8:11: *". . . Go and sin no more."*

Here we see the woman's final release from all past sin and the reality of a victorious future within her reach. The words that came from Jesus' mouth were some of the most incredible words ever to touch the ears of this young woman. She was free to go, to build a future, to have a family, to raise children, and to serve God. The very thought of sinning in the manner in which she had been caught was the furthest thing from her mind at this moment. She had been set free!

The ultimate goal of receiving His amazing grace should be to direct us to share it with others. I personally do not share my faith with others out of duty, but out of gratitude! His grace is sufficient for me, but it is also sufficient for others. His plan of grace didn't stop with me; it can begin in me.

People need "Jesus Today." They need you and I to share the simple message of His grace. They are looking for love in all the wrong places. Isn't it about time they found it in you? Let each of us believe God, not only for a greater measure of His grace in our own lives, but also grace to be poured out through us for others.

MY JESUS TODAY PRAYER

Dear Jesus,

I must admit there have been many times

When I have felt condemned.

There have been other times

When I have been guilty of condemning others.

I have been like the woman filled with a life of sin

And I have been like the Pharisees with a stone in my hand.

I have felt as if I should be judged

And I have felt as if I should judge.

Please forgive me for the times when I have acted as a Pharisee,

Judging instead of loving, condemning instead of compelling.

Help me to remember Your amazing grace,

So I can become a humbled vessel in which to contain it.

Teach me to love the unlovely,

Seeing them the way that You do.

Teach me to live with a grace-filled heart,

Not a heart filled with the Law.

I want to thank You again for those ever-precious words,

"Neither do I condemn you."

The words that flowed so freely from Your heart,

Let them flow freely from my lips.

Let the end result of this prayer be

That I might be a dispenser of Your grace

To a world that desperately needs

To see "Jesus Today."

Amen

CHAPTER SIX

HIS
FAITH:

ACCOMPLISHING

THE IMPOSSIBLE

WITH NEW LEVELS

OF FAITH

JOHN 11:1-44

A s the brisk East wind blew against the single-paned windows of Dave's studio apartment, the metallic sound of chimes outside the window became less annoying and distant—Dave was finally able to sink deeper into his early-morning prayer time with the Lord.

Suddenly, what sounded like a fire alarm startled him with a jump. His old rotary phone had the loudest ring of any phone he had ever heard and always caught him off guard. During that quiet morning hour lost in prayer, the ring seemed loud enough to be heard from across the street.

"Oh my God! Oh my God, Dave! It's Phil—he has been in a head-on collision. It's bad . . ." Cindy, Dave's older sister, broke into hysteria.

"Hold on, wait a minute! What happened?" As Dave waited for a response, he could feel a lump in his throat beginning to form.

Cindy took a gasp of air and continued, "He was on a back country road . . . outside of Pineville . . . slid on some ice on the way to work . . . and was hit head on by a logging truck coming the other way . . . Oh God, they think he is going to die!"

Because the rest of his family was already in Pineville for the holidays, Dave promised to catch the next plane to fly out West. He slowly hung up the phone. He felt numb as he thought of his childhood, playing with Phil at the pond catching frogs, throwing rocks at Mr. Nelson's dog, sleeping out on the hammock, and talking about becoming firemen when they grew up— something that at least Phil had accomplished. He couldn't bear the thought of losing his brother.

Dave sunk to his knees and immediately began to pray, "Lord, save my brother! Don't let him die!" Tears began to stream down his face until his words of desperation gave way to deep sobs.

As he cried out to the Lord, a supernatural peace came upon him. The resulting stillness of the moment allowed him to hear God. He was not prepared for what he heard as God said, "Be still and know that I am God, Dave. I am in charge. I will take care of your brother. Wait here and pray for the next forty-eight hours."

"Two days? What? God, that can't be You. I promised that I would . . ." Dave's thoughts were interrupted by a gentle whisper of the Holy Spirit.

"I am the God of all flesh, including Phil's. Nothing is too difficult for Me." Those powerful words ended the debate between Dave and God.

———————————— ▬▬▬▬ ————————————

Dave pulled his seatbelt tight as the MD-80 roared down the runway of The City's airport. As the plane broke through the fog that smothered the city, he felt catapulted into another world, detached from reality.

It was the longest flight of his life. Every minute seemed like an hour. He thought of the accident, his family's reaction to it, and imagined their response to his prayer vigil. He imagined seeing his dad again, and was taken to the point of overload. He leaned his head rack and tried to get comfortable for the eight-hour flight to Bumento. In order to relax, he tried to focus on the small town he would eventually arrive at.

Pineville was a beautiful, rural community in the foothills, made famous by the California Gold Rush of 1849. The town had grown and declined rapidly as the gold rush ran its course in the immediate area. After the mines were shut down, many of the remaining residents turned to the lumber industry as the Northern California forest became a rich commodity.

Dave's dad had a great-grandfather who had settled there in the first months of the gold rush. When he left to find gold further south, he wrote a letter to his family back east describing the beauty of the area. Since receiving that letter and making their first trip to California, the Finleys had always loved Pineville and tried to see it as often as possible. When the Finley children would vacation there in their youth, they felt like they were entering the Paradise of America. It was no surprise to anyone that Phil had wanted to give his life to saving the town by becoming a firefighter there. Besides, Cindy lived close by in Bumento.

As the plane hit the runway in Bumento, Dave tried to gather his thoughts. As the plane pulled in to the gate, he felt his anxiety level rise dramatically. With a duffel bag over one shoulder and a briefcase in the other hand, he slowly walked up the ramp into the airport terminal. As he did so, he thought to himself, *Who is going to be there? What will I say? Will my dad be there? Lord, help me.*

As he turned the corner and looked out upon the mixed group of people waiting to see their loved ones, he saw Cindy. His sister's face stopped him dead in his tracks. He knew that something was wrong.

Cindy grabbed her brother tightly and let loose her well of mixed emotions. She was so glad to see her distant brother again, but she was devastated by the tragedy of Phil.

As they rounded the corner to the only funeral home in town, Dave's heart began to race. The very thought of seeing his parents, especially his father, caused a level of anxiety severe enough to make him wonder if he was going to have a heart attack. Dave was not one for confrontation, but this would be one that he would have to face. He would have to face his father's disapproval of the prayer vigil, face the questions of why he *again* had let the family down, face the death of his brother, and do it all with a faith in God that he had yet to exercise.

As the door opened, Mr. Dawson, the owner of the funeral home, greeted Dave and Cindy. They stepped inside and Dave's eyes connected with his mother's.

"Davey! Oh, I am so glad you could make it. I am so glad to see you." His mom jumped up and ran to give him a hug.

His father's response was exactly the opposite. Cold. Sterile. Distant. Silent. It was something that Dave had grown accustomed to.

His mom took a step back while still holding his hands and softly whispered, "Your father is devastated. He's angry and confused. He is not happy with you showing up two days later. What could have been more important, Son?"

The same lump in his throat from two days earlier returned once again and was met with a prompting of the Holy Spirit and a racing heartbeat. "Mom, can we sit down?"

As they sat on the old, burgundy velvet couch, his dad immediately got up and marched out the front door. Dave could see him walk out to the car and light up a cigarette. Michael, who had been in a chair opposite the couch, rose to accompany his Dad outside. He was not able to look Dave in the eyes.

"Mom, I know that everyone has had a hard time with my decision to become a Christian, but I believe in the power of prayer and faith in God.

"On the plane I read a scripture that I want to share with you. For what it is worth, here it is." Dave grabbed his Bible as his mom put her head down.

Dave turned to the tear soaked page of John 11:25-26 and read, *"I am the resurrection and the life. He who believes in me will live, even though he dies; and whoever lives and believes in me will never die. Do you believe this . . . ?"*

"Son, Phil is dead! While you were praying, your brother died. If you had only come right away—maybe your prayers would have been heard and Phil would not have died!"

"As unbelievable as it may sound, I believe this to be true, Mom. God has a plan for me. God has a plan for you. God has a plan for Dad. And God has a plan for Phil." His words of authority began to stir up the faith within him. "I didn't come all this way to join with everyone's party of gloom and depression. I came to do exactly what God told me to do!" With that, Dave rose and looked straight into the eyes of Mr. Dawson.

"Where is he? Where is Phil lying?"

"Right this way." Mr. Dawson slowly walked down the hallway to the back room. Cindy followed close behind them, wondering what her crazy Christian brother was going to try now.

———————————— ▬▬▬ ————————————

"He is right over there, in refrigerator door number one." Mr. Dawson said as they entered the room. "The state requires refrigeration after twenty-four hours of death if the process of burial is not begun."

As Dave pulled on the handle of refrigerator door number one, he was met with the disturbing words of his sister. "You might not want to look, Dave. He looks pretty bad. You probably don't want to remember him that way."

Out of the innermost part of his being came an unusual burst of love and faith. As he stood with one hand on the sheet ready to pull it back, he began to weep. These were not human emotions, but the emotions of God. The prayer vigil had not been for nothing. What God began through these prayers would be realized in a matter of moments. For the first time in his walk with Christ, he actually felt faith for the impossible. It wasn't something that he mustered up. It wasn't some formula he followed. It was a gift, a supernatural gift given to Dave for this divine moment . . . and Dave knew it was God!

Slowly, he pulled the sheet back.

As he looked down, it was just as Cindy had said. There lay a pile of distorted flesh. Bruised. Mutilated. Swollen. Cold. Blue. *It doesn't even look like him,* he thought.

Dave took a deep breath and closed his eyes. It was the moment he had been praying for. It was a special moment. An appointed moment. A divine moment.

Silence filled the room as Dave took the sheet entirely off of Phil. He leaned over his body, put his warm hands on the cold, stiff chest of his dead brother and prayed, "Father, I thank You that You have heard my prayers. I know that You always hear me, but I say this for the benefit of the people standing here, that they may believe that You sent me."

Then with a voice that was not his own, he loudly quoted from John chapter eleven, "PHIL . . . COME FORTH!"

Dave began to shake. What seemed to be light and heat was coming from his hands and changing the body of his brother. Mr. Dawson stood in utter disbelief and Cindy screamed in terror.

"What is happening here? Dave, what are you doing?"

Dave didn't say a word. His eyes remained closed, his hands remained in place, and his faith remained strong.

Life itself was flowing from Dave's fingertips. The longer he stood there, the wider the circle of light upon Phil's body expanded. A miracle was taking place. The cold, blue, dead flesh was being transformed into warm, pink, living flesh.

Dave finally exhaled a deep breath of completion, as Phil's chest shuddered with a cough. He had come alive! Alive after two days!

Phil turned his head, and with glossy eyes and a raspy voice he muttered, "Where . . . where . . . am I? What . . . hap . . . hap . . . penned? Where did He go? Where did Jesus go? He was just with me! I was just with Him! Why am I not in that light tunnel? Dave? Cindy? What are you doing here?"

Dave had exercised faith for the impossible. He had seen a need and heard the voice of the spirit concerning it. His heart had been torn in two. As he prayed for Phil, he displayed grace to his family as he chose not to react to their negative words. The building blocks were in place, but there was still more to learn.

JOHN 11:1-44

A man named Lazarus was sick. He lived in Bethany with his sisters, Mary and Martha. This is the Mary, who poured the expensive perfume on the Lord's feet and wiped them with her hair. Her brother, Lazarus, was sick. So the two sisters sent a message to Jesus telling him, "Lord, the one you love is very sick."

But when Jesus heard about it he said, "Lazarus's sickness will not end in death. No, it is for the glory of God. I, the Son of God, will receive glory from this." Although Jesus loved Martha, Mary, and Lazarus, he stayed where he was for the next two days and did not go to them.

Finally after two days, he said to his disciples, "Let's go to Judea again."

But his disciples objected. "Teacher," they said, "only a few days ago the Jewish leaders in Judea were trying to kill you. Are you going there again?"

Jesus replied, "There are twelve hours of daylight every day. As long as it is light, people can walk safely. They can see because they have the light of this world. Only at night is there danger of stumbling because there is no light." Then he said, "Our friend Lazarus has fallen asleep, but now I will go and wake him up." The disciples said, "Lord, if he is sleeping, that means he is getting better!" They thought Jesus meant Lazarus was having a good night's rest, but Jesus meant Lazarus had died.

Then he told them plainly, "Lazarus is dead. And for your sake, I am glad I wasn't there, because this will give you another opportunity to believe in me. Come, let's go see him." Thomas, nicknamed the Twin, said to his fellow disciples, "Let's go, too—and die with Jesus."

When Jesus arrived at Bethany, he was told that Lazarus had already been in his grave for four days. Bethany was only a few miles down the road from Jerusalem, and many of the people had come to pay their respects and console Martha and Mary on their loss. When Martha got word that Jesus was coming, she went to meet him. But Mary stayed at home. Martha said to Jesus, "Lord, if you had been here, my brother would have not died. But even now I know that God will give you whatever you ask."

Jesus told her, "Your brother will rise again."

"Yes," Martha said, "when everyone else rises, on resurrection day."

Jesus told her, "I am the resurrection and the life. Those who believe in me, even though they die like everyone else, will live again. They are given eternal life for believing in me and will never perish. Do you believe this, Martha?"

"Yes, Lord," she told him. "I have always believed you are the Messiah, the Son of God, the one who has come into the world from God." Then she left him and returned to Mary. She called Mary aside from the mourners and told her, "The Teacher is here and wants to see you." So Mary immediately went to him.

Now Jesus had stayed outside the village, at the place where Martha met him. When the people who were at the house trying to console Mary saw her leave so hastily, they assumed she was going to Lazarus's grave to weep. So they followed her there. When Mary arrived and saw Jesus, she fell down at his feet and said, "Lord, if only you had been here, my brother would not have died."

When Jesus saw her weeping and saw the other people wailing with her, he was moved with indignation and was deeply troubled. "Where have you put him?" he asked them. They told him, "Lord, come and see." Then Jesus wept. The people who were standing nearby said, "See how much he loved him." But some said, "This man healed a blind man. Why couldn't he keep Lazarus from dying?"

And again Jesus was deeply troubled. Then they came to the grave. It was a cave with a stone rolled across its entrance. "Roll the stone aside," Jesus told them. But Martha, the dead man's sister, said, "Lord, by now the smell will be terrible because he has been dead for four days."

Jesus responded, "Didn't I tell you that you will see God's glory if you believe? So they rolled the stone aside. Then Jesus looked up to heaven and said, "Father, thank you for hearing me. You always hear me, but I said it out loud for the sake of all these people standing here, so they will believe you sent me." Then Jesus shouted, "Lazarus, come out!" And Lazarus came out, bound in graveclothes, his face wrapped in a headcloth. Jesus told them, "Unwrap him and let him go!"

LEARNING ABOUT FAITH

You have just been presented with two incredible accounts of someone being raised from the dead, one scriptural and one fictional. We seem to have difficulty embracing the impossible, as it defies common sense. When I read the story of Jesus and Lazarus, I can believe that this is a true account because I believe the Bible and have learned through both tragedy and triumph to trust the miracle-working power of Jesus. But when I read about Dave Finley, though it is a fictional story, the possibility of such an occurrence is much more difficult to embrace. I want to believe, I am supposed to believe, but it is hard to get past my Western mindset and accept that this type of dead-raising faith could apply to someone other than Jesus.

A few years ago, the Lord used the miraculous conversion of my grandfather to reveal His ability to accomplish the impossible through my faith. For over a half century, my grandpa was resistant to the Gospel. He was a hardworking, full-blooded, hotheaded Italian, who was not open to discussing any new ideas beyond his set opinions.

After my conversion in 1982, I began to pray daily for my family members, including my grandfather, to get saved. Although I had hope that he would some day turn his life over to Jesus Christ, I really didn't have the faith to believe it could happen—but I prayed anyway.

After six years of consistent praying, I received a call from my mother informing me that Grandpa had been diagnosed with lung cancer and was given six months to live. I immediately went to my knees to pray, harder than ever before, for God to save his soul. For the first time in six years of praying for him, I felt the Holy Spirit drop a seed of faith into my spirit to believe for his salvation.

This mustard seed of faith prompted my wife and I to eventually travel six hundred miles and visit him in a convalescent hospital. I was filled with expectation and excitement at the possibility of sharing the Gospel with my grandpa. Upon arrival, my plans were crushed by my grandfather's harsh rejection of any discussion about the condition of his soul. I felt as if someone had smashed my mustard seed into the pavement. I left discouraged and defeated.

Six months later I received the dreaded phone call from my mother, "Son, your grandpa has slipped into a coma, and they have given him one day to live."

Just as I had six months prior, I went to my knees. Not with faith, but with anger and resentment toward God's seeming lack of concern for my grandpa's physical and spiritual welfare. However God, in His infinite grace, sent a sense of peace and I once again felt a fresh deposit of faith as I heard the voice of the Holy Spirit saying, "You didn't hear her! She said, 'He has one day left to live.'"

Immediately, I sensed a complete change in my soul. My emotions turned from sorrow to joy, my mind shifted from doubt to expectation, and my will changed from giving up to getting up.

Within a few hours, I was on a plane with my mother, only to be met at the hospital by a room full of crying relatives and a priest sprinkling the bed. As my grandpa laid there, gasping for his last few breaths, my mother knelt down by his side and together we began to pray that the Lord would reveal Himself to my grandpa.

We were both encouraged to see the expression on his fear-filled face change as he experienced a supernatural peace that filled the room. We believed that God was touching my grandpa. I was seeing my prayers answered and my faith activated right before my eyes. We led him in the sinner's prayer. He then squeezed our fingers and, immediately, with a smile on his face, went home to be with his newfound Savior!

I left that day having learned something about myself and about God. As far as I can recall, it was my first major lesson on faith. I realized that much of my life is really out of my control and in the hands of the Almighty. However, I also began to understand that God is excited about faith and loves to respond to those who exercise it. What seemed impossible to me was a small thing for God. This new deposit of faith wasn't something that I had earned, mustered up, or could even create. It was a gift from my Father in heaven, a very special gift that I treasure to this day.

THE NEED FOR JESUS FAITH IN LAZARUS TIMES

The incident with my grandfather, coupled with many other faith-stretching opportunities since that time, has helped expand my faith and the way I view circumstances in everyday life. Each situation moves me one step closer to enlarging my faith that I may accomplish the impossible for God. Faith allows us to see the fulfillment of God's purposes in our lives. The more faith we have for our lives, the more our potential is released. What hinders us most from accomplishing extraordinary exploits is not the way God sees us, but the way we see God. God views us with unlimited potential, while we see ourselves in quite the opposite way. Let us be encouraged by Mark 10:27, *"Everything is possible with God."*

The account of Jesus and Lazarus holds some shocking parallels to the Church and her current condition. The lost people surrounding us are like Lazarus. They are dead in sin, bound by their habits and lifestyles, and are a stench in the nostrils of God.

The Church has taken on the role of Mary and Martha, either crying at the feet of Jesus, or busy doing church-related work, but not possessing the faith needed to bring change to the Lazarus generation.

What is needed is a Jesus faith, not a Martha and Mary faith, or we will never be capable of impacting our Lazarus society.

Do not lose sight of the fact that God has placed you exactly where He wants you to be! Your neighbors have been carefully selected and placed in your life by the hand of God. Your co-workers are set by your side as part of the Lord's master plan to bring them to salvation. He now desires to impart to you a new faith that you might become "Jesus Today" for all those around you to see.

God is just waiting for you to have faith that He can use you like never before. Whatever expectation level you have is too small. Ephesians 3:20 ensures us, *"Now glory be to God! By his mighty power at work within us, he is able to accomplish infinitely more than we would ever dare to ask or hope."* His thoughts are higher than your thoughts (see Isaiah 58:11), and He thinks you can do extraordinary exploits as His co-partner.

Not only does He believe that you can touch your neighbors and relatives but that you can be instrumental in touching nations . . . that's right, nations! If it weren't true, He would not have put it in His Word. He challenges us to ask Him for our inheritance in Him, *"Only ask, and I will give you the nations as your inheritance, the ends of the earth as your possession"* (Psalm 2:8).

It is only with this level of faith that we will see God's plan fulfilled in our lives, our churches, our cities, and our world. Reaching your friends and relatives requires great faith. Touching your city demands a greater faith, and reaching the over six billion people that span the globe cannot be accomplished through human strength, thoughts, or strategies, but only through complete faith in God. God desires that each of us would have abounding faith to turn the "I cant's" into "I cans."

MOVING FROM A MARY/MARTHA FAITH TO A JESUS FAITH

Mary and Martha clearly portrayed the inadequacy of mankind's ability to generate faith. Lazarus was dead, and there was nothing they could do about it in their own strength. What they needed was a God-induced faith that could only come through Jesus Himself. So they cried out to the Lord!

Christians often struggle in their own strength to muster up faith that does not exist. God's faith can never be manufactured through a fleshly process. Faith is not birthed through rigid determination or by reciting doctrine. Faith will never exist until one has a personal encounter with God.

We must be careful not to misinterpret belief as faith. One can believe in the Bible as truth, but that will not generate faith. One can believe that God will never leave him or her, but that still will not create trust in God. Attempting to will something into existence cannot be interpreted as faith either. One can quote Scriptures, recite creeds, make statements with great conviction, and still not have faith that moves him from the natural to the supernatural realm.

In his book, *The Lost Passions of Jesus*, Donald L. Milam, Jr. eloquently describes faith and its true source:

> Faith does act, but faith does not come from the act. The act comes from the faith. Positive confession is not the kind of faith that the Son of Man is looking for, the kind that taps Heaven's inexhaustible resources. It is a Divine Word, a heavenly touch, and an encounter with Heaven that ignites faith that produces a passion of conviction and resignation to the Divine Will and Purpose. Faith can never be attained or produced by the ingenuity or efforts of the human mind and will. It is the faith of God. There is a big difference between the faith of man in God and the faith that God gives to the man of God.[35]

JESUS FAITH FOR JESUS TODAY

Jesus modeled a God-induced faith. It was only with this type of faith (even though He was the Son of God) that He could accomplish the impossible task of raising Lazarus from the dead. This scriptural account is rich with insight concerning biblical faith. This is the type of faith we need to become "Jesus Today" and to the raise the Lazarus generation around us. Let's briefly review some of the nuggets of faith found in this portion of Scripture.

A God-Centered Faith

John 11:4: " . . . *it is for the glory of God. I, the Son of God, will receive glory from this.*"

The first words that Jesus spoke here were words of deflection. The glory was not intended for the building up of a man or a ministry, but solely for God. Jesus knew that the death of Lazarus would furnish an opportunity for a spectacular display of the glory of God and would ultimately furnish standing proof of the truth of His mission. The ministry of Jesus is filled with miracles that point directly to the glory of God.

What an unbelieving world needs to see in us is a faith that points them to the Author and Finisher of our faith (see Hebrews 12:2). Our faith can never be used as a steppingstone for building our identities, our positions, or our ministries. As we step out in faith to those in need, we must be sure to direct our faith and actions to the glory of God. The ultimate goal is that they might know *Him*, not just His works or the works of those who labor for Him.

An Unwavering Faith

John 11:4: *"Lazarus's sickness will not end in death . . ."*

Jesus chose to ignore the lies of the Enemy planted in the minds of His followers. He used the challenge to demonstrate the position of faith over circumstance.

How easy it would have been for Jesus to be caught up in the emotions of the moment. Impossibilities seem to test the true levels of one's faith. The measuring rod of faith is not calculated when everything is going well, but when one has reached the end of human reasoning and resource.

The famous healing evangelist, Smith Wigglesworth, known for his tenacious faith, once said, "If you really believe, you will ask God only once, and that is all you need because He has abundance for your every need."[36] Although God is not bothered by our continual asking, He is concerned if we are asking out of doubt and disbelief. Remember the challenge in James 1:6, *"But when you ask him, be sure that you really expect him to answer, for a doubtful mind is as unsettled as a wave of the sea that is driven and tossed by the wind."*

Another great man of faith, George Müller, added further insight into the dangers of wavering in our faith, when he said, "The beginning of anxiety is the end of faith, and the beginning of true faith is the end of anxiety."[37]

Once we have received the promise of God regarding the salvation of a loved one or the provision of God for a certain circumstance, we must not waver in our faith, regardless of what difficult factors may present themselves. He is the God of *all* flesh and *nothing* is too difficult for Him (see Jeremiah 32:27).

A Patient Faith

> John 11:6: *". . . he stayed where he was for the next two days and did not go to them."*

Jesus chose to be patient, knowing very well that His faith would challenge his followers. I am sure that if Lazarus were to have remained dead for another year, Jesus still could have raised his decomposed body from the dead. Jesus, in His infinite wisdom, chose this passing of time to model complete dependence on His Father in heaven.

George MacDonald has said, "The principle part of faith is patience."[38] Patient faith believes that the fulfillment of the promise is a "when" issue and not an "if" issue. Paul admonishes the Philippian church about being patient, *"Always be full of joy in the Lord. I say it again—rejoice! Let everyone see that you are considerate in all you do. Remember, the Lord is coming soon. Don't worry about anything . . ."* (Philippians 4:4-6). Patience is one of the fruits of the Spirit (see Galatians 5:22) and is a major component of faith.

George Müller prayed for a man for fifty-two years, totally convinced that the man would give his life to Christ. At the funeral of George Müller the minister gave an altar call and after fifty-two years of patient faith, he got saved beside the coffin of his friend.

If God has given you the faith to believe Him for the salvation of a friend or co-worker, then don't give up. If God has promised you a financial breakthrough, a miracle of healing to your body, or the return of a prodigal child, don't give up! Trust in His Word and allow faith to give you strength.

An Offensive Faith

> John 11:7: *". . . he said to his disciples, 'Let's go to Judea again.'"*

I appreciate the tenacity of Jesus to confront his accusers head-on. From a natural perspective, a trip back into Judea, following the most recent opposition against Him, would have ended in disaster. His disciples tried to discourage Him. Other Scriptures show that Jesus sometimes healed from a distance, praying for the sick in other cities. Why not now?

Jesus took an offensive position, facing this obstacle head-on as a way to demonstrate that faith is active, not passive. Faith confronts opposition. Faith laughs at impossible situations. Faith is offensive.

A Supernatural Faith

> John 11:9: *"Jesus replied, 'There are twelve hours of daylight every day. As long as it is light, people can walk safely. They can see because they have the light of this world. Only at night is there danger of stumbling because there is no light.'"*

Jesus used this opportunity to reveal the difference between the natural and the supernatural. Jesus knew that if His followers walked in the ways of their own hearts or the in ways of the world, they would rely on their own carnal reasoning rather than on God. As His followers often made this mistake, they fell into temptation and snares, resulting in great uneasiness and frightful apprehension to fulfilling the mandate before them.

St. Augustine defined supernatural faith by stating, "Faith is to believe on the Word of God what we do not see, and its reward is to see and enjoy what we believe."[39] Our human tendency is to desire to see proof about something before we believe it to be true, but faith is believing it to be true before proof is seen, resulting in that which we can now see.

William Newton Clarke said, "Faith is daring the soul to go farther than it can see. For what is faith unless it is to believe what you do not see?"[40] Faith, therefore, relies on the supernatural. Faith must find its source in God, not in man.

An Ever-Increasing Faith

> John 11:14-15: *"Lazarus is dead. And for your sake, I am glad I wasn't there, because this will give you another opportunity to believe in me. Come, let's go see him."*

If Jesus had chosen to heal Lazarus' sickness it would have done little to increase the faith of His disciples since they had seen the sick healed many times before. Jesus knew that greater levels of faith would be needed for greater levels of service. For the disciples to accomplish the task of reaching the world, they needed ever-increasing faith.

The task before us, reaching the lost for Christ, is only possible as we grow in our faith. With an ever-increasing faith, God can use each of us to impact our part of the world. Let us take on this principle, just as the late D.L. Moody, the famous evangelist in the nineteenth century, said, "A little faith will bring your soul to heaven, but a lot of faith will bring heaven to your soul."[41]

A No-Limits Faith

John 11:23: *"Jesus told her, 'Your brother will rise again.'"*

The ministry of Jesus helps us, as His followers, to see that there are no limits to what God can accomplish through us. Nothing is impossible with God (see Luke 1:37).

Any time we put a limit on faith, we rob ourselves of further blessings. If you have a vision to win one neighbor to Christ this year, I am here to say, your vision is too small. God may give you your entire block! Maybe you have been thinking, "I would like to see my church grow to 500 or 1,000 people in the next year." Again, too small. Faith stretches beyond every imagination and dream of man. He who is small in faith will never be great in anything but failure. Many have been cheated by believing for nothing. Never be embarrassed by believing for too much.

A no-limits faith can believe God to convert the entire homosexual community of your city. A no-limits faith can feed, house, and convert the homeless population of your town. A no-limits faith can provide you with the finances to fulfill your ministry dreams. Let us take on the challenge of a familiar statement used by many great preachers, "If God is your partner, make your plans big."

A Christ-Rooted Faith

John 11:25-26: *"Jesus told her, 'I am the resurrection and the life. Those who believe in me, even though they die like everyone else, will live again. They are given eternal life for believing in me and will never perish. Do you believe this, Martha?'"*

Christ reminded Martha that He is the foundation for all life and the author of all faith. I can only imagine that this must have caused her to remember His past words in John 5:25, *"And I assure you that the time is coming, in fact it is here, when the dead will hear my voice—the voice of the Son of God. And those who listen will live."*

To paraphrase, Jesus was saying, "Hey look, as God I have the power to cause even the dead to hear My voice. And if I can raise a world of men, dead for many ages, what stops Me from raising up one that has been dead a few days? Just keep your faith in Me. Understand?"

A faith rooted in Christ will never fail. There is great assurance in knowing that He is in charge. Let Him take all the pressure. Although we may fail, He will never fail us. Our faith must remain in Christ, not in ourselves.

A Spirit-Birthed Faith

John 11:33: *". . . he was moved with indignation and was deeply troubled."*

Jesus Himself never performed any miracle without the direct assistance of the Holy Spirit. In every recorded ministry situation of Jesus, the Holy Spirit initiated and Jesus responded. In this particular verse, it is important to note that Jesus was "moved in spirit" *before* Lazarus was moved in the tomb! The voice of the Holy Spirit initiated the faith!

Faith needs a focus. The voice of God is that focus. The voice stimulates the spirit, creating the response that we call faith. That voice is imperative to the true operation of faith. As Donald L. Milam, Jr. put it:

The cripple will remain at the pool of Bethesda unless the voice is heard. The demoniac continues to roam the mountainside, tormented by evil spirits, until the voice roars forth from the mouth of God. The adulteress remains in her bondage to sin and at the mercy of spiteful religious men until the voice exposes her sin and sets her free.[42]

Responding to the voice of the Holy Spirit is the first step in exercising true faith. That which is first birthed by the Spirit can be activated through our prayers and actions and result in the focus we need for faith.

An Activated Faith

John 11:39: *"'Roll the stone aside,' Jesus told them."*

Jesus activated His faith by confidently proceeding with the natural steps necessary to fulfill the supernatural promise. In order for our faith to be activated, we need to respond to God's voice with visible action that will remove any natural barriers to the promise. For Jesus, it was removing the tombstone. For Dave Finley, it was prayer.

Faith responds and then waits for the evidence, while hope waits for the evidence and then responds in faith. Faith acts, while hope waits. Activated faith takes the position that whatever one is believing for has already happened in the spiritual realm and, therefore, one must follow it through in the natural.

Such activated faith is illustrated by this story from the life of Hudson Taylor, the famous missionary to China. While on a sailing vessel off the coast of the Cannibal Islands, he was asked by the captain to pray for wind, to keep them from the savages that were eagerly awaiting their oncoming feast. Hudson responded, "I will, provided you set your sails to catch the breeze before I pray."

The captain declined to make himself a laughing stock by unfurling the sails in a dead calm sea. As the ship drifted closer to the shore, their only hope was to put up the sails.

"Mr. Taylor, the sails are now up. Would you now please pray?"

Hudson Taylor went to prayer. While he was praying, there was a knock at the door of his stateroom.

The captain asked, "Are you still praying for wind?"

Hudson replied, "Yes!"

The captain shouted, "Well, you had better stop praying, for we have more wind than we can manage." [43]

Whatever it is, we must act to remove any natural barriers that could thwart the fulfillment of God's promise.

A Thankful Faith

John 11:41: *"Then Jesus looked up to Heaven and said, 'Father, thank you for hearing me.'"*

The gesture Jesus used was very significant. It was an outward expression of gratitude toward His heavenly Father to show those who stood by Him from whom He derived His power and faith. Jesus modeled such gratitude throughout his ministry.

A thankless faith is a short-lived faith. Our response to a current victory can greatly affect whether God would use us again in the same fashion. Let us always be reminded of the words of Jesus in John 15:5, *". . . apart from me you can do nothing."*

A few years ago, while ministering at a crusade in Mexico, the Holy Spirit impressed upon me to pray for the sick. I, by no means, claim to be a great healing evangelist, but on this occasion people were being miraculously healed. I went to pray for a woman who was plagued with a disease for more than ten years. She was literally hunched over, as this was the only posture in which she could find relief from the pain. As I went to pray for her, I sensed the Holy Spirit say, "Get your daughter Heather to pray for her."

With a perfect track record of successful healing prayers that night, I tried to offer God my counsel to straighten Him out on His foolish request. I replied, "Lord, am I not the one praying for people here? Besides, my daughter is just eight years old and is over in the front row spacing out!"

However, I called my daughter over to pray. As Heather placed her hands on the woman, she immediately sprung up and began to jump, cry, and scream. The entire place began to celebrate!

Well, good ole' Marc did not feel like celebrating. I immediately realized that I was in error. I had made a mistake, and a big one at that. Then the Lord gently whispered to me words that I will never forget, "Don't ever think again that you had anything to do with it!"

I got the point! How thankless of me! How prideful I was! How insensitive I had been! God gently and lovingly set me back on course. He requires that we have a thankful faith.

A Praying Faith

John 11:42: *"You always hear me, but I said it out loud for the sake of all these people standing here, so they will believe you sent me."*

Jesus' faith was evident in His prayer. Prayer without faith is vain repetition. Notice that Jesus was praying as if the miracle had already taken place! He triumphed before the victory! He had faith in the promise that was given and knew that it must be activated through a praying faith.

Jesus understood that His Father always heard Him, and every act was dependent upon His intercession. To this day, *"...he is the one who died for us and was raised to life for us and is sitting at the place of highest honor next to God, pleading for us."* (Romans 8:34).

When it comes to praying for loved ones who do not know the Lord, our prayers must be driven by faith to see them as they will become, not as they currently are. It doesn't matter how impossible the situation looks while on your knees, pray with faith.

Joy Dawson, the great prayer warrior, makes this point very clear in her book, *Intercession*. She says:

> There are times when we are particularly burdened for the welfare of the unconverted and the circumstances are outside of our control or ability to help them. To have peace of mind, we need to put Psalm 37:5 into action: *"Commit your way to the Lord; trust in him and he will act."* [RSV]
>
> The Hebrew word for "commit" literally means "to throw." We "throw" the ones for whom we are concerned at God, asking only that He act to bring the greatest glory to His name in their circumstances. He knows how to work on them for their best interests. He knows the best methods and timing, and will do only the right and just things for everyone concerned, and longs to catch them. . . . God promises to act.[44]

A Militant Faith

John 11:43: *"Then Jesus shouted, 'Lazarus, come out!'"*

Throughout Scripture we see extensive evidence of militant faith confronting and overcoming the powers of darkness. David *"ran over"* to Goliath (1 Samuel 17:51). Shadrach, Meshach, and Abednego boldly faced the king and proclaimed, *"We will never serve your gods"* (Daniel 3:18). Elijah *"cried out"* that the widow's boy might be raised from the dead (1 Kings 17:21-22). Jesus said to the young boy in the coffin, *"Get up!"* (Luke 7:14-15). Peter, with the lame man at the gate, shouted, *"Get up and walk!"* (Acts 3:6). Peter, again with Aeneas, demanded him to *"Get up and make your bed!"* (Acts 9:34). Once more Peter told Tabitha, who was dead, *"Get up!"* (Acts 9:40).

God requires us to exercise this type of militant faith to confront the powers of darkness that surround us and mock us daily. The Enemy is attempting to take all he can get. Revelation 12:12 reminds us of the Enemy's plan, *"For the devil has come down to you in great anger, and he knows that he has little time."* We can no longer sit back and watch our children be destroyed by the Enemy's tactics. We cannot sit back and allow the Thief to come and rob us of seeing our friends and neighbors set free from bondages that paralyze their souls. We can no longer allow our neighborhoods and cities to be under the control of the great Deceiver. We must receive and activate a militant faith.

We must ask the question, "Is my life like a thermometer or a thermostat? Do I affect or am I affected by the world around me?" A thermometer is affected by its surroundings. A thermostat changes its surroundings. God is looking for people with a militant faith to become change-agents for the kingdom of God. We must arise with a "Jesus Today" faith.

A Living Faith

> John 11:44: *"And Lazarus came out, bound in graveclothes, his face wrapped in a headcloth. Jesus told them, 'Unwrap him and let him go!'"*

Jesus knew that the end result of this act of faith was not to satisfy the curious or to quiet the critics, but to dispense a living faith in one who was dead that the recipient might be a reproducing carrier of that same faith to dispense in others.

Our faith is to be a living faith, one that is not our own. It is a gift given to us to use for the glory of God and to pass on to all those with whom we come in contact. There are people around us every day who are in desperate need of Jesus faith. They are searching and looking for someone with the answers to their problems and challenges. You have the opportunity to be that person. Take your living, Jesus faith and spread it wherever you go.

MY JESUS TODAY PRAYER

Dear Jesus,
As I look around at all of the needs,
I confess that it seems overwhelming.
So many needs numb me
Into becoming a part of the problem, not part of the solution.
Daily, I can see the Lazarus generation dead and tied up
And I feel incapable of offering any help.
I realize that if I continue with a Martha/Mary faith,
I will never change anything.
Right now, I ask for an impartation
Of Your faith in exchange for my Martha/Mary faith.
I want to take this newfound faith, which You give me,
To a world that desperately waits.
Help me to always bring You the glory
And to never waiver, despite my circumstances.
Teach me the balance of being patient,
Yet remaining on the offense.
I ask that You would daily remind me
To never be satisfied with the faith level of today.
But help me to work to increase my faith for tomorrow,
Rooted in You, with no limits attached.
Let the fruit of this special prayer
Be the releasing of Your faith in me
Into a world that desperately needs Your truth,
As I become more like You, "Jesus Today."
Amen

CHAPTER SEVEN

HIS GIFTS:

RELEASING

SPIRITUAL GIFTS

FOR GREATER

FRUIT

LUKE 6:6-11

Since the miracle at Dawson's Funeral Home, things just weren't the same in Pineville. Phil's resurrection seemed to have a lasting impact on everyone involved. Mr. Dawson was a main contributor to the opposition, having labeled it a demonic act. As for the Finley family, they each reacted differently, just as they had on every other family matter. Dad was glad to have a second chance to see his son Phil, but still despised the mystical lifestyle of his fanatical son, Dave. Even the raising of the dead didn't reunite their relationship; it only pushed them further apart. After all, how was he going to explain it, especially as a politician?

Michael and Cindy returned to the East Coast with Mom and Dad, Cindy's husband having obtained a long-awaited job transfer. But Dave just couldn't shake himself loose from Phil or the leading of the Lord to stay in Pineville. Besides, who else was going to disciple Phil in his Christianity?

Dave flew home with his family to gather his belongings. As he drove off for Pineville, he prayed a simple prayer, "Lord, you have done much for my family, may you now use these events to soften their hearts toward you."

It looked as if the annual church picnic would be a smashing success. It was a citywide event that very few people in town were willing to miss. This year was a special year, the 50th anniversary, and the entire town was praying for a warm July day. Flyers were placed in all the business windows and a large vinyl banner hung across Main Street from Maple's Diner to the courthouse. No other events were scheduled.

Seventy-six ladies had entered the baking contest. It brought the smell of apple pies, peach cobbler, and chocolate cake drifting through the side streets of the 2500 person town. Most of the ladies in Pineville were buried in their kitchens, trying to find that special final touch that would give them the edge in winning the prestigious honor of "Pineville Community Church

Baking Queen." It was an honor that earned them bragging rights at most church and town functions throughout the year.

The picnic talent show was the largest on record and the rumor buzzing about town was that Mr. & Mrs. Thompson's famous duet "Amazing Grace" and their five-year winning streak would be beaten out this year by some new talent. As for Mr. Dawson, it would be a year to sit out from participating in anything. He had his hands full with the church board, trying to decide what to do about those Finley boys who had come to the church services.

The county fairgrounds were all set up and the finishing touches put on the many booths. Balloons were hung, hay bales were scattered about, the food booths were stocked with mouth-watering barbecue and all the fixin's, and the dunk tank, the most popular attraction, was being filled with cold water. Each year Pastor Ed would sacrifice himself in the dunk tank to raise money for the youth group's annual mission trip. The picnic would soon begin.

———————————————— ▬▬▬ ————————————————

Jim McCarther had risen early that morning for his daily devotions, and he sat intently reading the last chapter of the book, *Christianity with Power*. Ever since graduating from Bible College five years ago, he had a deep-seeded hunger for God to use him in the area of signs and wonders, healing, and miracles. He had refrained from sharing this passion, as the subject of healing was taboo at the Community Church, even if one of the town's people had been raised from the dead! Deacon Bob Matthews had made it very clear that there wouldn't be any of that "crazy stuff" from the charismatic Bible College accepted at the church. Jim was ecstatic to hear about Phil Finley and to meet him, but because he was also a member at the church, he had kept his opinions to himself. Besides, the Finley boys had only just begun to attend the Community Church a few weeks ago after they were unable to find a favorable reception at any other church in town.

Although Jim couldn't talk about his dreams and vision for the church to the church board, it didn't stop him from talking with Dave and Phil. It had been six months since Phil's miracle and commitment to follow Christ. Jim's passion for the supernatural coupled with his heart for discipleship made a great match and prompted a developing relationship with the two newest additions to the church.

At noon, the church service was dismissed by Pastor Ed. On this particular Sunday, few people stayed around for the usual after-service fellowship—they all raced home to change into their picnic clothes, hoping to reserve a table in the limited eating area at the fairgrounds.

Since Phil had to cover for some older firefighters who would entertain the kids at the church picnic, Dave was alone. He stayed after the service for a while, hoping to find someone who would at least become a casual acquaintance and show him around at the picnic. He stood in the foyer and attempted to strike up conversations with other church members, only to be overlooked as they rushed to talk with neighbors they hadn't seen all week—or so he thought. The reality was that the Finleys were off limits to everyone in the church. Pastor Ed had made that clear to the congregation the Sunday after the "Finley Phenomena." Unfortunately, that did not change with Dave and Phil's attendance at the church.

Unaccustomed to all the picnic hype, Dave casually strolled home to fix himself a sandwich and slip in a quick nap before walking over to the fairgrounds for this grandiose event.

Over at the fairgrounds, the crowds were already gathering and great excitement filled the air. Mr. Olson had on his usual clown outfit with the eight-foot stilt legs and greeted every child with free balloons, while the ladies' Bible study group quickly gathered the admission tickets from the growing lines of eager attenders. The good weather made the attendance swell to a new high.

Inside, the smell of barbecued hamburgers and hot dogs was everywhere. Every table in the picnic section was filled, and blankets covered the grassy area where families were finishing up their plates of food. Music drifted from the main stage, as the church choir began to sing the specials they had been working on all spring. Children ran to line up for the pony rides, and Pastor Ed was already wet from the first pitch at the dunk tank.

The wind blew through the narrow hallway and caused the bedroom door to slam. Dave rolled over, awakened from his nap. He had intended to shut his eyes for a moment, but had slept for more than two hours. He jumped up, threw some water on his face, and ran out the door to the fair-grounds.

As he arrived at the picnic, he saw the masses of people, even more than he had expected. He didn't realize that so many people actually lived in Pineville. He had never seen more than one hundred people at one time in any place.

Dave thought this would be a great time to get to know some people. He walked around and inspected all the booths and games and even paused to listen to some of the music. He looked for someone who was just relaxing and seemed ready for a casual conversation. Everywhere he looked, small cliques had formed, and it seemed as if none of them were penetrable.

He made his way over to the big oak tree and leaned up against it to secure his spot for the much-awaited talent show. This was an event he was not going to miss, even if he had to enjoy it by himself.

Act after act entertained the mellowing crowd. The warm July sun had left many sunburned, and the games and rides had worn out even the most energetic children. Coats and sweatshirts were pulled from the picnic bags to cover the shorts and tank tops. Even some of the ground blankets were used to fight off the early evening chill.

Just as a quartet was taking its place on stage as the final act of the evening, Dave saw something that would give him the opportunity to live life like Jesus would. He began to see differently. He noticed a rather homely looking man making his way into the crowd. He had never seen this man before, and by the looks of the others who had noticed him, no one else knew him either. He was dressed in worn-out clothes, covered with patches and dirt. It was apparent that this man had been wearing them for some time. His large, floppy hat covered his lengthy and matted dark red hair and shadowed most of his aging face, making it difficult to see his expressions. He moved along with a noticeable limp, and it appeared as if his right arm were hidden inside his corduroy jacket.

The quartet began their song and drew the attention back to the main stage. Their heavy practice schedule was evidenced by their flawless four-part harmonies. Their final song ensured them the vote for first prize among even the largest skeptics.

Suddenly, Dave *heard* the all-familiar voice of the Holy Spirit, speaking into his ear. "Dave, I am about to answer the desires of your heart. You have been praying and seeking My face concerning this town. I want you to go pray for the man I have brought to the picnic tonight. He is not here by accident and neither are you. I will heal this man's paralyzed arm right before this crowd."

His heart began to beat with conflicting pulses. With one beat he could *feel* compassion for this unfortunate man, while the next beat brought fear. The erratic beating caused his heart to race at almost twice its normal pace as Dave was flooded with doubt, "Why me? Why now? Why here?" But just as quickly as the doubting thoughts surfaced, he recalled a Scripture he had just read the night before. *"And let the peace that comes from Christ rule in your hearts"* (Colossians 3:15). He then felt the Holy Spirit say, "Go ahead. I will be with you."

As the peace of God began to dilute any fear, there was also a wave of *grace* to love this unlovely man. Dave no longer saw the outward condition of this man's circumstances, but the inward beauty that Jesus saw.

With all the crowd's eyes still on the quartet finale, Dave began to pick his way from the oak tree to the man who had settled directly in front of center stage.

Dave and the homeless man could not have better choreographed the meeting in front of the stage together. Dave reached the man as the final notes of the quartet were being sung. Pastor Ed bounded on stage to announce the conclusion of the show and the results from the judges. However, attention was not on Pastor Ed, but on Dave and the outcast man.

Dave cleared his throat and turned to the crowd. As he did so, he was met with the same feeling he had had as he stood over Phil's body in the funeral home. A *faith* for the impossible boosted his confidence and loosened his tongue.

"Friends and neighbors, I really don't know how to share with you what is about to happen, so I will just get to the point. I have been praying for you and for this town ever since my arrival a few months ago. I know that there has been an uproar as to the validity and source of my brother Phil's miracle. But the Lord wants to show you His will and thoughts concerning healing and miracles. I know that most of you here have not had any experience with miracles. In fact, most would be opposed to the thought that a miraculous healing could take place in this day and age, much less right now at the end of this fine picnic. But as I was sitting back under the oak tree, I sensed the Holy Spirit tell me that he had brought this man to us tonight to show us that He can and will heal those with diseases."

An uneasiness began to permeate the crowd, and many looked intently at Pastor Ed to see how and when he was going to stop this heresy. Deacon Bob Matthews stood up from his blanket and began to shout with his thirty-eight years of leadership authority, "We ain't looking for any of this spooky demon stuff from you or from anybody. Can't you see this ain't the time or the place? We are here for this picnic and talent show. Today you have come into our little community, into our church family, and messed up the most special picnic in fifty years!"

With that others started shouting, "Sit down! Go home!" Even Mr. Dawson joined in, screaming at the top of his lungs, "Leave us alone!"

As the crowd's annoyance and hostility grew, Dave's determination mounted. He had nothing to lose. He was already marked as a heretic. And he knew that he had heard from God. Filled with holy indignation, Dave grabbed the microphone and shared with the crowd in a confidant, yet caring tone, "What is more important to you all tonight? Is it more important that we are able to crown this year's talent show winner or that this man's paralyzed arm is healed and his life restored?" Dave dropped the microphone on the stage, and in what seemed like slow motion, reached over to pull the man's lame arm from his coat, looked toward heaven, and said, "In the name of Jesus Christ of Nazareth, be healed!"

The jolt of power through the homeless man's body was met with gasps from all over the audience. Young and old jumped to their feet to witness the shaking man in front. Dave himself bowed his head and closed his eyes as the power of God took control. People raced to the front to see the miracle-working power of God with their own eyes. It was a scene that could never have been rehearsed and definitely could not be debated. Everyone knew that this man was once lame, but now was healed.

As the crowd dispersed from the greatest show in the town's history, Dave stayed to lead the homeless man to Christ. It was his day of salvation. It was a day when all the angels in heaven rejoiced. On this day, another one of God's creation entered into the Lamb's Book of Life.

Dave leaned over to turn off the lamp next to his bed. It was now three a.m., and he needed some sleep.

His final thoughts before slipping away into a deep sleep were words to his Savior, "Lord, I thank You for what You are doing in my life. I thank You for taking me on this journey to make me more like You. I thank You that I can see the way You see. Lord, I thank You that I can hear the things You hear. Thanks, Jesus, for giving me Your heart of compassion as well as a supernatural grace to love people just the way they are. Although I don't deserve it, I thank You for this new impartation of faith, for You have truly shown me the impossible. . . . But Lord, how are You going to change this town? How are You going to change this church? How are You going to change Your people?"

HIS GIFTS

LUKE 6:6-11

On another Sabbath day, a man with a deformed right hand was in the synagogue while Jesus was teaching. The teachers of religious law and the Pharisees watched closely to see whether Jesus would heal the man on the Sabbath, because they were eager to find some legal charge to bring against him. But Jesus knew their thoughts. He said to the man with the deformed hand, "Come and stand here where everyone can see."

So the man came forward. Then Jesus said to his critics, "I have a question for you. Is it legal to do good deeds on the Sabbath, or is it a day for doing harm? Is this a day to save life or to destroy it?"

He looked around at them one by one and then said to the man, "Reach out your hand." The man reached out his hand, and it became normal again! At this, the enemies of Jesus were wild with rage and began to discuss what to do with him.

A LACK OF GIFTS PRODUCES A LACK OF HARVEST

Many of the lessons I have learned in life have come unexpectedly through my children. God has a way of using the simplest circumstances to reveal the most significant eternal truths. Such is the case with my little boy, Kyle.

One day I was observing my son out on the lawn, squirting the neighborhood boy with his battery operated squirt gun. They were both laughing and running, as Kyle proceeded to drench little Drew. Soon, however, I noticed that Kyle had stopped running and was now focused on his squirt gun that had broken. Without waiting another moment, he came flying in the door, ran to the tool drawer, pulled out a Phillip's head screwdriver, and proceeded to the dining room table to quickly fix his squirt gun so that he could continue "the hunt."

The seconds turned into minutes, as he grew increasingly frustrated with his inability to fix the problem. I noticed that the screws were actually standard head screws and required a different screwdriver. With great wisdom and insight, I leaned over and said, "Hey, buddy, let me help."

Quickly he lashed back at me, "No, daddy, I fix!"

He then proceeded to continue down the sure road of failure. He had great determination and a single focus, yet he lacked the proper tool to successfully accomplish the task at hand. In addition to lacking proper tools, he was also unwilling to humble himself and listen to what his father had to offer regarding the challenge at hand.

As I stood back with an "I told you so" smirk and a feeling of superior fatherly wisdom, the Lord quickly humbled me by allowing me to realize that often my responses to His plans for my life are exactly the same as my son's response to his toy. I learned a great lesson that day.

Sheer determination to share my faith is not the primary ingredient for winning the lost to Christ. Although my resolve may be the spark needed to engage me in an evangelistic mindset, it is the work of the Holy Spirit, to both guide me in sharing the right words in due season and to open the eyes and ears of the lost person to receive the Gospel message, that will bring success.

What I have realized is that when I am willing to humble myself and respond to the Holy Spirit, He is always willing to give me the exact tool (or gift of the Spirit) necessary to accomplish His will in that situation. Understanding this simple truth has allowed me the privilege of leading many people to Christ and has saved me from many frustrating witnessing situations.

On the other hand, I have also found that getting locked into a programmed mindset places my reliance upon the program or method, rather than the Holy Spirit. This is not to say that programmed evangelism is not a useful means of leading people to the Lord. I have been involved in hundreds of programs, resulting in many new converts. The real issue is this: Who is running the program, man or God?

If you were to analyze your own witnessing experiences, would you say they were fruitful or fatal? Do you find yourself in endless debates or God-directed conversations? Do people lean further away or closer to God after your encounter? Are you filled with fear or with faith? Is there a sense that the Holy Spirit is in your midst or does he seem to be in the next county? Whatever your results may be, God desires that you bear much fruit, and He wants to make you fruitful by giving you every tool (every gift of the Spirit) necessary to successfully win your neighbors and relatives to Christ.

Unfortunately, many Christians have been unfruitful in their witnessing experiences. Statistics show that ninety-five percent of all Christians in America will never lead one person to Christ! Eighty percent of all churches have plateaued or are declining in growth, and those that are growing are increasing due to church transfers (Christians being added to a local church who once attended another church). Fifty percent of all churches in America will not add one new convert to their congregation in an entire year. This is not to speak negatively about the Church, but the facts paint a real picture of the Church's condition regarding the harvest. It seems as if we have inverted the Scripture in Acts, where it says, "five thousand were added in one day," to "one was added every five thousand days."

Please understand my heart. My intention is not to put down any type of evangelistic event, as I am excited anytime someone is sharing the Good News. However, we must make sure that the Holy Spirit is actively participating if we want to see any long lasting fruit.

It is time to analyze our methods and programs to find out why we are not bearing much fruit. Is it possible that our wonderful programs, attractive productions, quality literature, and polished methods are lacking in that which is needed most? Could it be that we have forgotten to include total reliance on the Holy Spirit, allowing Him to direct our steps in reaching those in our lives? Is it possible that our great frustration and lack of fruit has been caused by using the wrong tool or by not using any tools at all?

JESUS AND THE GIFTS OF THE SPIRIT

Jesus Christ was the most successful evangelist of all time. It is interesting to note that every recorded witnessing event in the Scripture involving Jesus (128 total in the Gospels) was accomplished using at least one of the gifts of the Spirit. In eighty-two cases there were multiple gifts operating through Jesus at the same time. Jesus Himself did not rely on a familiar method, a flashy program, or even His own strength, but used a combination of the Word and the power of the Holy Spirit.

This is the example He used to teach His disciples and the pattern He left for us to follow:

> Matthew 24:14: *"And the Good News about the Kingdom will be preached throughout the whole world, so that all nations will hear it; and then, finally, the end will come."*

The Greek word for witness is *maturion*. It means "something evidential, with proof, with evidence." Jesus was saying that Christians should preach the Gospel with proof to verify its authenticity, such as the nine spiritual gifts listed in 1 Corinthians 12:8-10:

> *"To one person the Spirit gives the ability to give wise advice; to another he gives the gift of special knowledge. The Spirit gives special faith to another, and to someone else he gives the power to heal the sick. He gives one person the power to perform miracles, and to another the ability to prophesy. He gives someone else the ability to know whether it is really the Spirit of God or another spirit that is speaking. Still another person is given the ability to speak in unknown languages, and another is given the ability to interpret what is being said."*

To help illustrate the need for the gifts of the Spirit in witnessing, let me describe a witnessing situation involving a young Mormon woman and myself. I had approached this woman purely out of a determination to share my faith. I did not sense this was a divine appointment, nor did I feel direct instructions from the Holy Spirit to approach her. In the natural, this seemed to be just another random encounter.

After introducing myself, I found the conversation quickly moving into a debate on the identity of Jesus. For over thirty minutes I tried to intellectualize my way through the conversation to win the debate, but the more we talked, the more frustrated we both became. I was quickly becoming like Kyle using the wrong screwdriver.

Finally, I decided to ask the Holy Spirit to help me. I began to pray silently as she talked, and then sensed the Lord giving me the right tool for the job! I sensed the Holy Spirit giving me a word of wisdom, one of the nine gifts of the Spirit, and He said, "Don't tell her of my power—show her my power. Tell her to raise her hands."

As soon as she was done sharing her concept of "Jesus, the Polygamist" (Mormons believe that Jesus had three wives), I calmly responded, "You know, we could sit here all day trying to convince each other which of us is right. But I believe that the Holy Spirit just told me that if you would raise your hands, He would reveal His power to you and show you the true identity of Jesus." At that moment the Holy Spirit had given me the gift of faith.

No sooner were the words out of my mouth, when she mockingly threw her hands in the air and followed with a sassy, "You mean like this?"

The Holy Spirit immediately took over the witnessing situation. The power of God hit her and she flew back onto the floor and began shaking violently. While lying on the ground, she also began to speak in another tongue. After ten minutes of meeting with the Almighty, she calmed down long enough to allow me to lead her in the sinner's prayer.

God still desires for us to exercise the gifts of the spirit that are available to us. We need to rely more on the gifts than simply trusting in our own intellect to reach the lost. When that is applied practically in our daily lives, the level of fruit reaped in your witnessing experiences will only increase.

REASONS FOR THE GIFTS OF THE SPIRIT

The needs for spiritual gifts are as numerous as the needs of the Church, both inside (pastoral) and outside (evangelistic). The Bible gives special attention to the various spiritual gifts in 1 Corinthians 12, Ephesians 4, and Romans 12. However, our focus will be primarily on the reasons for the gifts of the Spirit in relationship to the lost.

The Use of the Gifts Brings Glory to God

Our scriptural text for this chapter portrayed Jesus healing the man with the withered hand on the Sabbath. It is quite sad to see that the Pharisees missed the opportunity to celebrate the healing of a man in need. Their focus was on their own agenda and not on the agenda of God. They desired to bring glory to the Law and not the Lawgiver! Their shortsightedness caused all their attention to center on upholding the fourth commandment, eliminating the possibility of being dispensers of His glory.

The goal of everything we do, including the use of spiritual gifts, must be to glorify God. Colossians 3:23 says, *"Work hard and cheerfully in whatever you do, as though you were working for the Lord rather than for people."* The purpose of leading someone to Christ is not to add to your credentials, build your self-worth, or make a name for yourself in your local church. It is to bring glory to God. I have found that when the primary focus in using the gifts is to bring Him glory, He will trust you in using them. God does not want His gifts to misrepresent Him in any way.

One of the most frequented public locations for myself, my wife, and our son, Kyle, is the local emergency room. It never ceases to amaze me the ways in which a young boy can physically punish himself. On one occasion, Kyle, who was supposed to be asleep at the time, had fallen out of bed with a Lincoln Log in his mouth. The result was a deep laceration in the back of his throat.

While rushing him from the triage counter to one of the beds in the back of the emergency department, we passed by one of the other beds, and I *saw* a frantic young boy and a crying mother. Later I found out that he had been run over by a car. As we sat Kyle on the bed, I *heard* the Holy Spirit say, "Go and pray for My peace to fill their room." Like usual, I found myself in an awkward position, trying to reason with God. After all, my son was seriously hurt too, right?

My heart began to fill with compassion as I *felt* the pain of the boy and his mother. I walked over and pulled back the curtain, only to find a doctor talking with the mother, which made my mission all the more difficult. Without hesitation I looked into the teary eyes of the mother and *graciously* said, "I am a minister, and I came to pray for you and your boy." Immediately the doctor excused himself, leaving the three of us in the little room.

Filled with *faith* that God was about to do something significant, I laid my hands on the little boy and prayed for the presence of God to come fill the room. I prayed for the "peace that surpasses all understanding" to enter their circumstance. Immediately, a hush fell over the room, and both the boy and the mother stopped crying.

The mother looked at me with a big smile and asked, "Who are you?"

Now, don't ask me why I said this (maybe I had seen too many *Touched by an Angel* episodes), but I said, "I am an angel." As silly as it sounds, that is what I heard the Lord telling me to say. Remember, if we do the ridiculous, He will do the miraculous.

Afterwards, I found myself thinking, "Boy, are you a real moron!" But after giving it some thought, I realized why the Lord had asked me to make that crazy statement. He wanted all of us in the room to understand that it wasn't about me. It didn't matter who I was. It was all about Him. He was the one who deserved the glory. I was just the messenger.

The Use of the Gifts Builds Faith in God

The crowd of onlookers in the synagogue, who witnessed the show-down between Jesus and Pharisees, most likely had different levels of faith in

God. Some were convinced that Jesus was the Messiah, others were still investigating the possibility, while a few remained in the camp with the Pharisees.

The Scriptures say that the Pharisees were furious. This baffles me! The man's hand was restored right before their eyes. They should have been amazed and astounded, but instead they were angry.

Regardless of the response of the Pharisees, many that day had their faith in the living God increased. Jesus used miracles to build faith in God. The miracle was not an end in itself, but a means to accomplish an end. These signs and wonders were to ultimately draw unbelievers into a personal relationship with Jesus that they might eternal life.

> John 20:30-31: *"Jesus' disciples saw him do many other miraculous signs besides the ones recorded in this book. But these are written so that you may believe that Jesus is the Messiah, the Son of God, and that by believing in him you will have eternal life."*

Late one night last summer, my wife, my sister, my brother-in-law, and I drove up to a lookout on top of a hill in Portland to enjoy the view of the city lights. While spending a peaceful evening under the stars, we ran into two teenage girls who had run away from home. As we tried to help them understand their foolish choices, we also attempted to share the Gospel with them.

It was clear that neither one of them believed in God or had any desire to pursue Him as an option for her life. While my brother-in-law continued to share, I asked the Lord for direction. I was immediately given a word of knowledge concerning one of the young girls. I knew that it was from God because I would have never thought of something like that on my own.

The Holy Spirit spoke very clearly and said to me, "She is suicidal and very depressed. She was sexually abused as a child, and it haunts her to this day." I understand that this is not an easy message to share with someone, and I would have never shared it if I didn't feel the Lord directing me to do so.

With much grace and sensitivity, I shared with her that God loved her so much that He would even use a stranger at midnight to reveal her pain that she might believe in Him and be healed once and for all.

She was totally shocked and began to cry. I didn't know what to do, other than to just pray. After a few minutes, she looked up at us and said, "How did you know? It is like you have known me all my life."

As a result of using this spiritual gift, faith in the living God was built, and both girls accepted Jesus Christ as their personal Savior that night.

The Use of Gifts Brings Freedom to the Bound

The ministry of Jesus initiated the Messianic Kingdom, which meant that the Holy Spirit would be poured out on all people, without preference to nationality, religious background, or financial status. The prophecy in Joel 2:28-29 speaks of God pouring out His Spirit upon all flesh, resulting in a new release of spiritual gifts upon men and women, young and old.

These gifts were not just to be a sign of the Church in her splendor, but they were to be an essential part in fulfilling all that God had intended the Church to be, including her rule over all principalities and powers.

We find Jesus in numerous situations exercising authority over those who were bound. Never before had there been a ministry or a man who operated with such power. The benchmark Scripture for His ministry includes the use of spiritual gifts. Luke 4:18 says, *"The Spirit of the Lord is upon me, for he has appointed me to preach Good News to the poor. He has sent me to proclaim that captives will be released, that the blind will see, that the downtrodden will be freed from their oppressors, and that the time of the Lord's favor has come."* In 1 John 3:8, we are assured that His mission was to set people free from the works of the Devil, *"But the Son of God came to destroy these works of the Devil."*

Here are some of the main works of the Devil:

– The Devil comes to steal, kill, and destroy (see John 10:10).
– He employs supernatural power to blind the minds of unbelievers (see 2 Corinthians 4:4-6).
– He holds people in bondage through the fear of death (see Hebrews 11:24-25).
– He causes physical illness (see Luke 13:11; Matthew 9:32; 12:22).
– He causes mental illness (see Luke 8:26-29).
– He even can cause demons to enter and dwell in a person (see Matthew 12:45; John 13:27).[45]

Upon His ascension, Jesus passed the responsibility of ministry to his disciples—including you and me. His post-resurrection command to us is found in Mark 16:15-17, where He tells us, *"Go into all the world and preach the Good News to everyone, everywhere. Anyone who believes and is baptized will be saved. But anyone who refuses to believe will be condemned. These signs will accompany those who believe: They will cast out demons in my name, and they will speak new languages."* The word "they" in this Scripture means you!

The Use of the Gifts Offers Comfort to the Afflicted and Affliction to the Comfortable

Jesus always had a way with words. He always had the right words to speak and was never caught off guard. It is safe to assume that His eloquence was due to His total reliance on the Holy Spirit for direction.

The story of Jesus healing the man with the withered hand is a classic example. The word of wisdom, shared in the midst of the crowd, comforted the healed man, yet afflicted the Pharisees standing by. Another example is Jesus with the prostitute (see John 8:1-11) as described in a previous chapter. His words comforted the prostitute and afflicted the Pharisees.

There are many times when you may have the opportunity to minister to someone in need. Stop and think for a moment of how many people God has put in your path the last month that have significant problems. Maybe they were having marriage problems. Maybe their financial situation was bringing great stress. Maybe they were facing a great tragedy such as the death of a loved one or a terminal illness.

Now, apply this truth to that situation. Did you pray and ask God to give you a word of wisdom for their situation? Did you pray with them or use the situation as an opportunity to direct them to the Master Comforter?

On the opposite side of the equation, think of how many people you have relationships with that feel as if they have no need for God. By all outward appearances, their lives are great. They are successful in that they have cars, houses, toys, and tons of money in the bank. Maybe instead of needing a little more comfort, they need a little more affliction to drive them to their knees in search of Christ. Didn't Jesus do this with the rich young ruler to cause him to repent (see Mark 10:17-22)?

The Use of the Gifts Gives Holy Spirit Direction and Insight

Once again, Jesus became the model for illustrating this point. He was the Master Communicator. Not only did he understand to whom he was to minister, but He also understood the timing and the manner in which it was to be done.

On some occasions we find Jesus remaining silent, allowing the Holy Spirit to convict His prospects, like with the prostitute (see John 8:6). On other occasions we see Him quite vocal and adamant about making a point, like when He shouted at the moneychangers in the temple (see John 2:16). There were times when He slept through tempest storms, and other times when He remained awake, spending quiet evenings on hillsides or in the Garden. We also see Him, on occasion, requesting that the multitudes be brought to Him, while other times He demanded that the multitudes leave Him alone. In every case, the Holy Spirit gave him direction and insight in order to properly carry out His plan.

The Use of the Gifts Brings Salvation to God

In his book, *Surprised by the Spirit*, Jack Deere does a masterful job in defining the relationship of the gifts of the Spirit to salvation:

> Miracles can lead people to repentance. When Jesus led Peter, James and John to a miraculous catch of fish, Peter, *"fell to his knees before Jesus and said, 'Oh, Lord, please leave me—I'm too much a sinner to be around you.'"* (Luke 5:8). This miracle served to convict Peter of his sinfulness and lead him to repentance. Jesus said this is what would have occurred in the cities where he had done most of his miracles ([see] Matthew 11:20-24).
>
> Miracles open doors for evangelism. Many times the Gospels record that after a miracle the report of that miracle went out through the land. It caused people to wonder greatly about Jesus and to want to hear him for themselves ([see] Matthew 9:26,31; Mark 5:20; Luke 5:15; John 4:30, 42; 6:2; 12:9-11, 17-19).[46]

Just imagine the Lord directing you to someone at work who is sick.

You feel the Lord leading you to pray for him or her, and this person is miraculously healed and saved. How do you think that situation will affect all those who have mocked you or made fun of your faith? It just may be the open door God will use to reach your coworkers!

CULTIVATING A "JESUS TODAY" LIFE FILLED WITH THE GIFTS OF THE SPIRIT

After reading and praying through this chapter, I am sure that you are asking the question, "How?" Please understand that many a difficult time could be had in humanly trying to develop a gift that is supernaturally empowered.[47] It is easy to see how a person can develop the gift of teaching or enhance his or her apologetic abilities through diligent study, but how do I develop something so intangible as the word of knowledge or discerning of spirits?

The truth is that every person can effectively develop a successful, gift-filled existence. Actually, there are some very simple steps each person can take in becoming more like "Jesus Today."

Believe that the Gifts are for Today

You must first be convinced that spiritual gifts are for today; otherwise, there is no reason to pray for God to plant them in your life. After much research, I am convinced that no person will ever come to Christ through the appeals of man, but only through the power of God. If there are any doubts in your mind, let me recommend one of the most thorough books on this subject, *Surprised by the Power of the Spirit* by Jack Deere.

Believe that the Gifts are for You

God desires that everyone become a carrier of His divine tools. Each of us has a purpose and plan. We all have been called to the ministry of reconciliation (see 2 Corinthians 5:17). The only way to fulfill our individual destinies is through the implementation of the gifts in our lives.

Actively Pursue the Gifts

Once you have determined that the gifts are for today and that they are for you, immediately begin your pursuit of the gifts of the Spirit. The apostle Paul encouraged the Corinthians to pray for the gifts (see 1 Corinthians 14:13). Begin to pray, stir yourself up, and ask God to show you which gifts He has given you. Make this a daily part of your devotions!

Exercise the Gifts Regularly

It has been said that those who plan to accomplish nothing will surely attain their goal. Exercising your gifts requires risk. The only way you will ever learn to use the gifts effectively is through practice! Hebrews 5:14 admonishes us, *"Solid food is for those who are mature, who have trained themselves to recognize the difference between right and wrong and then do what is right."* In other words, spiritual maturity and effectiveness will be given to those who practice using their spiritual gifts.

Increase Your Understanding Concerning the Gifts

The Bible tells us in 2 Timothy 2:15 to *"Work hard so God can approve you. Be a good worker, one who does not need to be ashamed and who correctly explains the word of truth."* Revelation and understanding of spiritual gifts lead to greater fruitfulness and less embarrassment.

Surround Yourself with Others Who Move in the Gifts

I have had the wonderful privilege of being surrounded by some of the most mighty men and women of God. Much of what has been birthed in me has come through careful observance. One of my greatest hobbies in life is to "hang around godly individuals." Proverbs 13:20 says, *"Whoever walks with the wise will become wise;"* Pray that God would lead you to mature Christians who have similar giftings.

Never Quit Using Your Gifts

Once you have developed your gifts, continue to use them. Gifts aren't dispensed with a warranty for life. Just as one can lose muscle tone from the lack of regular, healthy exercise, so can one lose spiritual alertness and gifts through the absence of spiritual use.

It just might be possible that you could be the next Dave Finley! God is counting on you to touch all those whom He has divinely placed in your path. However, you will never do it on your own. You need the gifts of the Holy Spirit to become more like "Jesus Today." His wonderful partnership plan makes you a key part of the team. You have a bright future, working together with the Holy Spirit, and can be assured of greater fruitfulness in the days ahead.

MY JESUS TODAY PRAYER

Dear Jesus,
I am beginning to realize
Just how much I still have to learn.
I have come so far,
Yet I have so far to go.
My desire is to be like Jesus,
Using the gifts You have given me to touch broken lives.
But, if I am real with myself,
I realize I am more like the Pineville crowd of doubting onlookers.
I need You to help me see
That the lack of winning people to Christ in my life
Is greatly due to the lack
Of using the gifts in my life.
Impart to me today Your spiritual gifts
That I might bring glory to Your name,
That I might build faith in others,
And that I might partner with You to set people free.
Let the end result be
That the afflicted are comforted and the comforted are afflicted,
And that every person I share with
Would be compelled to put their faith in You.
Lastly, I ask that You remind me daily
That the gifts are for today
And that You have given gifts
To me for today.
Provoke me to actively pursue enhancing my gifts
And to find others who can help me.
Give me opportunities to practice using my gifts
That I would never give up pursuing "Jesus Today."
Amen

CHAPTER EIGHT

HIS AUTHORITY:

DISCOVERING A NEW POWER TO FIGHT

MARK 1:21-28

The early-morning sound of hungry baby birds could be heard over the instrumental worship that played on Phil's CD player. The few remaining pieces of bacon and syrup-covered plates proved that these three guys were not shy when it came to food. Their conversation at breakfast seemed light and casual, despite the heaviness of their spirits. It had been a rough few months to say the least.

With their bellies full, Dave, Phil, and their new friend, Jim, moved into the living room for their Saturday morning prayer meeting. It was the only meeting that brought each of them the strength and confidence they needed to face the opposition they experienced the other six days of the week. The increased tension in Pineville over the Finley's unusual acts had brought new meaning to the word "prayer." For these three guys, the Saturday morning accountability and prayer was a time to be themselves, to share their hearts and feelings, and to discuss what the Lord was *really* doing, without the fear of being completely ostracized.

Despite feeling the constant pressure from all of the town gossip, they were still able to rejoice in some recent victories. Dave shared about his recent phone call from Amy Jefferson and how she had left the law firm to take a job working as a receptionist at a church back home. The news of her love for Christ and the Church overshadowed their current dilemma. Also, the exciting turnaround of Herb Allen, the homeless man who had been healed, also relieved some of the tension and brought further encouragement to them.

Jim opened the Bible to Luke 10:19 to share some thoughts that the Lord had placed on his heart. He had been back in Pineville for five years, much longer than the Finleys, and he sensed that the Lord was helping him to put a finger on the *real* problem facing the town.

He began reading, *"And I have given you authority over all the power of the enemy, and you can walk among snakes and scorpions and crush them. Nothing will injure you."* The words seemed to bounce around the room and grow with intensity and meaning, *"I have given YOU authority . . . given YOU AUTHORITY . . . GIVEN YOU AUTHORITY."*

"I think we haven't tapped into the authority we have been given," Jim continued. "There is so much more available. For the most part, I think we operate on our own strength and not His. I looked up the original meaning of the word 'authority' in the concordance and it means that we have been given the lawful right to enforce obedience and power.

"The Bible also says, *'we are like Christ here in this world'* (1 John 4:17). And, *'The truth is, anyone who believes in me will do the same works I have done, and even greater works, because I am going to be with the Father'* (John 14:12).

"For too long, the devil has been in charge of our town, in charge of the people, even in charge of church. There has been no life in our church, no miracles, no salvation. Just the same people week in and week out. Nothing ever changes!" They all nodded their heads in agreement.

Dave leaned forward and said with confidence, "The only way we can change the situation is to begin to recognize our authority and *use it!* Let's begin to pray that God would break this blindness and apathy off of our church and that people in the town would begin to get saved."

Pillows were thrown on the floor to facilitate their praying positions. The lights were dimmed and the music was turned off. They began to venture into a new territory in prayer that would change their lives. They would soon begin to understand *authority* and how to use it, and the results would be astounding.

"In the name of Jesus, we ask today that You would . . ."

———————————————————————————————

On the opposite side of town, in his little study on the backside of the sanctuary, Pastor Ed sat huddled up at his desk. The piles of commentaries, lexicons, word study guides, and dictionaries were a sign that he was digging for some deeper truth.

The rattling of the old water radiator used for heat seemed to go unnoticed as Pastor Ed rolled up the sleeves on his flannel shirt and reached forward for another commentary. This new set of commentaries had gone untouched, as if they were set aside for an appointed time. Page after page, he slowly read, *God, Revelation, and Authority* by Carl F. Henry, soaking up every word.

After two hours, he jumped up with great excitement. "I got it! I got it! Uh . . . but do I want it?! Oh, this is great! But, oh God, what will this mean to our church, to the people, to my . . . job?"

The church sanctuary was filled to maximum capacity. Every dark pine pew was crammed with restless people who waited to hear what this "special meeting" was all about. Others stood along the white paneled walls in the back, making sure that they too wouldn't miss out.

The church now held the most people that had ever attended the church at one time. Never before had Pastor Ed, or any other pastor for that matter, called a special mandatory Tuesday night meeting. Every church member was called, and it seemed that almost one hundred percent were in attendance. Even the mayor and the town sheriff stood along the back wall to scan the crowd as they quietly whispered to each other.

The tension was as thick as the homemade peanut butter from Crockett Grocers. Everyone was waiting for the entrance of Pastor Ed. What would he say? How would he handle this heresy? What would happen to the Finleys and their little following? Would the Finleys have the audacity to show their presence? And if so, would they even survive the out lash of anger from the other church members?

"Hello?" Dave leaned over the kitchen counter and picked up the phone.

"Dave, this is Pastor Ed." His voice was met with an uncomfortable silence. But Pastor Ed continued anyway, "Dave, I know this may sound like suicide, but I need to ask you a favor. I need you to get your brother, Phil, and Jim and get down to the church right away. We are getting ready to start a church meeting and I need you to be there."

"What? Do you think I'm crazy?" Dave quickly blurted in return.

"You have to trust me on this one. Please come at once! I have to go. I will see you there." Pastor Ed hung up the phone, leaving Dave's heart racing and his mind buzzing with questions.

The side door opened and Pastor Ed walked in carrying his Bible in one hand and his notes in the other. The loud chatter in the room came to an immediate halt. All eyes were on him as he stood behind the pulpit. He pulled his wire-rimmed glasses to the edge of his nose, and the crowd could see that there was something different about Pastor Ed. His countenance was different. He stood erect, broadening his shoulders with a look of fire in his eyes. This wasn't the soft-spoken pastor they had known for years.

As Pastor Ed opened his Bible and set the notes on the pulpit, the back sanctuary doors opened from the foyer and all eyes turned in amazement to see Dave, Phil, and Jim. They stood in the entry as shocked as the rest of the crowd, not knowing what to expect. The silence of the crowd was broken immediately by gasps and hostile accusations as many pointed their fingers at the unwelcome guests.

"Can I have your attention, please," Pastor Ed said politely, as the crowd continued to rumble about the intruders.

"I said, CAN I HAVE YOUR ATTENTION, PLEASE!" It was the loudest they had ever heard Pastor Ed talk. His tenacity silenced the crowd.

He continued, "Thank you. Dave, Phil, and Jim, why don't you come up front and sit down here."

All eyes focused on the three. As they came forward, they felt as if they were about to be sentenced at a murder trial. They sat down in the last remaining chairs as Pastor Ed focused his eyes on the crowd.

He cleared his throat and began his speech, "I have called this meeting here tonight, after much prayer and fasting, because I felt that as a church we needed to address the recent events in our town."

Mr. Dawson stood up and blurted out, "It's about time!" His outburst was met with a host of confirmations from other disgruntled members.

Pastor Ed looked him in the eye and said, "Sit down! Please, just sit down." His tone validated that this wasn't the Pastor Ed they were used to. Silence fell on the crowd.

"I have been in this church for over twenty years, and I believe that my character and ability to lead this church has gone unscathed. I have served you faithfully and cared for your families. I have married many of you, buried your family members, and have brought you the truth week in and week out, the best that I know how." The crowd began to nod their heads in agreement.

He leaned over his pulpit, pulled off his glasses and said, "These past few weeks have been the roughest days of my life."

As he looked over at the Finleys, he continued, "The recent unusual events with Phil Finley supposedly being raised from the dead and the miracle of Herb's arm at the picnic has caused even the most religious to reconsider their beliefs. As far as Herb's arm is concerned, I would have never believed it, unless I had witnessed it with my own eyes."

"Tonight, as your pastor, I need to confess and repent that for too long I have led you astray. This may come as a shock to most, but after spending many days on my knees and many sleepless nights studying, I have come to the conclusion that I no longer want to live a powerless Christian life." The faces of the people substantiated their state of confusion.

"We as a church have grown introverted, stale, and dead. We have lost our focus and the reason for our existence. And at the risk of being fired by the board, I have come here tonight to say that I believe there is a religious spirit that has controlled this church and this town for a long time." He cleared his throat and stood up straight.

"For the first time in my life, I realized the authority that I have in Christ. I realized that He lives in me. I realized that I *can* do *all* things *through* Christ. I realized that greater is He *that is in me*, than he that is in the world. I realized He has given *me authority* over *all* the power of the Enemy." His passion was clearly evident as he began to cry.

Tears rolled down his cheeks, he hit the pulpit with his fist and declared, "Things are going to change! I am going to change! This church has to change!"

Pastor Ed leaned forward and began to sob. Dave and Phil put their heads forward and began to silently pray. Jim looked over his shoulder at the rest of the room to check out the pulse of the crowd. Many heads were facing the floor. Others just closed their eyes.

To everyone's surprise, Mr. Dawson stood up. He too had tears pouring down his face. He too had a new look on his face. He had been touched by the Holy Spirit, just like Pastor Ed. He took a deep breath, closed his eyes, and began to clap.

All eyes were now focused on the "Chief Pharisee" as he applauded in agreement. Right next to him was Dale Stanley, owner of the hardware store and a fellow church board member. He stood up with the same look of passion, stared straight at Dave Finley, and began to clap as well.

One by one, the crowd rose to their feet. Something out of the ordinary was beginning to happen. Something unusual, something supernatural, something sovereign, something historical.

In a matter of moments, the entire crowd was on its feet clapping. Their clapping was met with different individual outbursts of praise. Soon, the whole place was filled with shouts of agreement.

It was the first time in the one-hundred-year history of the church that an entire room filled with people stood together in unity. Broken. Humbled. Hungry. Eager. Anticipating something more. The Holy Spirit had broken through. Broken through their religiosity. Broken through their apathy. Broken through their narrow-mindedness. Broken through the Enemy's strongholds.

The more they clapped, the more it pleased the Lord. The entire experience went against the grain of their century-old theology. But now everyone knew that they were in the presence of almighty God.

Without any direction from the pastor, people began to sing spontaneously. Some knelt and prayed, while others lay on the floor and wept. The Holy Spirit had taken over, and no one complained.

As the night wore on, the Lord began prompting people to stand and pray out loud. One by one they prayed for their church. They prayed for their town. They prayed for the lost. They prayed against the darkness over their region. It was evident that they too had corporately received the revelation of their authority in Christ, a new power to fight.

———————————————————

As Dave put his head on his pillow, he reflected back on his Saturday meeting with the guys and how God had orchestrated his week. With a sense of gratification, he looked up toward the ceiling and laughed, "God, You did it again, didn't You?"

As he closed his eyes, he pondered the revelation that Christ was living *in* Him. He was overwhelmed with the understanding of his new authority in Christ. He whispered, "Just as He is, so *am* I in the world. . . . So am I in the world."

"What now, God? What are You going to do next?" It was a question that only the Lord could answer and would in due time.

It was another lesson along the pathway of life; another step in living life as Jesus would.

HIS AUTHORITY

MARK 1:21-28

Jesus and his companions went to the town of Capernaum, and every Sabbath day he went into the synagogue and taught the people. They were amazed at his teaching, for he taught them as one who had real authority—quite unlike the teachers of religious law. A man possessed by an evil spirit was in the synagogue, and he began shouting, "Why are you bothering us, Jesus of Nazareth? Have you come to destroy us? I know who you are—the Holy One sent from God!"

Jesus cut him short. "Be silent! Come out of the man." At that the evil spirit screamed and threw the man into a convulsion, but then he left him.

Amazement gripped the audience, and they began to discuss what had happened. "What sort of new teaching is this?" they asked excitedly. "It has such authority! Even evil spirits obey his orders!" The news of what he had done spread quickly through that entire area of Galilee.

Once again, we are taking another step toward becoming "Jesus Today." At this point, I hope that you are prayerfully implementing these principles along with our fictional character, Dave Finley. It should be clear that each attribute plays a crucial role in your daily living; all attributes are necessary, and one cannot be substituted for another.

Authority in Christ is no exception to this rule. Once we have seen what the Lord desires us to *see*, and we *respond to His voice* with a *compassionate heart* filled with *grace* and *faith*, we must then stir up the *gifts* within us in order to move forward with confidence and *authority*. Let's carefully review the issue of authority modeled by Jesus.

The scriptural account in Mark 1:21-28 places Jesus in the synagogue with a curious crowd, some hardened Pharisees, and a most unusual situation. Just like many other temple gatherings, the order of the meeting had turned into an all-out spiritual boxing match; with Jesus in one corner, the Devil in the other and a crowd of anxious onlookers waiting to see who would reign as champion.

It seems that the purpose of His continual confrontation with the Pharisees was to break off the religious molds that bound them and rendered them powerless and incapable of pleasing God. His purpose was not to resist them, but to open their eyes and ears that they might receive Him as Lord and attain their God-given destiny. The challenge that Christ faced with the religious leaders of His day is one that many Christians currently face.

As the intensity of this first century battle heightened, the crowd of onlookers quickly moved to the winning side, as those watching were able to discern who was really in charge: not the Pharisees, nor the evil spirits, but Jesus. Mark 1:22 states, *"They were amazed at his teaching, for he taught them as one who had real authority—quite unlike the teachers of religious law."*

Unfortunately, the Pharisees repeatedly made the same mistake. They believed that their authority was attained through a series of religious acts and observances. They thought their strict adherence to the Law and their special title, "Pharisee," earned them a position of spiritual authority. However, the crowd in the synagogue realized that the Pharisees held influence in title only. They based their authority on what they did, not on who they could be in Christ.

AUTHORITY: BEING OR DOING?

It is interesting to note that the Pharisees encountered little or no supernatural activity. Their sense of authority through "doing" did not intimidate or move the demonic forces in any way. However, we see that once Jesus came on the scene, the evil spirits confronted Jesus, hoping to find a way of escape. His very being scared the evil spirits and stripped them of their power in the life of the demonized man. They knew exactly who He was and identified Him as the *"the Holy One sent from God"* (Mark 1:24). He didn't *do* something in order to establish His authority; it was simply inherent in *who He was*. Jesus understood the difference between being and doing.

One of the most embarrassing moments in my life happened as a freshman in high school. This incident taught me an important lesson about authority. I was involved in a fight with another freshman and ended up winning. The only problem was that my opponent had an older brother who was a senior at the time. Upon my arrival to school the next morning, I was stopped by a stranger.

He said with a hint of anger, "Are you Marc Estes?"

Being a little low on common sense, I said, "Yep, that's me."

Immediately I found myself falling backwards as his fist met with my chin. He then shouted, "If you ever touch my brother again, I will go crazy on your face!"

You know, I actually believed him! For the next three days he would meet me in front of the gym as I went into P.E. and would punch me, each time telling me how much he hated me. Every day brought greater fear and anxiety. I found myself not sleeping at night, and I was even scared to go to school. He was huge and powerful, and my skinny, 145-pound physique was no match for this star football player.

On the fourth day something changed. At the time, I didn't realize what was taking place, but it was the beginning of an authority shift. As he had for the past few days, he walked up to me and shouted the same words, but this time he didn't hit me. Then he said, right before walking off, "And by the way, if you ever tell your cousin that I hit you, I'll kill you!"

Duhhhh! Why didn't I think of that? My cousin was one of the toughest guys in school and had a reputation as a great fighter who had never been beaten. I bet you can guess what happened next. I called my cousin and told him about the crazy nut who was picking on me.

The following day marked the beginning of my newfound freedom. While walking to the portable classrooms during lunch, the bully and a bunch of his cronies surrounded me and proceeded to inform me of my impending doom. While feeling very helpless and nervous, I looked over the shoulder of this rabid senior football player, only to see my cousin running full speed to my rescue.

Something happened. I realized, at that moment, that my size had little to do with the situation. I knew that nothing I could *do* would bring me victory, but *who I was* made all the difference. I was Rich's cousin! The closer my cousin got to me, the more confident I became. And once he arrived on the scene, I was forever released from this bully's harassment. You can only guess what happened next. The end result brought freedom and liberty!

While I don't recommend fighting in school as a means to overcoming an obstacle, the point is still clear. When we are fighting with the enemy, it's not what we do that bring victory—it's who we are in Christ that matters! And when he comes to our rescue, freedom and liberty are the results!

AUTHORITY: FEELING OR FACT?

If I were to ask if you felt that you had all authority over the Evil One, what would your response be? If you are like most of us, you would immediately respond with a resounding, "You bet I do!" Now let me probe one step further. How did you feel the last time you heard the Holy Spirit tell you to witness to someone? How did you respond? Did your heart begin to race? Did your palms begin to sweat? Did you feel a loss of words? Again, if you are like most Christians, you would reply this time a little more sheepishly, "Yes, in fact, I did feel nervous!"

As I have talked with many Christians about their spiritual authority, I have found them to be the first to admit they possess this all-powerful, eternal gift from the Father. But they are also the first to come running to the pastor for help when they are involved in a situation in which they are confronted by demonic forces. I believe their intentions are pure and they intellectually understand authority, but they fail to walk it out practically because of a lack of revelation of their true identity in Christ.

For the most part, many base their spiritual authority upon what they feel or what they do, not on *who they are in Christ*. But the foundation of our authority is not our personality or feelings. It is not a by-product of relentless study or consistent religious practice. It is not even determined by our maturity or the duration of our Christian walk. It comes solely from our position in Christ as an heir in the kingdom of God.

As Dean Sherman put it:

> Our spiritual authority is a legal issue. It is a legal reality that does not waver because of our unbelief, and is as real as any transaction. In fact, it's a legal arrangement much like marriage. When I ask people if they are married I never hear, "Well, I'm not sure. Sometimes I feel married, and sometimes I just don't know." They will always say, "Yes" or "No." If we are married, we are totally convinced of it at all times, and have a legal document to prove it. Feelings, thoughts, and personalities do not change the reality of that legal arrangement.[48]

We need a fresh revelation of our identity in Christ to transition from the mindset of "who I am is determined by what I do" to a more biblical perspective of "what I do is determined by who I am." Our understanding of who we are in Christ is the most critical in exercising authority over the Enemy.

WHAT IS REAL AUTHORITY?

Let's take a brief moment to define this important concept. The word "authority," as illustrated in our pilot text, Mark 1:21-28, is defined as "the power or right to do something, particularly to give orders and see that they are followed." The word "authority" in the Bible usually means "a person's right to do certain things because of the position or office that he holds." The word emphasizes the legality and right more than the physical strength needed to do something.[49]

The Bible has much to say on the subject of authority:

> Supreme authority is God's alone (see Romans 13:1) and is unconditional and absolute (see Psalm 29:10; Isaiah 40:1), making Him supreme over nature and human history alike. From this intrinsic authority comes that of governments (see Romans 13:1-7), employers (see Ephesians 6:5-9), parents (see Ephesians 6:1-4), church elders (see Hebrews 13:7,17), and others in positions of power. Similarly the angels function under divine authority (see Luke 1:19-20), and evil spirits are also subject to God's power (see Ephesians 6:11-12).
>
> Because Jesus was God, His authority was not merely derived from the Father but was also intrinsic. His power knew no limitations (see Matthew 28:18) and was the ground of His commissions to His disciples (see Mark 6:7; John 20:22). A preeminent source of derived authority is the Scriptures, inspired by God Himself (see 2 Timothy 3:16; 2 Peter 1:20-21) and therefore by His supreme authority.
>
> For this reason we are required to obey them. . . . Christians are given the authority to become children of God (John 1:12) and have the right to pursue certain forms of behavior (see 1 Corinthians 6:12).[50]

Jesus Has All Authority

The coming of Christ to this earth marked the largest military invasion in the history of mankind. His arrival on this planet overthrew Satan's rule here. During Jesus' temptation in the wilderness, Satan said to Jesus, *"I give you the glory of these kingdoms and authority over them—because they are mine to give to anyone I please"* (Luke 4:6).

Although Satan may have been given authority, he has never been given ownership. God is the Creator and, to this day, still holds the deed of trust (see Psalm 24:1). Therefore, the kingdom of darkness and its authority consists only of the control Satan possesses over the lives of lost people through deceptive acts, also referred to in Scripture as *"strategies and tricks of the Devil"* (Ephesians 6:11).

Because God, in His redemptive plan, never intended that Satan would continue to reign over His precious creation, He sent His Son to break off the authority of the Enemy, once and for all. Therefore, the kingdom of God that Jesus came to establish was not a land that has territorial boundaries, but a kingdom that exists in the hearts and lives of human beings.[51]

At Calvary, Satan went to the mat as a defeated foe—his fate sealed forever. Colossians 2:15 reveals the stripping of his power, *"In this way, God disarmed the evil rulers and authorities. He shamed them publicly by his victory over them on the cross of Christ."* Once he was disarmed, his keys were taken, and he was no longer legally in control. Revelation 1:18 says, *"Look, I am alive forever and ever! And I hold the keys of death and the grave."*

Jesus Transferred All Authority to Us

You might be wondering, "If Jesus took away all authority, then why is the Devil still in control of people's lives?" Because the war is still not over. Although Jesus took away the Enemy's authority, there are still over three billion people who have not yet surrendered their lives to Christ and who remain under the kingdom of darkness. Christ's authority over one's life is only complete as long as he has a personal relationship with God, through Jesus Christ. Many have not yet made that decision. The apostle Paul says in 2 Corinthians 4:4, *"Satan, the god of this evil world, has blinded the minds of those who don't believe, so they are unable to see the glorious light of the Good News that is shining upon them. They don't understand the message we preach about the glory of Christ, who is the exact likeness of God."* Peter further validates this point in 1 Peter 5:8, *"...the Devil, your great enemy.*

He prowls around like a roaring lion, looking for some victim to devour."

Although Jesus has all authority and has conquered Satan, there still is work to be done! There are lives that still need to be delivered! There are still people who need Jesus! That is why He has given us the authority, so that we might be victorious in fulfilling His mission.

Luke 10:19 says, *"And I have given you authority over all the power of the enemy, and you can walk on snakes and scorpions and crush them. Nothing will injure you."* The word "all" means *"all!"* He has given us authority over *all* the combined forces of darkness—every demon, every spell, every stronghold, every religion or cult, every attack, every influence, and every atmosphere. They are *all* subject to Christ who lives within us (see 1 John 4:4).

Dean Sherman puts it this way:

> By destroying the works of the Devil on the Cross, He also enabled us to do the same—to reach out to the oppressed, the downtrodden, and the brokenhearted. Before ascending back to heaven, He gave us a mandate to reverse the works of the Devil. Included in the Great Commission were the statements: *"They will cast out demons in my name . . . They will be able to place their hands on the sick and heal them"* (Mark 16:17-18). This is our stewardship of the authority Jesus retrieved on our behalf.[52]

UNDERSTANDING YOUR AUTHORITY

In the past decade, Christianity has been flooded with books, seminars, and ministries devoted to spiritual warfare and the doctrine of our position of authority over the Devil and his legions of demons. From this emphasis, two extremes of thought have emerged. On one end, many believe that the Devil has been completely relinquished of all of his power and authority and doesn't have any influence or persuasion over a Christian's life. On the other end of the spectrum, some would teach that a great deal of focus and energy should be spent fighting the Devil, as he has extreme power to assault anyone at any time.

There are two important truths to consider when trying to find a balanced perspective on this vital issue. Both are necessary in properly understanding your God-given authority as a follower of Jesus Christ and allowing you to see great fruit in sharing the love of God with a needy world.

Satan Has Been Stripped of All Legal Rights over Your Life

First of all, Satan and the forces of hell have no legal right over your life. You have been given the right and power to resist the Devil and, in doing so, he must flee (see James 4:7). The important part of this Scripture that many forget to apply is the opening statement, *"humble yourselves before God."* Resisting the Devil is not accomplished by spontaneous shouting, but through daily surrender and total submission to the Lord. Shouting at the Devil, without having your life aligned to God and the Scriptures, is like shouting at a mountain to be moved—nothing happens! Resisting the Devil is not what you confess, but what you possess!

The Sovereignty of God

The sovereignty of God is another issue that often brings confusion because it is an aspect of God's being that cannot possibly be understood by the human mind. There are times when God, in His infinite wisdom, will actually allow seasons of affliction for our own good. There are other times when He will ask us to share with a loved one, only to be resisted. In my own life, there have been many times when I have felt rejection while sharing my faith, and I found myself asking, "Why Lord?" only to find out years later that it was an instrumental turning point in that person's life. We must allow the Lord to be sovereign in all situations and understand that He has specific reasons for allowing the Enemy to attack us.

There are many scriptural examples of God's people confronting the powers of the Enemy to advance the kingdom of God, only to be met with opposition. Joseph endured years of affliction in jail before he saw any rewards. Daniel was thrown into the lion's den before he experienced great favor and godly influence. Shadrach, Meshach, and Abednego's fiery furnace forced a nation to evaluate their idol worship. Elijah's three-and-one-half-year journey to Mount Carmel ended with victory over the prophets of Baal. Hosea was commanded to marry a prostitute named Gomer in order to bring the word of the Lord to God's drifting people through his life story.

We have authority over Satan and the legal right to force him to leave our life circumstances alone. Yet at the same time, there must be a willingness to accept the fact that God, in His sovereignty, may allow us to face battles with the Enemy. This not only will strengthen us, humble us, and mold us more into becoming "Jesus Today," but it will also give us the grace to believe that He is working out His perfect plan in the lives of those to whom we are ministering.

Our Authority is "In Christ"

Being "Jesus Today" means that you are "in Christ!" This one statement is the overwhelming theme of the New Testament. How well we understand this concept of being "in Christ" will determine the level of maturity and freedom we experience. It will also determine how the Enemy will respond to our Spirit-led demands. Being "in Christ" is foundational for exercising our authority.

Neil Anderson says this about being "in Christ":

> In the six chapters of the book of Ephesians alone there are forty references to being in Christ and having Christ in you. For every reference for Christ being in you there are ten for you being in Christ. Being in Christ is the most critical element of our identity. . . . Understanding your identity in Christ is absolutely essential to your success at living the Christian life. No person can consistently behave in a way that's inconsistent with the way he perceives himself. If you think you're a no-good bum, you'll probably live like a no-good bum. But if you see yourself as a child of God who is spiritually alive in Christ, you'll begin to live in victory and freedom as He lived. Next to the knowledge of God, a knowledge of who you are is by far the most important truth you can possess.[53]

Realize that your authority comes from being "in Christ." Allow that truth to sink deeper that you might understand it with your heart, not just your head. Once this truth is assimilated, you must learn to apply it to everyday life.

APPLYING OUR "JESUS TODAY" AUTHORITY

Take a moment to reflect on what you experience when prompted to share your faith. Most of us would answer *fear*, some would say *anxiety*, and still others would express that they feel *confusion* about what words to share. Statistics show that you are not alone! Eighty-five percent of all Christians say they don't share their faith due to fear, while others don't share because of a sense of inadequacy. These subtle attacks of the Enemy are invoked to paralyze the advancement of the Gospel to those in need of hearing it.

My own experience in the following witnessing situation is a prime example of how the Enemy uses intimidation tactics to keep us from sharing the Gospel.

While my flight was delayed in the airport at Salt Lake City, I left the crowded seating area to stretch my legs and get something to drink. I happened to glance toward the gate and noticed a Middle Eastern family, whom I would later find out were Hindus.

Immediately, I looked at them through the eyes of Jesus and sensed that they needed Christ. I then heard the Holy Spirit say, "Go tell them about my love." I felt as though I had compassion to share this love, and even the faith to believe that the message would be received, but I was unexpectedly met with another challenge . . . the authority challenge.

I stood there looking at them, as the Enemy brought the first subtle wave of fear. Without even realizing that my focus had changed, I found myself thinking of all the things that could go wrong: "They could yell at me. They could tell me to get lost. They could tell the gate agent that I was harassing them."

So I went to plan B. I set out a fleece for God. "God, if this is your will that I share with these people, when I get back from getting a soda they will still be there."

Of course it was His will, but I proceeded to find the furthest restaurant and stand in the longest line, hoping that my procrastination would eliminate the possibility of sharing and save me from the increasing pressure of the Enemy.

I walked at a snail's pace back to the gate, only to find the lady looking at me and smiling!

"Oh great! Now what?" I thought. "I know . . . I'll go to the bathroom, and if they are still here when I get back, it must really be you, Lord, right?"

I was again reminded of Colossians 3:15, *"And let the peace that comes from Christ rule in your hearts."* As I meditated upon that Scripture, the fear subsided, the anxiety disappeared, and a fresh release of confidence came over me. I once again realized, "I am *in* Christ, and Christ is *in* me! And He has never lost a battle!"

I then engaged His authority, along with my other "Jesus Today" attributes, and immediately sensed the Enemy disappear from the area! I was filled with His grace and faith. Next, I asked Him to stir up the gifts in me. Suddenly, I couldn't wait to talk with this wonderful couple. A fresh revelation of my authority gave me the ability to overcome the Enemy's resistance and allowed me to share the Gospel with this Hindu family. The interesting part of the story is that they were excited to hear about Jesus and welcomed my conversation. The father even allowed me to pray with the entire family!

Friend, you and I were brought to the kingdom of God for such a time as this, to once and for all displace the long-standing rule of Satan over the lives of the lost. Satan will do whatever he can to distort your perception of who you are in Christ and rob you of the revelation of your legal authority. You are no longer under his control because you are in Christ! Let us make the commitment today to activate this important truth in our lives and start releasing His authority through our actions. May this truth be added to our daily walk and take us one step closer to becoming "Jesus Today."

MY JESUS TODAY PRAYER

Dear Jesus,
Today I come knowing
That I am in need of further adjustments.
My heart desires to please You,
Yet I feel paralyzed from mistaken authority.
Help me to break through
Any religious traditions or mindsets
That have caused me to believe
That my authority comes from what I have done or felt.
Lord, please help me to see
That my authority exists
Because of who I am,
As I am "in Christ."
Give me the revelation and strength
To overcome the Enemy
And to be used by You to enforce
Your will and Your ways.
I am an overcomer and will overcome
The obstacles and snares of the Enemy
And proclaim that the Enemy has no legal right in my life,
As I take a step closer to becoming "Jesus Today."
Amen

CHAPTER NINE

HIS PRAYER:

UNLEASHING

INTERCESSION

FOR HARVEST

BREAKTHROUGH

MATTHEW 26:36-46

D ave rolled over and looked at the alarm clock, "Three a.m.? Not again!"

For the past seven days, Dave's eyes were wide open at three o'clock in the morning. He knew that the Lord was partnering with him in prayer. His flesh didn't like the new rendezvous time, but his spirit was willing. Each night the Lord would meet him in a very special way. It was their quiet time.

Dave rolled over on his stomach, tucked his pillow under his chest, pulled out his journal, clasped his hands and began to pray through the long list of names that were stored on the pages. At the top of the list was his father. Then his mother, Michael, and Cindy followed. Mr. Browski. Amy Jefferson. Herb. Pastor Ed. Mr. Dawson. Jim. Phil. From that point forward were the names of just about every person in Pineville. Little notes were scribbled next to different names, and, on some names, the ink was smeared from the tears shed during moments of compassionate prayer.

As Dave prayed, he could see what Jesus saw. He heard the voice of the Lord directing him to pray for certain names, and he felt their hurts and pains as if they were his own. He even felt an overwhelming grace for the unlovely of Pineville, for both the down-and-outers *and* the up-and-comers.

His prayers began to take on new levels of faith as he believed each word would be answered by the Almighty. He exercised a new level of authority, as he commanded charge over the principalities and demonic influences governing the lives of lost people.

God was bringing him to a new level of prayer. A new foundation stone, just like the others. So subtly, yet so strategically, a new gene of soul travail was being placed deep into his spirit each night. It was a Holy Spirit gene. A breakthrough gene, one that would be necessary to accomplish the will of God for their town. One that would bring great joy, but at a great price.

"Hey, Jim, this is Dave." Jim wiped his eyes, put on his glasses and tried to gain his composure.

"Why are you calling me so early? It's four-thirty in the morning!" Jim cleared his throat and waited for a valid response.

"Something is happening to me. I was awakened this morning again at three, but this time something is different. It is so real, but . . ."

Jim interrupted, "What are you talking about? . . ."

"It's like I buckled over in pain as I prayed for people, and as I pray it's like the Lord takes over and won't allow me to stop praying until there is a release of some sort. . . . I think this is a God-thing. I think you should join me. You and Phil. . . ."

Jim sat up in his bed and offered some insight, "You know when I was in Bible college I took a class called 'Intercession and the Church.' What you are describing to me was explained in detail in a few of the books that we were required to read. Dave, God is using you to break through Satan's hold on the lives of those who are bound!"

"You really think so?" Dave questioned him even though he already knew the answer.

"Yep! I really think so."

———————————— ▬▬▬▬ ————————————

Dave and Jim agreed to increase their prayer time by meeting consistently at a scheduled time. Immediately following the Sunday night service, Dave, Phil, and Jim met together at Dave's house to pray for whatever the Lord put on their hearts. Each meeting took on a different flavor. There were nights when they sensed the presence of God so thick that they would lie silent for hours; other nights it seemed as if they were there out of pure obedience. Some nights they would pray from nine p.m. until three or four a.m. Other times they would finish at eleven o'clock. It just depended on what the Lord was doing that night.

One particular summer night was different altogether. The warm summer air blew through the screens as the hum of crickets drifted in from the field behind Dave's home. The late sunset interrupted by the rising of a full moon was a picturesque backdrop to the night. As they lowered the lights in the living room and took their normal positions, the atmosphere was immediately energized with unified expectancy.

"Lord, we believe You are here tonight! We ask that You would do more than we could think or ask," Jim prayed as he remembered Ephesians 3:20.

Dave followed right behind with his own prayer of faith, "*Tonight* we want a breakthrough! *Tonight* we ask that You answer our prayers! Tonight we ask for revival! *Tonight* we say to the enemy, *give them up*!"

Prayer after prayer was offered to God like a sweet-smelling aroma. Passionate prayers. Faith-filled prayers. Holy Spirit-directed prayers. Soul-travailing prayers. Silver bullet prayers.

"Guys, it is happening again . . . uhhhhhhhhhh!" Dave began to moan. "The Lord is impressing upon me right now to pray for the lost!"

Both Jim and Phil looked at Dave as he rose to his knees and lifted his hands in the air.

The atmosphere was contagious. The Holy Spirit was close. Their assignment was clear. Intercession for the lost! Both Jim and Phil began to receive this burden to pray for the lost as well. Within a matter of moments all three were crying out to the point of agony for their town.

"God save them!" Jim cried.

"Take the blinders off their eyes that they may see You!" Phil groaned.

Dave added, "Save my dad, my mom, my siblings. God save Mr. Browski! Save the sheriff and the mayor!" He had memorized his prayer list. His pleading with God turned into an uncontrollable sob.

Suddenly, a sense of calm descended on the little room where they prayed. Peace saturated each one. Rest and joy settled them. Silence filled the room as the presence of God permeated every atom.

"RIIIIIIIIIINGGGGGGGGG!" Dave's rotary phone blasted through the room, shaking everyone back to their natural minds.

Jim looked at Dave and said jokingly, "Who would be calling at this time of the morning? It can't be you—you're here!" They all laughed as Dave raced to the phone.

"Dave, you are never going to believe what is happening! You gotta get down here quick." It was Pastor Ed.

"Where are you?" Dave responded.

"I am at the church! Come now!" With that, Pastor Ed slammed down the phone.

Cars lined the dimly lit street outside of the church building. In both directions and around the corners cars pulled in, one after another. Dave, Jim, and Phil jumped out of the Mustang around the corner and began to run down the sidewalk to the church.

"What in the world is going on here?" Phil said, gasping for breath.

Dave answered back, "I don't know, but at four a.m. it's gotta be good!"

"No, it's gotta be God!" Jim responded.

As they drove closer to the church, the scene before them was nearly unbelievable. People were crowded around the building as it was already full. People knelt out on the lawn, others sat on the steps, and many stood in circles praying. Cries of repentance, prayers for mercy, evidence of sorrow covered the entire property. It was as if they were entering a divine radiation zone, a God zone.

The three guys pushed their way through the crowd, stepping over people on their way up to the podium. Pastor Ed leaned over the pulpit with his hands raised, praying silently. Each person in the room was having his or her own personal encounter with God.

Dave reached Pastor Ed and whispered to him, "What is happening?"

Pastor Ed lifted up his tear-stained face and said, "Can't you see? It's God! He has broken through. People are getting saved!"

With a puzzled look, Dave said, "Who called them and told them to come?"

"That's my point! It's God. No one called them! Evidently, God is waking people up all over town and directing them here. Others are getting saved and then calling their loved ones. Oh, it's beautiful!" Pastor Ed put his head back down on the pulpit.

As Dave looked around, he could see the faces of so many new people. People he had been praying for. In one corner were Mr. and Mrs. Fields, holding hands, crying, and praying aloud. In the pew to his right was Mr. Maple from the diner, kneeling and begging God for forgiveness. Halfway back, standing against the wall with his head down and hat in his hand, was the sheriff. Right next to him the mayor was praying as well.

A revival was taking place right before their eyes. People were getting saved by the hundreds. God had touched the town of Pineville. It was something they all had been praying for, but something they didn't really expect to happen. At least not like this.

The sun began to rise as Dave lay on his bed and closed his eyes. Just as he drifted off to sleep, the phone rang once more.

"Dave?" It was a familiar, yet distance voice.

"Dad? Is that you?!" Dave's heart began to race.

"Son, please forgive me! Oh, I am such a failure! Please forgive me." Mr. Finley began to sob.

Dave cautiously prodded, "Dad, what is going on?"

Mr. Finley cleared his throat and said, "I don't know what's going on. All I know is that I was awakened this morning at six a.m. as if God had shaken me awake. And suddenly I felt this overwhelming conviction come over me as He showed me everything I had done wrong in my life. I cried out in fear thinking that He was going to kill me on the spot. Dave, I need your God. Would you tell me how to get your God?"

With that, Dave would enjoy a moment that was long overdue . . . leading his father to Christ.

The price had been great—lost sleep and months of dedication without tangible results. But in the end, the intercession worked and the reward was great. For Dave, leading his father to Christ was the crowning moment of his life to that point. Nothing seemed as important or satisfying as he explained Salvation to his father and felt a measure of restoration in their relationship. Prayer had unleashed the power of breakthrough.

MATTHEW 26:36-46

Then Jesus brought them to an olive grove called Gethsemane, and he said, "Sit here while I go on ahead to pray." He took Peter and Zebedee's two sons, James and John, and he began to be filled with anguish and deep distress. He told them, "My soul is crushed with grief to the point of death. Stay here and watch with me."

He went on a little farther and fell face down on the ground, praying, "My Father! If it is possible, let this cup of suffering be taken away from me. Yet I want your will, not mine." Then he returned to the disciples and found them asleep. He said to Peter, "Couldn't you stay awake and watch with me even one hour? Keep alert and pray. Otherwise temptation will overpower you. For though the spirit is willing enough, the body is weak!"

Again he left them and prayed, "My Father! If this cup cannot be taken away until I drink it, your will be done." He returned to them again and found them sleeping, for they just couldn't keep their eyes open.

So he went back to pray a third time, saying the same things again. Then he came to the disciples and said, "Still sleeping? Still resting? Look, the time has come. I, the Son of Man, am betrayed into the hands of sinners. Up, let's be going. See, my betrayer is here!"

AN APPOINTED MOMENT WITH JESUS

No one could ever imagine the intensity Jesus felt at that moment. It was the night of His betrayal and the beginning of a lonely journey to the Cross. His earthly ministry was almost complete, but a few more items had to be put into place. He had just left the warm, comfortable, intimate setting of the Upper Room and the Last Supper, to lead His confused disciples down the dark, chilly path of the Kidron Valley to a very familiar place, the Garden of Gethsemane.

Jesus knew that it was not just another day, but that it was an appointed day. While in the garden, He said to His disciples, *"the time has come"* (Matthew 26:45). It was not just another time in the garden, but an appointed time, a divine time. Jesus would take on the sin of humanity at the Cross. In that most difficult moment he had yet faced, he turned to deep intercessory prayer. Prayer would be the key to receiving the grace and strength needed to endure this horrific experience. Prayer would be the weapon to break the power of the Enemy. Prayer would pave the way for the Gospel to be preached so that those in the world might know Him as their Savior.

This principle is illustrated in the story of our friend, Dave Finley. Dave was being tutored in the school of prayer. He too came to realize that his prayers would be the key to unlocking revival in his town. Night after night, he obeyed the Holy Spirit and partnered with Him in his own late-night "Garden of Gethsemane," standing in the gap for his loved ones. The result was a massive breakthrough in his community as well as in the life of his distant father.

We must realize that God wants to work through us to meet the many needs of the lost, but a breakthrough must occur for the lost to be ready to receive our help. That breakthrough comes only by intercessory prayer.

AN APPOINTED MOMENT FOR THE CHURCH

We are living in momentous times, and God is looking for momentous people, like you, who will partner with Him in bringing about the end-time harvest. As we move closer to the return of Christ, I can sense the Lord saying to us all, *"the time has come"* (Matthew 26:45). The fields are ripe and ready for harvest, and our prayers will bring the harvest time into existence.

It is no wonder that we are experiencing a global prayer awakening like never before in the history of the Church. Peter Wagner states in his book, *Churches That Pray*, "A prayer movement that greatly surpasses anything like it in living memory, perhaps in all of Christian history, is rapidly gaining momentum. In all the years I have ministered to pastors all over . . . I have never seen prayer so high on their collective agendas."[54]

This prayer momentum is sweeping through every country, every culture, every state; reaching cities, homes, neighborhoods, churches, public schools, and even our governmental offices. Here are some exciting testimonies to inspire you to join the church in this appointed time:

– October 1993, the United Prayer Track of the AD2000 prayed for the 62 countries within the 10/40 Window. Over 21,000,000 Christian leaders from 100 nations agreed to pray for revival in these spiritually needy countries.

– October 1995, the United Prayer Track prayed for 100 gateway cities into the 10/40 Window. Approximately 36,000,000 intercessors from 120 nations prayed every month for revival.

– October 1997, the United Prayer Track targeted the 1739 least evangelized prayer groups worldwide. They calculated that between 40 and 60 million Christians participated.

– "See You At the Pole" has mobilized 3,000,000 young people to pray for their schools.

– "Mom's in Touch" is mobilizing record numbers of parents to pray for all the schools.

– Bill Bright, in his book Fast America, challenged 1,000,000 leaders to fast for 40 days in November 1998. The result far exceeded his expectations.

– "Pray USA!" hosted an event in 1998, "Pray America Back to God." CBN reported it to be the largest fasting and prayer initiative in history.

– Networking of worldwide ministries to establish prayer for every person is now taking place worldwide. Ed Silvoso with Harvest Evangelism, the National Prayer Committee, Global Harvest, AD2000, U.S. Prayer Track, Promise Keepers, Mom's in Touch, Aglow International, and Lydia Fellowship are among hundreds of other ministries that are working together with prayer as a main emphasis.

– A huge increase in the number of conferences on intercession and spiritual warfare has swept every nation.

– City pastors and citywide prayer meetings are flooding many cities in our nation.

- The number of books, magazines, articles, and sermons that address the subject of prayer and intercession is drastically on the rise.

- National prayer walks, prayer marches, and lighthouses of prayer are taking place daily, as well as on-site prayer for businesses and government.

Entire cities are being marked off in grids for strategic prayer walking so that every person is being prayed for. The effects of this ongoing prayer for the lost can be measured objectively. Prayer is unlocking the chains that have bound lost people. The prayers of the saints are having an astonishing effect worldwide. Here are some staggering results:

- In Washington DC, 237 churches have been involved in 24-hour prayer watches, which have produced a seventeen percent drop in crime.

- The crime rate in America has dropped twelve percent in America's ten largest cities.

- The murder rate in America has dropped to a thirty-year low, according to the FBI.

- The number of abortion providing facilities has decreased markedly in the 90's.

- Approximately fifty-six percent of Americans now say abortion is wrong. This is the highest percentage in fifteen years.

- Sexual promiscuity has dropped eight percent among the teenagers of America.

- There has been a nine percent drop in those teenagers who approve of premarital sex.

- The Houston Prayer Movement has been effective in bringing down the number of violent crimes committed in their city by fifty-nine percent. The overall crime rate is down seventy-four percent.

– Major revivals are beginning to break out in our nation's prisons. Every prison in Alaska is seeing revival.

– Over 190,000 people a day are coming to Christ worldwide, resulting in almost 70,000,000 conversions this year alone!

– Approximately 30,000 per day are praying to receive Christ in Russia since the fall of Communism. This equates to almost 1,000,000 per month.

– In Africa 20,000 per day are being converted.

– In China, up to 35,000 per day are giving their lives to Christ, regardless of extreme opposition. The underground church is now three times the size of the Communist Party.

– With the strong emphasis on prayer over the past few decades, South Korea now reports that one out of every two people in their nation is born again.

– In India, there are reports of 15,000 per week getting saved. One recent crusade reported that 1.7 million people came to hear the Gospel in just six nights! Another crusade had 500,000 in attendance and reaped over 120,000 conversions in just five days.

On one hand, I am excited about these statistics, but on the other hand, I am cautious not to let these testimonies derail me from the urgency of the times in which we live. There still is much more that needs to be accomplished. There are many lives that need Christ. It is imperative that we play our part by maintaining our "Garden of Gethsemane" experiences.

JESUS BROKE THROUGH WITH PRAYER

Jesus was the ultimate intercessor. His earthly ministry was saturated with effective examples of breakthrough intercession. Not only was prayer the foundation to His entire ministry on earth and a key tool in winning the lost, but it is still one of the primary ministries of Christ today. Hebrews 7:25 declares, *"Therefore he is able, once and forever, to save everyone who comes to God through him. He lives forever to plead with God on their behalf."*

The Garden of Gethsemane was no different. Jesus was partnering with the Father in paving the way for all humanity to experience eternal life through His death, burial, and resurrection. It is not by accident that Christ ended up praying in Gethsemane before the Cross. His actions during this time of trial were very intentional and methodical. With these actions, he left the perfect model for intercessory prayer.

As you review this model, be thinking of people you know who need Christ.

Revelation Prayer

Matthew 26:36: *"Then Jesus brought them to an olive grove . . ."*

This place was not just a simple olive grove, but a divine place, a super-natural place. Not only did He take them to a natural place, which represented a place of crushing (speaking of the olive press), but He also took them to a spiritual place. He desired that they might experience a spiritual breakthrough and come out with a new mindset. He took them to a place where they might tap into a newfound revelation necessary for future ministry. This was truly a prophetic place, an anointed place, a place of breakthrough.

Our prayers for our friends, neighbors, and loved ones must begin with an understanding of Jesus' Gethsemane experience. We must realize that people's lives are standing in the balance. Gethsemane is not a casual or careless experience but one of utmost importance.

For years I have used this analogy when preaching about passionate prayer. It has challenged me every time I have shared it.

As a young man walked along the beach every morning on his way to school, he would pass an old man standing on the beach, arms stretched out in prayer and intercession. Every afternoon as he headed home, the old man would still be standing there. Intrigued by this man's dedication and passion for prayer, he stopped one day and asked him, "Sir, will you teach me to pray like you?" The old man proceeded to grab the young man by his shirt, drag him into the ocean, and push his head under the water. He held the young man's head under until he began to flail about wildly, and then he jerked his head back up. The boy gasped and filled his lungs with air, just as the old man pushed his head back under the water for another minute. Again, as the boy kicked and struggled, the old man pulled the boy's head back up and allowed him to desperately suck in a lung full of air. Finally, the old man released him. Shocked, the young man shouted at him angrily, "Why did you do that? All I did was ask you how to pray!" The old man looked at the boy and said, "Son, until you want God as badly as you just wanted that breath of air, I cannot teach you to pray."

Our first need is to desire God more than anything else in life. It is through this pursuit that we are pulled close to the Father and receive a revelation of His heart toward lost people. It is this revelation that provokes us to pray!

Anointed Prayer

Matthew 26:36: *". . . called Gethsemane . . ."*

Once we have received a fresh revelation of the need for intercessory prayer for the lost, we must make sure that we pray an anointed prayer. The place where Jesus went was called "Gethsemane," which is of Aramaic origin and signifies "an olive press, like a winepress, where they trod the olives." In the garden were many olive trees that were used, during the time of Christ, to extract oil. Scripture clearly uses oil and the olive tree symbolically as a type of the Holy Spirit anointing (see Luke 4:17; Isaiah 61:1; Psalm 23:5; Acts 19:38; 1 John 2:20,27; 2 Corinthians 1:21; Leviticus 2:1-2; Deuteronomy 33:24). Just think of how he was bruised and crushed that fresh oil might flow to all of His followers, including you and me, in order to intercede as he did.

The anointing of God upon our prayers is an essential ingredient to seeing our requests come to fruition. Jesus had warned His disciples earlier not to offer up vain repetitions as did the heathen (see Matthew 6:7).

Arthur Wallis describes it this way:

Some prayer is nothing more than activity from the lips; it is praying in the realm of the body. It is possible, however, for our praying to be thoughtful and intelligent, and even scriptural in its phraseology, but nothing more. Such is praying in the realm of the mind, and this can never prevail with God.[55]

In prayer it is better that your heart is without words, than your words are without heart. Without the anointing of the Spirit, there can be no praying in the Spirit. We must contend for what the Spirit is anointing us to pray, rather than ask the Spirit to anoint whatever we feel like praying. The most important thing in prayer is not what we say to God, but what God says to us. Be careful not to finish praying without giving God a chance to answer or direct you as you pray.

Burdened Prayer

Matthew 26:38: *"He told them, 'My soul is crushed with grief to the point of death.'"*

Never has there been an event, in the history of humanity, in which one has borne such pain as Christ did from Gethsemane to the Cross. It was there that He was faced with every sin ever committed by every person ever created. It was there that He alone faced all the powers of darkness. It was there that He became the sacrificial lamb for the world. The burden was of such intensity that He actually sweated blood (see Luke 22:44).

This supreme example of burdened prayer demonstrates an important act called "soul travail." Those who make themselves available to carry the burden for the lost can expect to experience intense moments in which they pray so intensely that they travail over it like a woman giving birth. Such was the case with Jesus in the garden, as He travailed to the point of sweating blood.

David Brainard, a missionary to the Housitonic Indians on the Massachusetts frontier, was a man who clearly lived as a vessel fit for the Master's use. In his diary record of late winter 1742, he shares his experience of carrying the burden for lost Indians:

It was the middle of the night in the dead of winter, snow hip high in Western Massachusetts. I was stirred with a burden of the Lord. I rose out of my bed and went outside so that my groans would not awake my wife and young baby. I walked outside the village and huddled under a tree. By morning the snow had completely melted an eight-foot circle around me because of the intensity of the burden placed on me by the Lord. About dawn the burden had lifted and the call to intercede had been pushed through. So I walked back to the village, and saw people from all over the village walking down the streets to the town square, all with hot tears pouring down their cheeks. And when I put my foot onto the soil of the city street I felt a warm wind of God's presence blow and immediately men, women and children all fell prostrate before the Lord, crying out in repentance before the Lord.[56]

This type of burdened prayer cannot be fabricated or worked up but comes as we make ourselves available to receive His burden and handle it with the utmost concern. Once it is received, it can become such a consuming desire that one feels that he or she must pray until the prayer is answered or perish in the attempt.

We are now in a time when God is not just looking for men, but for *"a man"* (Ezekiel 22:30)—individuals who will take personal responsibility and begin to partner with Him in carrying the burden for the lost. Like the revivalists of old who used to cry out in prayer, "Give me children or I die," so let us make ourselves willing vessels to carry the same burden for those whom God has placed in our lives, that we might see them birthed into His kingdom.

Patient Prayer

Matthew 26:38: *"Stay here . . ."*

Once we have received the revelation to pray anointed prayers and to carry the burdens of the lost, we must learn to be patient for the results of our prayers. We can see this patience carried out in the life of our fictional friend, Dave Finley. He patiently carried the burden of his father's salvation until God broke through. Dave knew that it wasn't a question of "if," but "when."

Jesus made the decision to tell His disciples to wait for Him as He prayed. One can only imagine the restlessness the disciples must have felt, knowing that something big was about to take place. Like a child separated from its parents in a strange place, so the disciples were separated from the comfort and protection of their Master. Though momentarily separated from Him, they missed the meaning of Christ's words when He said, "Stay here."

The phrase, "stay here," is also translated in the New King James as "tarry here," which means "to abide, to continue, to dwell, to endure, to remain, and to stand."[57] Jesus had every intention of including them in His prayer time. His desire was that they would continue to pray until He gave them further notice.

Often our prayers aren't answered because we don't continue to stand in prayer until the breakthrough comes. After a few short weeks of praying for a loved one, we can become discouraged or distracted, resulting in less than desired results. The waiting period, whether it is for weeks or years, is the divine incubation time in which God is preparing us for the outpouring that He has purposed. His timing and ways are different than ours. We must be careful not to let our "microwave mentality" dictate the manner in which we pray.

I prayed for over twelve years for my oldest sister, Dawn, to give her life to Christ! Now that she is serving God and has become a wonderful woman of God, I look back on those years of praying for her and believe that it was worth every minute. There are other loved ones that I still believe God will bring into His kingdom. I have now prayed for some of them nearly twenty years. They will come to Christ! It is not a question of "if," but "when." Don't give up on those God has placed on your heart.

Alert Prayer

Matthew 26:38: *". . . watch with me."*

Jesus knew that this moment in the garden was not the time to let down His guard. He could sense the angels in the distance, ready for war. He felt all the demons of hell craning their necks in anticipation. He knew He was in for the fight of His earthly life. It was with this revelation that He exhorted His disciples to be vigilant, to watch their back, and remain alert to anything that might bring harm.

If there has ever been a time in the history of the Church to keep watch, it is now! Prayer for the lost is the single most resisted activity on the planet! Anyone who comes into the garden with Jesus can expect to find himself in the center of the bloodiest spiritual battle known to man. It is a real battle in which both sides are playing for keeps. It is now time for each of us to remain alert and sober-minded.

Daring Prayer

Matthew 26:39: *"He went on a little farther . . ."*

If you could ask of the Lord to save anyone, regardless of his or her spiritual or physical condition, being assured that your request would be answered immediately, who would you pray for? Would you pray for that child who has run away from home or turned his back on God? Would you ask God to save your unsaved spouse? What about your parents who have become callused toward God and really have no interest in "religious things"? How about that grandparent who is dying of cancer and is now in a coma at the hospital?

In the natural, it seems as if these situations are just too far out of our reach, and we don't really believe that God will answer when we pray for them. What we need, as we continue to become "Jesus Today," is a "go a little farther" prayer attitude. We need to go a little farther in asking Him for specific people. We need to go a little farther in asking Him for specific timing. We need to go a little farther in asking Him to save our entire block, not just our next-door neighbor. We need to go a little farther in asking Him to pour out His Spirit on our entire family, not just on one member. We need to go a little farther in asking Him to save every kid on the high school campus, not just the friend in Biology class.

Your daring prayers do not embarrass or irritate God. He is not bothered by unusual or extraordinary prayers. In fact, I think He gets excited when we begin to ask Him to do things that, to us, seem impossible. He wants us to make that daring request as He assures us of His promise, *"But with God everything is possible"* (Matthew 19:26). It has been said, "Prayer is dangerous business. Results will come." Let this be our confession and our goal as we offer up daring requests.

Humbled Prayer

Matthew 26:39: *". . . fell face down on the ground, praying . . . "*

The very act of falling to the ground was an outward indicator of Jesus' inward heart condition. It is impossible to know what was racing through His mind, but Scripture points out that He positioned Himself in a posture of humility. Maybe He recalled the parable He had told, regarding the arrogant Pharisee and the humble tax collector (see Luke 18:13-14), when He had shared that those who would exalt themselves would be humbled and those who humbled themselves would be exalted. Possibly He reflected back on His masterful Sermon on the Mount, when He shared, *"God bless those who realize their need for him,"* (Matthew 5:3-4). Perhaps He remembered the words of the prophet Isaiah when His Father said, *"I will bless those who have humble and contrite hearts,"* (Isaiah 62:2). Whatever the case may have been, He knew that the key to receiving the blessing of His Father upon His prayers was humility.

There is but one road that leads to God, and it is the road of humility. All other ways only lead us astray. Without this virtue, we keep all our defects crusted over with human pride, making it nearly impossible to enter the throne room of God. Each time we pray, our heart's posture must be one of reverence and honor. In doing so, we can be assured that the blessing of God will reside upon our petitions.

Selfless Prayer

Matthew 26:39: *"My Father! If it is possible, let this cup of suffering be taken away from me. Yet I want your will, not mine."*

With this prayer of supplication, Jesus clearly modeled the importance of selfless prayers. I will never be able to comprehend how Jesus, though He understood the suffering He was to experience, was freely willing to offer Himself as my punishment! This is by far the greatest act of selflessness known to man.

Often we make seemingly good requests but neutralize the effectiveness of our prayer because we are driven by selfish motivations. When the motive of our prayer is to satisfy our own desires and pleasures, the prayer becomes unholy, and God cannot and will not fulfill our petitions.

It is possible to pray for the right thing with the wrong motive. It is vital to examine our hearts on this matter. Pause for a moment and ask yourself, "Why do I want to see people saved?" As a pastor, do you strive to build the Church, or do you desire a large congregation that brings self-identity and human applause? As a parent, is the salvation of your rebellious teenager for their benefit or to save the family name? As a teenager, is the salvation of your boyfriend or girlfriend the green light to continuing your emotional attachment, or do you really care about their eternal destiny?

When we become aware that the motive of our prayer is anything other than to bring glory to God, let us stop immediately and repent, that our prayers might once again become sharp, anointed, and effective weapons of humbled intercession.

Specific Prayer

The seventeenth chapter of John gives us another account of Jesus in the garden. However, this portion of Scripture focuses much more on the prayer He prayed, instead of the circumstances surrounding His prayer. This prayer was the most detailed and profound prayer of all those recorded in Scripture. In this account we see Jesus as the mediator, the intercessor, the gap-stander for all of humanity. We see Jesus model the ultimate prayer for the salvation of the world:

> John 17:20-22: *"I am praying not only for these disciples but also for all who will ever believe in me because of their testimony. My prayer for all of them is that they will be one, just as you and I are one, Father—that just as you are in me and I am in you, so they will be in us, and the world will believe you sent me. I have given them the glory you gave me, so that they may be one, as we are. . ."*

It is important to note that His prayer was very specific. He began by methodically praying for Himself and His specific situation at hand (see John 17:1-5). Next, He began pleading to the Father for His disciples, that all of their needs would be met (see John 17:6-19). Finally, He began to pray for all those who will believe, that they all would love Him as much as the Father has loved Him (see John 17:20-26). Each portion of His prayer is made up of very specific, targeted requests.

Frank Damazio discusses the issue of specific prayer as he writes:

> Intercessory prayer must involve a specific target. Spiritual enemies and circumstances that must be broken through often block the target. At times the target needs to be struck with accuracy and force. The force of intercession is one of the greatest weapons known to the Christian.[58]

What this teaches us is that our inability to see people come to Christ can often be attributed to the vagueness of our requests. Just as in a military battle, when the moment arrives for an attack, the success of the mission is directly proportionate to the concentration of force at strategic points.

Relating back to our fictional story of Dave Finley, his brother Phil, and his friend Jim, their prayers in their living room were quite specific. They were daring, anointed, specific prayers, "*Tonight* we want a breakthrough! *Tonight* save my family!" And breakthrough is what they got, primarily due to their specific petitions sent up to the throne.

Persevering Prayer

Matthew 26:42,44: *"Again he left them and prayed . . . So he went back to pray a third time, saying the same things again."*

I once heard a story about a man's dream concerning himself and His unsaved daughter who had run away from home. In the dream, the father saw his daughter being strangled by a demon with the word "death" written on his chest. As he frantically prayed in the dream, his prayers turned into darts, which struck the demon, and brought it great pain and discomfort. After a few minutes of sending darts at the demon, the man stopped praying and asked the demon, "Why won't you let go?" The demon laughed and with an eerie voice said, "Because I know that your prayers will soon stop!"

One of the most important lessons learned from Jesus' Gethsemane experience was that he went back and prayed a second and a third time. Even though He faced incredible opposition in prayer to the point of having blood seep from His pores, He went back and prayed until there was a breakthrough.

He communicated this same truth in His parable in Matthew 18. The widow, by continually coming to the judge and pleading her case, wore him out until he changed his mind and she won the dispute. What a beautiful parable concerning persevering prayer.

The principle that we must apply, not only in praying for the lost, but also in every prayer situation, is that we must pray in spite of delay and discouragement, knowing that each prayer applies additional pressure on the Enemy that will eventually cause his defenses to crumble and lead to victory.

As we continue to see the Lord bring people into His kingdom by the thousands, we can be assured that the Enemy will continue to resist our assault on his domain. It is imperative that we position ourselves securely in the garden, persevering until we see our prayers answered.

Breakthrough Prayer

Matthew 26:46: *"Up, let's be going. See, my betrayer is here!"*

The goal of every attribute of prayer mentioned so far is to activate this final element—*breakthrough*! Each aspect of prayer cannot become an end in itself, but all of them combined become a means to accomplish the end objective—breakthrough in the lives of those for whom we are praying.

It seems as if Jesus came to the point where He felt a release, and the extremity of His agony was over, or at least momentarily diverted. There was a breakthrough in the spiritual realm, and now the fulfillment would come through the Cross, in the natural realm. He stood up with an undaunted courage and prepared Himself for the next challenge at hand. Please note that He said, "Up, let's be going" to meet our accusers, not "Up, let's run" from them. He knew that the battle had already been won in the heavenlies, and now He would walk out the victory over the Devil, once and for all, through His march to the Cross.

Hopefully, we will learn from this Scriptural example that once we have received a breakthrough in prayer, we can face any trial, regardless of how extreme. There have been many occasions when I have prayed to the point of breakthrough for the soul of a loved one, only to be confronted with abnormal behavior that seemed to contradict God's clear promise. In these times, I quietly remind myself of the breakthrough and rise above the struggle. Like Christ, I face this person with love and peace, knowing that his or her time has come!

There is a place in prayer where we realize that our prayers have been accepted and heard. We actually become aware of receiving the promise, with great anticipation, prior to the event actually taking place. God wants us to pray until a breakthrough comes. Let each of us make the changes necessary to become effective intercessors and take our position in the battle for our loved ones and for our cities. It is up to you! Let us move one step closer to becoming "Jesus Today!"

MY JESUS TODAY PRAYER

Dear Jesus,

Thank You for Your journey

To the Garden of Gethsemane.

It was there that You were crushed

And became the burden carrier for my soul.

In times past I have read this Scripture,

Only to be relieved that it wasn't me.

However, today I realize that I am called

To Gethsemane to be a burden carrier for others.

Give me the revelation to see when the hour has come

And help me not to sleep as You are now pleading for my help.

Although the only path is through the olive press,

I desire to go a little further with You.

Strengthen me as I help carry the burdens

And make me alert as I wait patiently for the breakthrough.

Stretch me in asking You daring requests,

While keeping me humble and selfless in my approach.

Direct me to pray specific prayers that You are anointing

And birth in me the tenacity to persevere until I see breakthroughs.

Continue to develop in me every attribute necessary

That I might become "Jesus Today!"

Amen

CHAPTER TEN

HIS EMPTINESS:

ADJUSTING

PRIORITIES

TO BECOME

USEFUL

MARK 6:30-44

In a matter of weeks, the town of Pineville had been turned upside down. Due to the size of the town, news traveled very fast and created a curiosity to investigate the unusual services down at the Pineville Community Church. Pineville was quickly becoming "Jesusville."

The foundations of prayer, brokenness, humility, and unity in the church had created fertile ground for the Holy Spirit. Not only were most of the church members repenting from their sins and rededicating themselves to Christ, but scores of new converts were flooding the weekly services. Entire families were coming forward. Single mothers and their children, even groups of teenagers from the local high school were getting saved. There were more people coming to Christ each night than had been saved in the last ten years combined!

Church, as they had known it, had changed. Services had changed. Life had changed. The spiritual awakening in Pineville seemed to be "ruining" every prior aspect of community life! The initial excitement of the breakthrough was met with the reality that this kind of church vision had some huge responsibilities attached. Revival may have been free, but it was costing them everything they had.

The warm, sweet smell of Mrs. Maple's rhubarb pie wafted out of the kitchen into the family room where everyone had gathered. The weekly small group meeting had grown considerably in a matter of weeks, making the group a little too large for the Maple's house. It was a healthy group filled with many long-time church members who had been the backbone of the church for so many years.

"So what do you think about all the new people filling up our church?" Mr. Maple asked the group.

Mr. Dawson took another sip of coffee and responded, "Well, you know it is kind of exciting to see all the new faces and all that, but I get a little irritated with all the changes. It seems like we're letting everything go. Unruly kids are running around, new people come in wearing Levi's and t-shirts, teenagers hang behind the church. Even got some new folks smoking after the service!"

Mr. Thompson was nudged by his wife to speak up. "You know, I do understand that new converts bring new problems, but I think the bigger problem is that the church has lost its focus. All we care about is lost people. All we do is talk about evangelism. Doesn't Pastor Ed know that Jesus is looking for quality and not quantity?"

Mrs. Thompson continued her husband's thoughts, adding the details that she thought her husband had missed. "What he really is trying to say is that we liked our church the way it was. We didn't have to worry about our kids being influenced by all these new kids and their problems. We could come to church and enjoy a good message and worship, but now it seems there are more meetings than ever and we are constantly being asked to get involved in more programs. Can't these new people go to a different church?"

———————— ▬▬▬▬ ————————

"Alright, everyone, that will do it for tonight. Make sure to follow your Bible reading chart and let's all try and fill out the questions on water baptism for next week's class. Okay? Have a great night! We will see you next week, same time."

Dave looked over the crowd of new converts crammed into the tiny, multi-purpose room of the church, twenty-five in all. As he stood back and observed, a deep sense of satisfaction soothed his soul.

He began to talk to himself under his breath, "New people hungry for God. So many added to the church. So many saved. . . ."

His thoughts dissipated into the fatigue of another night out and the pressure of meeting all the needs of the people. He continued talking to himself, "So many problems, so many needs, so much to do."

The words of a good friend rang again in his mind, "Be careful what you pray for, you just might get it!" That he did! He got just what he had prayed for—revival.

"I feel like a juggler at the circus!" Dave said with a tone of exasperation as he pushed back the bill of his cap.

Pastor Ed leaned back against his chair, slid his plate of eggs and sausage aside, put his elbows on the table and then leaned forward, "What do you mean, Dave?"

Since the night God had broken through, something had clicked between Pastor Ed and Dave. There was a bonding of two souls, a bonding of vision. It was a partnership in the making. The Lord had sovereignly brought them together, just like Jonathon and David. Their weekly breakfast meeting had become a highlight and great strength to both of them. It was a time to reflect on the week's activities, a time to share what the Lord was saying; a time to encourage each other to keep fighting; a time to just to open up and dump.

Dave put his head down and proceeded to open up cautiously, "Don't get me wrong. I love what the Lord is doing. I am excited that God has allowed me to be a part. But I feel like one of the disciples telling Jesus to send them away. The load seems so heavy. I just can't seem to do it all anymore."

He took a sip of his coffee and continued, "My two jobs are draining me. Trying to disciple my family back home eats away at a good part of my week. My New Converts' Class with the follow-up phone calls and counseling is a load in itself. I also have all of the other things I am involved in, golf with the guys, Monday night football, and . . . "

"Dave, Dave, Dave, slow down for a second. Let's talk about it." Pastor Ed interrupted to keep Dave from falling apart. He began to share a proper perspective, like only Pastor Ed could.

"You know, there comes a time when we all must step back and look at things from a fresh perspective. God never intended anyone to kill himself with the work of the ministry. Furthermore, God never intended any of us to try to carry the whole load ourselves. It is His church, not ours. It is His people and His ministry, and I learned a long time ago, the hard way, that Jesus would always be my joy, *not* my job." Dave nodded his head in agreement.

"However, I have been looking at my own life as well. I have been asking myself plenty of questions like, 'What is most important to me? What is most important to God? Are they the same?'" Pastor Ed looked into Dave's eyes.

"Dave, I have even gone as far as to ask the hard questions like 'Does everything I'm doing have eternal significance? How much is for me, and how much is for Him?' You know, I have come to the conclusion that I am not my own. I was bought with a price. Jesus said it best, if I can paraphrase it, 'He who does not take up his cross, deny himself, and follow me daily, is not worthy to be My disciple.' Dave, there is an honor *and* a cost attached. The reality is that during times of God's outpouring there will be those who are willing to work and those who are not. It really is that simple! The key to survival is deciding what activities you can continue and which ones you need to eliminate in order to maintain your sanity."

Pastor Ed's wisdom penetrated right to the heart. Dave didn't want to hear it, but he knew he needed to. It was time to go back to the drawing board for Dave. Time to go back to prayer. Time to adjust his priorities. Although he was fully immersed in the current church programs, it was even time to adjust his attitude.

A three-day get away, alone with God, was just what Dave needed. Dave loaded up the trunk of his Mustang, packing in all the essentials needed for a long weekend of prayer and fasting.

"Bible? Check. Pad of paper? Check. Tape recorder? Check. Journal? Check. Open heart? Well . . . check. Ready to get creamed by God? Uh . . . I'll cross that off the list!"

The small cabin nestled along the side of Silver Lake was tidy. The lake was like glass, the sky crystal blue, the air crisp and clean. It was a perfect environment to meet with God.

Throughout the weekend, Dave read his Bible on a log by the lake, took long walks up to the top of the ridge overlooking Hope Valley, and just sat and prayed. The mountain ranges and many vistas brought a constant reminder of the majesty of God. It also reminded him of the seeming insignificance of his own existence.

As Saturday drew to a close, he sat at the table and lit the green oil lamp. He had disengaged from all the busyness long enough to slow down and re-acquaint himself with his Lord. The previous hours of prayer and Bible reading brought back the intimacy of relationship that he had so subtly lost. He opened the Bible to the Scripture reference given by Pastor Ed at breakfast earlier that week and read out loud to himself.

"Then he said to the crowd, 'If any of you wants to be my follower, you must put aside your selfish ambition, shoulder your cross daily, and follow me. If you try to keep your life for yourself, you will lose it. But if you give up your life for me, you will find true life. And how do you benefit if you gain the whole world but lose or forfeit your soul in the process?'" (Luke 9:23).

He paused, closed his eyes, and whispered, "Lord, speak to me through Your Word." He read it again.

"Then he said to the crowd: 'If any of you wants to be my follower, you must put aside your selfish ambition, shoulder your cross daily, and follow me. If you try to keep your life for yourself, you will lose it. But if you give up your life for me, you will find true life. And how do you benefit if you gain the whole world but lose or forfeit your soul in the process?'" (Luke 9:23).

He put his Bible down and began to pray, "Lord, I want Your will to be done in my life. I don't want to fight it. I don't want to dodge it. I don't even want to water it down. Jesus, I don't want to miss the reason why I exist. Help me! Lord, help me to deny myself. Lord, help me to take up my cross. Lord, help me to follow You, no matter the cost."

Those simple words of repentance were met with a sweet presence of the Holy Spirit. With gentle tenderness, He peeled back the dryness, the wrong priorities, the bad attitudes, the shallow-mindedness. His confession and repentance were met with the Lord's kindness and tender mercies.

Once the Lord had changed his heart, the attitude change came easy. He realized that life was much easier just doing it God's way and not Dave's way. With a desire to be used in a greater dimension, Dave picked up his new palm pilot organizer and began to review his schedule.

"Well, Lord, let's delete that!" With a stroke of his stylus, his weekly Saturday golf day was removed as if it had never existed.

"That wasn't so bad, Lord. Now what's next?" He scrolled down through the week-at-a-glance and then the month-at-a-glance. For each entry, he would ask the Lord if it was something the Lord would want him to do. One by one, he would remove or adjust his schedule to match his new desire to give his all to the Lord.

As he laid his palm pilot on top of his Bible, his checkbook caught his eye.

Immediately, Dave reviewed how he spent his money. "Well, it certainly is time to get on a budget. I know that I can be a better steward of my money and maybe even be a blessing to others."

Line by line, he prayed and asked the Lord whether he should spend his money in that fashion. There would be many changes concerning Dave's spending habits in the future. Less eating out, more money to missions. Less clothes shopping, more giving to the poor.

The final night of his trip was a night of thanksgiving. God had done more than Dave had expected. He rolled over on his bed, pulled up the covers and continued his talk with the Lord.

Dave slept well that night, he knew that God had spoken and his life was properly prioritized. The trip to Silver Lake helped Dave focus on God alone and allowed him to adjust his priorities in order to become useful to the kingdom.

MARK 6:30-44

The apostles returned to Jesus from their ministry tour and told him all they had done and what they had taught. Then Jesus said, "Let's get away from the crowds for a while and rest." There were so many people coming and going that Jesus and his apostles didn't even have time to eat.

They left by boat for a quieter spot. But many people saw them leaving, and people from many towns ran ahead along the shore and met them as they landed. A vast crowd was there as he stepped from the boat, and he had compassion on them because they were like sheep without a shepherd. So he taught them many things.

Late in the afternoon his disciples came to him and said, "This is a desolate place, and it is getting late. Send the crowds away so they can go to the nearby farms and villages and buy themselves some food."

But Jesus said, "You feed them."

"With what?" they asked. "It would take a small fortune to buy food for all this crowd!"

"How much food do you have?" he asked. "Go and find out."

They came back and reported, "We have five loaves of bread and two fish."

Then Jesus told the crowd to sit down in groups on the green grass. So they sat in groups of fifty or a hundred. Jesus took the five loaves and two fish, looked up toward heaven, and asked God's blessing on the food. Breaking the loaves into pieces, he kept giving the bread and fish to the disciples to give to the people. They all ate as much as they wanted, and they picked up twelve baskets of leftover bread and fish. Five thousand men had eaten from those five loaves!

ANALYZING OUR PRIORITIES

If you have been a Christian for any length of time, I am sure that you have gone through seasons in your life when the Lord has adjusted the way in which you live or think. Priority adjustments can be quite unpleasant but almost always result in making you a better Christian.

Many years ago, while talking with my dear friend, Gary Beasley, about priorities in the lives of other Christians we knew, I made the mistake of thinking that I was okay while they were all goofed up. With my arms crossed and a smile on my face, I said, "Well, I am sure glad my priorities are in order. Don't you think so, Gary?" He smirked, leaned forward and said, "Well, I don't know. Why don't you give me your DayTimer and checkbook, and we'll just see!" I started to laugh but slowly realized that maybe there was some room for adjustment.

These real life challenges that we all face are illustrated through our fictional character, Dave Finley, and his trip to the mountain cabin. He too came to a place where changes were necessary if he was going to move to the next level in his walk with Christ.

What about you? Are you happy with where you stand with Christ? Have you done all that should be done to fulfill your destiny and calling? Or would you admit that an annual checkup with the Master Surgeon, Jesus, is needed in order to cut off some of those habits and attitudes that have crept in?

Each of us must stop and reflect on where we are and where we want to be. We must be willing to make those uncomfortable adjustments to become more useful to God. It is time to pull out the scalpel of the Holy Spirit and begin cutting off the excess layers of flesh. Some things we do are really important, others just seem that way.

THE CONDITION OF OUR CULTURE

As we slow down our busy lives to reflect upon the culture in which we live, we discover that never before has a generation of people had so many possessions, yet feel so empty. In his book, *Evangelism that Works*, George Barna states, "Sociologists have described America as the loneliest nation on the face of the earth. Research suggests they may be right. Although we live in close proximity to tens of thousands of people and probably come in contact with hundreds of people every week, most have few real friends, few true confidants."[59]

The spiritual challenges facing our nation have reached epidemic proportions in every arena. The very fabric of our cultural and spiritual foundations is being scrutinized and torn apart at the seams. The constant onslaught upon biblical morals has created a battle to redefine the values of our nation for the next century. These pressures have had a profound effect on the spiritual climate of the nation and created unrest in those we are trying to reach.

Despite all of these challenges, people are hungrier for spiritual truth today than they have been in decades. We are witnessing a generation that has tried everything to fill the void felt inside, only to remain empty. Millions of people have turned toward the melting pot of religious beliefs that have flooded our country—the Psychic hotlines, New Age practices, and self-help seminars—hoping to find a cure for their emptiness. Our culture needs the truth of the gospel and is ready to receive it!

THE CONDITION OF THE CHURCH

Something exciting is definitely taking place throughout Christianity today. Everywhere I turn I hear testimonies, read e-mails or articles, and see signs that the Church of Jesus Christ is coming back to life. God is preparing us for a multitude of hungry people who will come running to find Jesus. Because of this, the condition of the Church becomes important; for as the Church is so the harvest will be.

As we review our scriptural text for this chapter, there is an interesting parallel between Jesus, His disciples, and the multitudes, and the Church today. Here are a few characteristics of the condition of the Church.

A Fresh Stirring to Return to Jesus

Mark 6:30: *"The apostles returned to Jesus . . ."*

Following the death of John the Baptist, and after a season of ministry, the disciples returned to Jesus. Their only hope for renewal would come through the reunion with their Master.

Over the past few years, the bad news that surrounds us daily has been used by the Holy Spirit to bring us back to Jesus. There has been a fresh passion birthed in the hearts of all believers to return to their first love. Jesus is drawing each of us back to an intimate relationship with Him. This return is bringing great healing, refreshing, and empowerment for every Christian and equipping us with all that is needed for the tasks that lie ahead. The Church is excited about knowing God more.

The Challenge to Look Toward Future Goals and Not Past Accomplishments

Mark 6:30: *" . . . and told him all they had done . . ."*

Although Jesus always took the opportunity to discuss past ministry situations with His disciples, He never intended to live His life on the basis of past accomplishments. He challenged His disciples to put their hands to the plow and not look back (see Luke 9:62). He reminded them that the harvest is at the end of the age (see Matthew 13:39). *"Do you think the work of harvesting will not begin until the summer ends four months from now? Look around you! Vast fields are ripening all around us and are ready now for the harvest"* (John 4:35). He knew that many still needed salvation, and urged the disciples forward in building the kingdom.

Though many Christians today are excited about tomorrow's possibilities, they are still camping on yesterday's dreams. This often happens to those Christians who have been saved for some time. Let us not be like the fifty-year-old man who still wears his letterman jacket from high school and is always talking about the good old days. Our challenge, at this critical time in the history of the Church, is to focus on our future. Let us be thankful for our past, but focus on the challenges ahead.

New Balances

Mark 6:31: *". . . for a while and rest."* (NKJV)

The disciples seem to misinterpret Christ's command. They assumed that it was time to call it a day and rest, period! But Jesus, as pointed out in the New King James Version, commanded them to rest *"for a while."* He wanted them to be refreshed for the multitudes, which were about to be fed and touched. We need to realize that there are times to rest. But that can't be all we do—there must be a balance between our rest and our work.

A popular definition used frequently in our church for the word insanity goes like this, "doing the same thing over and over again but expecting different results." We will never get a thousand dollars of results on ten cents of effort. There is an increased challenge from the Lord for us to learn new balances in every area of our lives. Let us not be like our fickle, fictitious friends, Mr. and Mrs. Thompson, who sat and gossiped about the disruption of their perfect little church, while being unwilling to adjust their lives for the sake of the harvest. Instead, may we be willing to work until tired and then balance that work with healthy rest.

Beginning to Recognize Signs of Harvest

Mark 6:31: *" There were so many people coming and going . . ."*

The hearts of His disciples were changing. On one hand, they were excited to see many people touched, but on the other hand, it wore upon their institutionalized religious foundation. However, they began to recognize the eternal value of having many people come to Jesus.

I have seen this personally in our church, as well as in the lives of many other Christians I know. God is bringing multitudes of people into the kingdom, and many have problems. They look a little funny, act really funny, and some even smell a little funny! Our members began to struggle with their attitudes toward these new converts as they were assimilated into the church. However, as they begin to recognize that God is doing something new, their restlessness slowly disappears.

Potential Risks of Isolation

Mark 6:32: *"They left by boat for a quieter spot."*

As with the disciples, many church members today find a place of isolated safety or, as they would define it, "a place of sanity." Their goal is to protect themselves and their families from the perverse people coming into the church, polluting the sanctity of God's house. Furthermore, they perceive that the church is moving too fast, and their only solution is to get away from the increasing burden of needs caused by these multitudes. They remove themselves to a solitary, stable environment, free from challenges. Don't give in to this temptation. God needs your help! You never know, maybe you hold the key to helping a new convert through their problems.

JESUS' APPROACH TO THE SITUATION

In this passage, Jesus had a clear understanding of the circumstances, just as He has a handle on every situation now. He illustrated two very simple, yet profound, truths for gathering the harvest and provided the example for how we are to position ourselves when the multitudes come. Let's review His approach.

He Recognized the Multitudes

Mark 6:33: *"But many people saw them leaving, and people from many towns ran ahead along the shore and met them as they landed."*

Jesus recognized that the multitudes were hungry for His presence. If He had desired to remain apart from them, I am sure that He would have done so. But recognizing their needs and the appointed time for the Holy Spirit to pour out on these desperate people, He willingly positioned Himself in their path. We must also position ourselves to recognize the multitudes that surround us and place ourselves strategically in their path.

He Made Himself Available for the Multitudes

Mark 6:34: *"A vast crowd was there as he stepped from the boat, and he had compassion on them because they were like sheep without a shepherd. So he taught them many things."*

We too must make ourselves available. As we feel the compassion of God for the multitudes, our first response needs to be that we make ourselves known to them. As we do so, we will build relationships with them and be blessed with a measure of trust as a result. That trust will open a door of opportunity for us to reach them for Christ.

MISTAKES OF THE DISCIPLES

Be assured that these same mistakes made by the disciples in this passage have been made by even the greatest of Christians. But that's not a good reason to continue making them now. Instead, let us learn from the disciples' mistakes.

The Disciples Missed the Potential of the Multitudes

Mark 6:35: *"This is a desolate place . . ."*

Due to the disciples' weariness and the overwhelming number of needy people before them, their focus was drawn to the seeming impossibility of the situation. They saw through temporal eyes and viewed the needs of the people as a natural impossibility. But what they didn't see, as with the woman at the well, was a supernatural opportunity to reach the multitudes of people.

I am reminded of the Hippie Movement that swept our nation during the 70s, when thousands of strange-looking, barefooted, long-haired young people flooded the quaint, orderly church buildings throughout America. To many, this group of foul-smelling, funny-looking people was a hindrance to their church services. However, these hippies would become some of the greatest leaders of the twentieth century. It is reported that Chuck Smith, pastor of Calvary Chapel in Costa Mesa, California, was confronted by disgruntled church members during this time. They were complaining about the filthy carpets and pews caused by the grimy hippies who occupied their church services. He replied with a "Jesus Today" response, "Then tear out the carpets and sit on the floor, but I will not tell them to leave." Thank God for great leaders like Chuck Smith.

Let us not repeat the same mistakes as we look at the individuals who are flooding our church buildings. On the outside, they may appear very unusual and their circumstances may be quite strange, but their hearts are wide open to the Gospel. You never know, one of them might become your pastor someday!

The Disciples Became Weary from the Multitudes

Mark 6:35: *". . . and it is getting late."*

The disciples assumed that their long day was coming to a close, whereas Jesus saw the day as just beginning. It was harvest time, and the last thing Jesus was going to do was miss an opportunity to touch the lives of thousands of people.

Many of us, myself included, have grown tired during momentous times of kingdom building. What keeps me going is the fact that the multitudes flooding into our church are the reason that I exist. I was born for this moment. I have prayed for harvest my entire Christian life. Now that it is here, I don't want to miss the appointed time! Jesus has given me a message to proclaim. He has given me an opportunity to be a part of the greatest organization in the history of humanity, the Church!

The Disciples Were Unavailable for the Multitudes

Mark 6:36: *"Send the crowds away . . ."*

The disciples moved that they should be sent home. When the day was not far spent, and night drew on, they said, *"Send them away to buy bread."* This, the disciples suggested to Christ; but this was not the suggestion of the multitudes.[60]

If we are not careful to analyze our heart condition and remove the wrong perceptions caused by weariness, we run the risk of hardening our hearts and making rash decisions that hinder our walk with God and the ful-fillment of our existence. Jesus never intended to send any person away. He desired that they would come after Him. May our decisions concerning those with needs be based upon principles and not emotions!

A few years ago, I read an interesting study conducted by Lloyds of London, a large insurance company known for insuring unusual things. The research focused on the life of a paper clip. Here are their findings: Out of every 100,000 paper clips that were made, 14,163 were bent and twisted during phone conversations; 5,434 were used as a tooth pick or an ear scratcher; 3,916 were used to clean pipes; 5,308 were used to clean finger-nails; 7,201 were used to hold together clothing; 19,141 were used as chips for card games; 25,010 fell to the floor and were swept away; only 20,004 were used for their intended purpose of holding together paper. [61]

If we are not careful, we could become one of God's wasted paper clips, never fulfilling the reason for our existence. We can slip so easily into the trap of building our kingdom rather than His kingdom. If we are not care-ful, we might begin viewing that irritating neighbor or arrogant co-worker as a problem rather than an opportunity. This produces a *"send them away"* attitude, as we forever miss the potential of the situation at hand. Don't let these famous words become our epitaph: "Of all the sad words of tongue or pen, the saddest are these, 'It might have been!'"

The Disciples Ignored the Needs of the Multitudes

Mark 6:36: *"Send the crowds away so they can go to the nearby farms and villages and buy themselves some food."*

The progression of the disciples' mistakes continued to escalate to the point that they were rendered useless. Only when Jesus shook them from their selfish mindset were they used to reap the harvest. Here is a poem that should challenge us all.

I knelt to pray, but not for long, I had too much to do,
Must hurry off and go to work for bills would soon be due.
And so I said a hurried prayer, jumped up from off my knees,
My Christian duties now were done, my soul could be at ease.

All through the day I had no time to speak a word of cheer,
No time to speak of Christ to friends, they'd laugh at me I feared.
No time, no time, too much to do, that was my constant cry,
No time to give to those in need, at last was time to die.
And then before the Lord I came and stood with downcast eyes,
Within His hands He held a book, it was the "Book of Life."
God looked into His book and said, "Your name I cannot find,
I once was going to write it down, but never found the time." [62]

E. Stanley Jones once said, "The most miserable people in the world are the people who are self-centered, who don't do anything for anybody, except themselves. They are centers of misery with no exception. . . . On the contrary, the happiest people are the people who deliberately take on themselves the sorrows and troubles of others. Their hearts sing with a strange wild joy." [63]

Before reading any further, ask yourself these questions: "What kind of person am I, miserable or happy? Am I irritated or overjoyed with the changes taking place in my church concerning the harvest?" Take a moment to seriously contemplate the answers and pray for God to reveal any changes that you need to make in your own life. Then take the initiative to apply the following principles to your life.

ADJUSTING OUR PRIORITIES TO BECOME "JESUS TODAY"

The final portion of this chapter contains keys that could very well change your entire life. Are you hearing what the Spirit is saying right now? Is your heart softened enough to receive His conviction and modify any areas that need adjustment? Is it time for you to have a "Silver Lake" experience and get away with God for a season of fasting and prayer? My prayer is that each of us would apply these six priorities and make any adjustments necessary—that we would become "Jesus Today."

Be Ready to Respond

Mark 6:37: *"But Jesus said . . ."*

One can have every other attribute mentioned in so far in this book but lack in this one area, resulting in complete uselessness to God. He is not necessarily looking for our abilities, God is more interested in our availability. Throughout history, those who were used most mightily by God were those who were willing to respond at any time.

A great example of someone who made himself available is one that should challenge each us of to examine our own willingness to respond. In communist Romania, a story is told of a man who was imprisoned for preaching the Gospel. Once imprisoned, his preaching only accelerated to his now "captive" audience. Eventually, after much torture and little compliance, the prison guards made the gruesome choice to cut out his tongue. This major setback did not stop this man's availability to be used by God. Since he could no longer speak, he chose another line of ministry: to stand in daily for the beatings of other Christians who were too weak to survive the torture. This is true availability!

Be Ready to Give Your Time

Mark 6:37: *". . . you feed them."*

The disciples knew that they did not have the food or resources to meet this need. All they had to offer Jesus was their time. It is interesting that Jesus focused His attention first on the laborers, and not on the multitudes. He could have handled the crisis on His own by calling manna down from the sky! But He chose to use His disciples as instruments of distribution.

It might be interesting to document how you have spent the last 1,168 hours given to you by God this week. How much time was spent in prayer? How much time was spent in front of the television? How much time was spent reading the Bible? How much time was spent reading the newspaper and magazines? How much time was spent witnessing or ministering to those in need? How much time was spent in front of the mirror, pampering yourself each morning? Pretty convicting? Well, here is a breakdown of how others spend their time over the span of their life.

20 years sleeping	20 years working
6 years eating	7 years playing
5 years getting dressed	1 year talking on the telephone
5 years watching TV	5 months tying one's shoes
2$\frac{1}{2}$ years miscellaneous	3 years waiting for someone
1$\frac{1}{2}$ years in church [64]	

Time is one of the most precious commodities given to man by God. It cannot be purchased, stored, or put on pause. Once this day is gone, it will never return. We won't regret the time that we devoted to Him and His service. Let us not squander the precious gift of time on our own selfish interests.

Be Ready to Give Your Resources

Mark 6:38: *"How much food do you have?' he asked. 'Go and find out.'"*

Jesus always had a way of getting to the core of the issue. The disciples knew what was available, a few loaves and a few fish, but Jesus gave them the opportunity to respond properly. It seems that no matter how they had answered, they would have been put into a corner. After all, there were thousands who were hungry, and there was only enough food for a few. Jesus hoped that they would return and say, "This is all we have, my Lord, take it and use it however you wish," but their response was less desirable. Jesus wished that they would be ready to give, not only of their time, but also of their resources.

As we move together to meet the needs of the multitudes coming our way, we need great liberality and freedom to give our resources. Our willingness to give is a great litmus test to our spiritual state. It is a tragedy when God's people carelessly spend their God-given resources on worldly items and are then unwilling to give to those in need. It is sad that we can spend money we haven't earned to buy things we don't need to impress people we don't like. Today, let's decide to be ready to give of our resources for eternal purposes.

Be Ready to Do Whatever He Asks

Mark 6:39: *"Then Jesus told the crowd to sit down in groups on the green grass."*

The task at hand seemed immense. Arranging five thousand men, not including the women and children, was no small chore. There must have been some reluctance on the part of the disciples. I can even hear them walking through out the crowds, whispering to each other, "Pete, what is He up to? I wonder if He will spit in all their ears? This is going to be really interesting to see how He pulls this one off!" Regardless of what they felt or said, Jesus' hope was that they would be ready to do whatever He asked. We also need to be ready to do whatever He asks.

One day, while witnessing with a team at the waterfront in Portland, Oregon, a young man flew by on a bicycle. Immediately the Lord prompted me to yell at the young man to get him to stop. There was no time to waste, so I shouted, "Hey you, come here!" After yelling, I felt pretty ridiculous and wondered what the end result would be. The young man turned around and pedaled back to my location. He looked at me, wondering if he knew me, and said, "Yeah?" I began to share the Gospel with him, only to find out the he had been crying out to God for someone to show him the way to heaven. He would spend the next twelve days with me, helping for more than ten hours a day in our summer outreach, "Operation Portland."

Be Ready for a New Way of Doing Things

Mark 6:40: *"So they sat in groups of fifty or a hundred."*

There was never a dull moment with Jesus. Whether He was spitting in a deaf man's ear, putting mud in a blind man's eyes, or casting demons into a herd of pigs, the disciples were always in for a surprise. He was always doing a new thing! In this particular case, He chose an orderly manner in which to distribute the food. It was rare that Jesus used this method of dealing with the multitudes, and to His disciples, it was another new experience.

As God is doing a new thing, be assured that He very well may be asking you to do things in a new way also. Often changes that affect our way of "doing church" create tension and cause us to be uncomfortable. How do you feel when your pastor changes the style of music to better reach the younger generation? What type of feelings do you have when people show up in church wearing Levis or shorts? How do you handle the change when you are asked to leave your friends in your small group to start a new one with newer people? The list of changes that come with the influx of new converts into our churches can be endless, but the point is that we need to be flexible and willing to move in new ways to accommodate the harvest.

Be Ready for Supernatural Provision

Mark 6:41: *"Jesus took the five loaves and the two fish, looked up toward heaven, and asked God's blessing on the food. Breaking the loaves into pieces, he kept giving the bread and fish to the disciples to give to the people."*

This miracle was not carried out by His disciples, but by Christ with the cooperation of the Holy Spirit. The bread and fish supernaturally multiplied; for they all ate and were filled, though they were five thousand. This miracle was significant, and it shows that Christ came into the world to be the Great Feeder as well as the Great Healer. He came not only to restore but also to preserve and nourish spiritual life. He showed them that in Himself there was enough for all who come to Him, enough to fill the soul, to fill the treasures; none are sent away empty from Christ except those who come full of themselves.

Oh, that we would only learn this important principle! There is never a lack with God. His hand is never short, His pockets are never emptied, and He is waiting for us to give Him the opportunity to reveal His glory through supernatural acts. The only way that we will ever meet the needs of those who surround us is through His supernatural provision. Isn't it about time that we move aside and allow Him to take control?

The next time you are faced with another person's need, pause and pray before you say no. Don't use your traditional response, "The least I can do is pray for you." No, don't stop there! Pray that God would give you the miracle, that God would provide the finance, that God would provide the job, that God would provide the food and clothing! God can and will show Himself true in every situation. Be ready to receive supernatural provision!

THE REWARDS OF ADJUSTING OUR PRIORITIES

For those who are willing to adjust their priorities and position themselves as ready and willing vessels, eternal rewards are theirs for the taking. Scripture gives us the privilege of seeing the end result of Jesus' lesson on adjusting priorities. Each of these is available to you today!

The Reward of Fulfilling Your Destiny

Mark 6:42: *"They all ate as much as they wanted,"*

Every need was met and every person satisfied. What an awesome experience it must have been for all those present to see thousands of needy people become recipients of God's blessing. The disciples must have gone to sleep that night knowing that they had fulfilled their destiny for that day.

There is no greater joy than to see the wounds of a hurting person healed, the mouth of a hungry person filled, or the life of a lost person found. This is the reason we exist. Make it your aim to daily fulfill your destiny and reap the rewards.

The Reward of Supernatural Blessing

Mark 6:43: *" . . . and they picked up twelve baskets of left-over bread and fish. "*

They had more in the end than when they had begun. We must learn to trust in Him. If He has called us to the task of giving of our time, energy, and resources, then *". . .this same God who takes care of me will supply all your needs from his glorious riches, which have been given to us in Christ Jesus"* (Philippians 4:19). He will multiply what we have given and bless us in return.

The Reward of Receiving Your Inheritance

Mark 6:44: *"Five thousand men had eaten from those five loaves!"*

The Bible identifies our inheritance as the lost people we bring to Christ. Psalm 2:8 says, *"Only ask, and I will give you the nations as your inheritance."* The lives of people whom we have brought to Christ and those to whom we have ministered during our lifetime will be our reward. Be a part of receiving your inheritance! Move beyond the needs of your own life and jump into the joy of reaching the multitudes. Let each of us become "Jesus Today!"

MY JESUS TODAY PRAYER

Dear Jesus,
I thank You for the fresh stirring in my heart
And for the challenges You have laid before me.
Help me to recognize the multitudes all around me
And make me available like never before.
I ask forgiveness for the many missed opportunities
And for complaining during times of weariness.
I too have been guilty, both in thought and deed,
In saying, "Send them away."
But today I am ready to respond
And dedicate all that I have to You.
My time is Yours, my money is Yours,
And I desire to do whatever You ask of me.
Give me the flexibility to change
And to understand that You are doing something new.
Build in me faith to receive
Any supernatural provision needed to win the lost.
Lord, I look forward to daily laying my head on my pillow
Knowing that I have fulfilled my destiny for that day.
Continue to bless me supernaturally
As I receive the reward of my inheritance in becoming "Jesus Today."
Amen

CHAPTER ELEVEN

HIS FRUIT:

MAKING
DISCIPLES,
NOT
DECISIONS

MATTHEW 28:18-20

The Sunday evening meeting ended abruptly. The tone of the meeting definitely wasn't what Pastor Ed had expected. As people filed out through the doors of the church, only a few of them stopped for their usual handshake. Like most services, the last ones to leave the church were Dave, Phil, and Jim.

"Tough night, Pastor Ed." Dave patted him on the back.

"That's an understatement!"

Jim piped up, "Hey, let's go get us some coffee and a slice of pie."

"Great idea! I could use some real friends at this point."

Pastor Ed knew that the direction of the church needed to change. The church needed to be re-educated on why it even existed. Despite all of the great meetings and recent miracles, there was still a need to change some philosophies. It would take everyone working together to keep the harvest that was coming their way. Up until this point, many new people were coming forward to the altars weekly, but the church wasn't growing the way it should. Some of the new converts remained in the church, but many more of them left. There were many decisions, but few disciples. Something had to change.

"So, was that what you hoped would happen tonight?" Dave asked Pastor Ed regarding the special meeting he had called.

Pastor Ed leaned back, loosened his tie and said, "Not really. The whole reason I called the special meeting was to get everyone's feedback on how we could work together on discipling all these new converts."

"Don't they see the need?" Jim asked.

Phil, wanting to be a part of the conversation, answered, "I guess not."

Dave leaned over and shared his thoughts, "You know, guys, I kind of understand what they are feeling. I have been excited to see God moving in our church. I am excited to see the signs and wonders. I am excited to see all the new people, but until last weekend, I was wrestling with the same things."

That grabbed the attention of his dessert companions. "It wasn't until I had a fresh encounter with God that I was able to see how my priorities had been distorted. I realized I wanted the glory but wasn't willing to sacrifice."

Phil looked at Dave, feeling a little convicted, and asked, "What did you do?"

"Well, I came to the conclusion that I had to make some changes. I realized that God couldn't use me as much as He wanted to because there was still a lot of 'me' in the way. After three days of prayer and fasting, I sat down and rearranged all of my schedule and reprioritized my life."

The pieces of pie seemed to lose their appeal. All forks were now on the plates and all ears were tuned in to Dave.

"I don't know what's next for me. I don't even know how God is going to use me. But I better at least be ready and willing. God has brought us a great deal of new people. These people are our responsibility. Each of them matters to God!

Pastor Ed jumped in, "That's right. The way I see it, our people genuinely want to see God move in our church and in their lives. However, they are being confronted with the reality that revival costs something. It's easy to see someone pray a prayer, but it is another thing to devote your life to see that person become an active, reproducing member of our church."

He concluded, "Guys, I need you. I need you to pray. I need you to support me. I need you to get involved like never before."

Within a matter of moments, the three of them mutually agreed to sacrifice their personal lives in helping Pastor Ed. It would be an agreement that would bring great sacrifice but would also reap great rewards.

"So where are you going to go from here, Pastor Ed?"

Pastor Ed thought for a moment and grinned, "Forward! Straight forward!"

Over the next few weeks, these four spent a great deal of time in prayer together—praying for guidance, praying for direction, praying for Pastor Ed, and praying for the church. It was through these times of prayer that Pastor Ed felt led to spend the next few months preaching on "The Cost of Being a Disciple," followed by another series, "The Cost of Making Disciples."

Both series had a profound effect on the church. Pastor Ed had the ability to steer the most hardened of hearts in the right direction. His anointed preaching penetrated deep, right to the heart of the church.

Through the preaching God had broke through and brought the change He was looking for. In just a few months, the entire atmosphere of the church changed. Attitudes changed, lifestyles changed, marriages and families changed, involvement in ministry changed. The church was now in the place to begin to reap *and* keep the harvest.

Pastor Ed had chosen this particular Sunday to emphasize small groups. In recent months, the birth and explosion of small groups in the church had been their saving grace. As the multitudes came, they were dispersed into small groups all over town. The results were staggering.

Pastor Ed began, "Fred and Sharon Maple, why don't you come forward and share what is happening in your small group." As they rose and came forward, everyone clapped.

Fred took the microphone, "All I have to say is that God is doing something big. After Pastor Ed's sermons on discipleship, our group realized we were introverted and needed to change!"

Sharon, eager to get her two cents in, grabbed the microphone, "It has been exciting to see that as we have given our lives to disciple others, the Lord has blessed our lives like never before."

Fred pulled the cord to get control again, "Honey, let's get to the point, tell them about the Rendall family."

"Alright, already! The miracles God has been doing with the Rendalls is amazing, to say the least. In fact, why don't you guys come forward and tell the church yourselves." She pointed to the Rendalls, who reluctantly came forward.

Art Rendall slowly walked up to the microphone and began his story, "It wasn't but four months ago when I got out of prison. My life was in shambles. During the three years while I was in the can, my wife and four children were on welfare, barely making it. Child Protective Services had taken our little ones at least twice on the account that my wife wanted to commit suicide. Getting out of jail only complicated matters." All eyes were riveted on the Rendalls.

Art proceeded, "We finally came to the end of our rope, and then we ran into this fine couple at the post office. The Maples invited us over for dinner and led us to Christ that very night." The congregation began to cheer.

"Through them, we've seen God's provision ever since. They helped me get a job. They allowed us to stay in the guesthouse on their property. They filled our fridge with food when we didn't have none. Every day Fred would pray with me. Every week he would meet with me and teach me about the Bible. We could have never made it without them." The church stood and clapped with fervor at the grace of God upon the Rendalls.

Pastor Ed then asked for Mr. and Mrs. Dawson to come forward. Bill took the microphone to share his story.

"In the past few months, the Lord has really been doing a number on me. Through a lot of prayer and some good preaching from our pastor, I came to the conclusion that I wasn't the Christian that God intended me to be."

With his dry sense of humor, which only came from being a funeral director, he quipped, "My small group was dead for a long time." Everyone laughed.

"But we too made the decision to make disciples and not just decisions. Over the past few months, each person in our small group has been working with at least one new convert, ten in all. And since it would take the rest of the service to share what the Lord is doing in each of these lives, let me tell you about just one—Rob."

Everyone knew about Rob. He was the town bum. He was always in trouble, always drunk, and always bumming for money and food.

"I made the decision that I was going to pray for Rob and lead him to Christ. That is exactly what happened. I asked him if I could get him something to eat one morning, to which he agreed. I put him into my truck and drove him three hours to San Pedro for lunch." Everyone laughed at the familiar story.

"He was seat-belted next to me for three hours! I told him I would be more than willing to give him a ride home if he would go to church with me the next Sunday, which he did, and he got saved." Everyone applauded.

Mr. Dawson continued, "And as Pastor Ed said, 'Praying a prayer isn't enough. They need to be discipled.' So that is just what I did. It has been hard, but it has been worth every minute of it. Look at him. He's got a job and a godly girlfriend. He worships and prays like nobody's business. To top it off, he is even wearing a suit!" Rob was the first of many to burst out in laughter.

The remainder of the service was filled with many testimonies of how

God had changed the lives of people in the church. One after one they rose and testified of the goodness of God. It was so evident, yet ever so subtle, that the church members had been transformed into discipling experts.

Dave sat back in the pew, and smiled from ear to ear. He had many testimonies to share, but he enjoyed listening more than trumpeting his own horn. He too had been transformed into a discipling expert. After making the decision to draw closer to the Lord and reprioritize his life, the Lord had blessed him with a part of his inheritance. His life was filled with many new converts.

Memories of the times of discipleship and early morning meetings with his discipler, Pastor Sean, were fresh in his mind. He realized he had become just like Sean. His new converts were becoming just like him—active, reproducing disciples!

MATTHEW 28:18-20

Jesus came and told his disciples, "I have been given complete authority in heaven and on earth. Therefore, go and make disciples of all the nations, baptizing them in the name of the Father and the Son and the Holy Spirit. Teach these new disciples to obey all the commands I have given you. And be sure of this: I am with you always, even to the end of the age."

BUILDING DECISIONS OR DISCIPLES?

The fictional story of the church in Pineville is enough to make anyone excited about discipleship. To see lives changed from the "guttermost" to the "uttermost" is one of the most enjoyable experiences that should be part of every believer's life. However, few Christians have ever experienced the joy of discipling someone from sinner to saint. The end product in the lives of new converts is often far from the desired goal established by Christ. We have filled the pews across our nation with many decisions, but few real disciples.

A few months ago, I decided to build some cabinets in my garage to organize all of my tools (very few) and all of the junk (a great deal) that I have accumulated over the years. Being the great craftsman that I am, I decided to borrow some tools from my neighbor across the street, who owns nearly every tool ever created. His large assortment of tools and on-going projects has earned him the neighborhood nickname of "Tool-Time Jeff."

Once I had all of my tools together, I headed off to the local Home Depot to pick up the materials needed. Upon my arrival, I was surprised to find that I could buy cabinet kits that were relatively easy to install and also looked beautiful on display. Without hesitation, the blueprints went into the trashcan, the cabinet kits went into my shopping cart, and I was off to show my wife, my kids, and the neighborhood that Marc was capable of building his own set of garage cabinets.

Ten hours later, my cabinets were complete, and I couldn't wait to fill them up with all of my stuff. I returned the tools and asked Jeff to come look at my superb handy-work. My wife came downstairs for the grand tour. My kids were escorted in to see the product of my labor. These cabinets were beautiful.

Two days later, my little boy, Kyle, decided that he wanted to get the flashlight out to play. As he slammed the cabinet door, it fell off its hinges to the counter below. As I arrived home from work and pulled my car into the garage, I noticed the door lying on the counter. From my reaction, you would have thought that the house had burned down! How could this be possible? What horrid trick had someone played on me? My precious cabinets had been destroyed!

Once I had finally calmed down, I tried to assess the damage. To my amazement, I realized that the cabinets were made of particleboard and were covered with a plastic veneer. In laymen's terms, that means these cabinets were not built to withstand much abuse. The construction of the cabinets determined their strength and durability.

Unfortunately, many Christians have been built out of a similarly poor product. The means by which they have been discipled has produced a lack of strength in their Christian walk—they are shiny on the outside and cheap on the inside. The slightest bit of strain upon the fabric of their Christian foundations generates complications and setbacks. Without much direction on how to fix the problems, they never learn to live as true disciples.

Many years ago, William Booth, the founder of the Salvation Army, made an alarming prediction concerning the Church and its direction. As he looked toward the beginning of the twentieth century, he said, "Six things will dominate the lives of Christians at the end of this century. They will have religion without the Holy Spirit, forgiveness without repentance, conversion without new birth, politics without God, heaven without hell, and Christianity without Christ!" [65] He wasn't far off in his predictions.

We have become a by-product of our society. We all want a fit body, but we won't work out and eat right. We all want to have Bill Gates' money, but we spend every dime we get on worldly pleasures. We all desire to have successful careers, but we won't discipline our minds to study or show strong work ethics. This mindset has affected our view and perception of discipleship. We would love to see people saved, set free, and become great Christians, but we are unwilling to pay the price necessary to get the desired results. This attitude among the majority of Christians has produced churches filled with decisions and not disciples.

Bill Hull, in his book, *The Disciple Making Church*, says,

> The church has seriously responded to "blue water" mission, while neglecting "in Jerusalem" or "at home" disciple making. Both foreign missions and the American church have suffered for

this mistake, because "at home" disciple making is the key to world evangelism. Unhealthy churches at home lead to weak missions abroad, but when the church makes disciples at home two good things happen: Christians become healthy and reproduce, and as they multiply, the world becomes evangelized God's way. . . In truth, almost any church does some discipling. When a pastor uses the Bible in a sermon or a teacher opens it to a Sunday school class, the church provides the initial phases of discipling. *But disciple making must go far beyond that.*[66]

That is where you and I come into the picture!

DEFINING A "DISCIPLE"

In His final words to the disciples, Jesus shared what was most important to Him. He didn't say, "Go and make decisions," but commanded, *"Go and make disciples"* (Matthew 28:19). This mandate was not given to pastors and leaders only, but to every person who claimed to be a follower of Christ. He knew that the only way the world would be won, and the needs of the multitudes fulfilled, was for every Christian do his or her part in discipling the harvest.

Let's take a moment to define exactly what Jesus had in mind when He commanded us to make disciples. The word disciple in the New Testament is the rendering of the Greek word, *machetes*, which means "learner," and occurs frequently in the Bible. The meaning applies to one who professes to have learned certain principles from another and maintains them on that other's authority.[67] In all cases it implies that the person not only accepts the views of the teacher, but that he is also in practice an adherent. The word has several applications. In the widest sense, it refers to those who accept the teachings of anyone, *not only in belief, but in life*.[68] We must be a disciple of Christ before we can disciple others. As we grow in our knowledge of God and emulate Him, we become a candidate for building disciples out of the new converts around us.

HOW TO BUILD DISCIPLES

We must first ask ourselves these questions before we can ask them of anyone else: "Am I a disciple of Christ? Have I taken my beliefs and applied them to my lifestyle?" If you were tried in a court of law for being a

Christian, would there be enough evidence to convict you of your crime?

These questions are critical because, in discipling another, you will reproduce who you are. The age-old myth, "Do as I say and not as I do," has never worked in raising children, or raising disciples. Adjusting your priorities and being willing to get involved is just one part of the plan. You must also have a lifestyle that radiates the principles learned from our teacher, Jesus Christ.

Here are twelve foundational truths to use as a test for your own life as well as a blueprint for the lives of others you will be discipling. Take a moment and ask yourself the question, "Are these attributes currently operating in my life?" Secondly, ask yourself, "Are these attributes present in the lives of those that I have discipled?"

1. People who are disciples of Christ and are in submission to Jesus as Lord (see Luke 14:25-35; 9:23-25).
2. People who are filled with and living by the Holy Spirit (see Ephesians 5:17-18).
3. People who are functioning in their spiritual gift(s) (see Romans 12:1-6).
4. People who are committed to and supporting the local church (see Acts 2:37-47).
5. People who are fervent worshipers (see Colossians 3:16; Ephesians 5:17-18).
6. People who are faithful prayers (see Luke 16:1-10).
7. People who are bold sharers of their faith (see 1 Peter 3:15).
8. People who are generous givers (see 2 Corinthians 8-9).
9. People who are family builders (see Genesis 1-2; 2:18; 2:24; Matthew 19:4-6).
10. People who are servants to others (see Matthew 20:26; 23:11; 25:21).
11. People who are overcoming their self-life (see Matthew 10:39; 16:25; John 12:25).
12. People who have a world vision (see Matthew 28:20; Acts 1:8).[69]

Use these principles to establish a plan for building disciples. Once your plan is in place. Remember these four things as you start your discipleship program.

Count the Cost of Discipling the Harvest

Before we begin, we must take the counsel of our Master and count the cost (Luke 14:28-35). As discussed earlier, the cost is our time, resources and money. Equate what you think it will cost you to be a discipler and set aside what you will need to meet those needs. Counting the cost just means to prepare yourself for the task at hand.

Maintaining a High Level of Obedience

Over the past twenty years, I have applied these truths and made them a way of life as a Christian. I could share countless stories of how I have failed in being the mentor that I have should have been. I could share some sad stories about opening our home to pregnant teenagers and others, only to be taken advantage of. However, I can also tell you many stories of people whose lives have been transformed and who are now great leaders in the kingdom of God.

Through it all, I have learned a principle that has kept me going. I am not called to be successful, only obedient. My reward is a result of my obedience, not my fruit. I am rewarded the fruit, but by no means am I measured by it. This one truth will help you in days of testing and will lift you up in times of discouragement.

Discipleship Requires Relationship and Follow Through

Jesus modeled the importance of intimate, lasting relationships with His disciples. During the ministry, He spent more time with those twelve men than with the rest of humanity combined.

Somewhere along the way, the Church has disengaged discipleship from long-lasting relationship. The hardest part of the evangelism process, and the most neglected, is the time from conversion to the point of maturity. It's called discipleship. For some, this process may take months, and for others, it can take a lifetime. As I have watched the discipleship process in the lives of many others, I have found that the length of time needed for the new convert to come to maturity often can be attributed to the discipler and not just the disciple.

It is no wonder that Jesus spent a great deal of time with His disciples. Discipleship is much more than going through a booklet or a course. Jesus wasn't interested in just exchanging information so that His disciples were intellectually equipped. He was after complete transformation of body, soul and spirit.

In order to accomplish the goal of producing healthy, active, reproducing members of the church, we must be ready to build lasting relationships with our disciples. In my own life, many of my closest friends were birthed out of the discipleship process. For example, Alex Hernandez and I have been together for eighteen years. Our relationship started while he was in seventh grade. He is now part of our pastoral team at City Bible Church.

My relationship with Paul Friederici, one of my closest buddies, started while I was working for his father in the carpet business, and our friendship led to his salvation. Paul is now very active in working with youth and has become a mighty man of God.

Another of my good friends, Anthony Wilson, came to a youth group service, gave his life to Christ, and then ended up in trouble with the law. I never gave up on him, and in one instance I drove four hundred miles to see him at a youth facility. My follow through touched his heart, and today he is a youth pastor at a thriving church in Lake Tahoe.

Mike Owen came into my life as a young man. Over the period of a few years, it was evident that our relationship would last for a lifetime. Mike currently has a great ministry to children and in music.

As you can see, there are two common threads in each of these cases: relationship and follow through. Each young man wasn't just a project, but a person, special to God and special to me. Each one spent time with me, went on trips with me, even went on vacations with my family so that he could learn biblical truths—not only at a scheduled weekly appointment, but through a modeled daily life of a real Christian. Long-term relationships are required to produce long-term results.

You Are Called to Work Hard

Not only are we required to build lasting relationships and follow through, but our desire should be to do it with excellence and with fervency. I have always said that evangelism is spelled, "H-A-R-D-W-O-R-K!"

It is not always easy for me to get out of bed for the Saturday morning meetings I hold. I expect my new converts to be there and I expect them to be on time. For that meeting I must prepare for teaching, encouraging, counseling, correcting, and caring. It's work! But the results are always worth it.

DISCERNING THE HARVEST
FOR SUCCESSFUL DISCIPLING

Through the last eleven chapters, we have made many adjustments to our lives in becoming "Jesus Today." In this chapter alone, we have defined what a true disciple is to be; we have chosen to count the cost, to be obedient, to follow through, and to work hard in making disciples. The next step is to "Go!"

Going requires direction and discernment. We must know something about the person whom we are discipling, and we must have a divine strategy in working with him or her. Without these two elements in the discipleship process, we may grow frustrated with it.

When discipling someone, we must also ask ourselves, "What type of background does this person have?"

The fact is that we now live in a post-modern, non-Christian nation. Once most people accepted basic Christian concepts. Now only a minority do. This moral and religious shift is not the only change we face. "We are experiencing enormous structural change in our country and our world . . ." Christians dare not be blind to change of this magnitude.[70]

This sharp decline in Christian exposure has opened the door to hundreds of different religions and the escalation of pluralism, humanism, secularism, atheism, agnosticism, religious syncretism, monism, and pantheism, to name a few. These philosophies have greatly influenced many of the people coming into the Church today.

Here are some interesting statistics, gathered by George Barna and Barna Research Group in Oxnard, California, concerning what people believe:

– There is only one God.	66%
– Jesus is God's Son and lives today.	50%
– The Bible is the Word of God.	44%
– All religions pray to the same God.	33%
– The Devil is not living, but only a symbol.	33%
– All good people will go to heaven.	27%
– Christianity is the only answer to life.	23%
– The idea of sin is outdated.	9%
– God only loves those who have earned it.	7%[71]

THE TOOLS NEEDED FOR BUILDING DISCIPLES

You may currently be working with someone in a discipling relationship, or God may be about to bring someone your way. In either case, it is imperative to discover who this person is and what he or she has been through. By taking the time to do that, you will find what tools are necessary to build him or her into a great Christian.

There is no limit to the number of resources available for working with new disciples. Every bookstore and every church staff can offer some great materials to use in giving the new disciple a biblical foundation. The twelve foundational truths, mentioned earlier in this chapter, are a great place to start.

However, keep in mind that foundational materials are only one half of the tools needed. The other tools are comprised of what you possess and can impart or model as a mentor. One can have the greatest materials, but the poorest character, and end the discipleship process with disastrous results. As a discipler, here are eleven character tools[72] that will help you in winning the hearts of your disciples and shaping them into healthy Christians.

Integrity

Building a trust relationship with your new disciple is vital. You are asking this person to trust you to lay a spiritual foundation of truth in his or her life. Make sure to saturate your example with integrity. In every aspect of your life, be sure that you are as good as your word.

Humility

It is necessary, while building trust, to show humility. Humility allows others to receive what you say. Realize that without Jesus you could not have made it as far as you have.

Sensitivity

Maintain a high level of sensitivity. Most people come to Christ because of a significant need in their life. Discerning their needs and being sensitive to them will help you offer comfort and counsel in the appropriate areas.

Patience

Working with new converts requires great patience. They do things they shouldn't do, say things they shouldn't say, and think things that are

not Christ-like. Remember, they are newborn babes and require special attention. Be patient and loving at all times.

Persistence

It is difficult for most new believers to talk freely about God, to pray, or
to worship. Because of this, you must be persistent, but not obnoxious.
Allow the Holy Spirit to show you the proper level of persistence needed,
while being careful not to turn your new convert away from you, the Church,
or God.

Respect

One of the quickest ways to repel people is to be condescending. In
doing this, you create a teacher/student relationship. You should instead create a friend/friend relationship.

Listening

It has been said, "Gain permission to speak by first listening." Once
you begin a conversation with someone, ask him or her open-ended questions about job, family, or social life. Try to find common ground and allow
the person to speak.

Graciousness and Understanding

There will be times when people will reject what you say. Often
Christians react negatively in these situations. Getting upset can cause confusion and bitterness in a new convert and make it difficult to move forward in
the follow-up process. When someone is unwilling to listen to you, smile,
love them, leave them with a positive, caring perception, and wait for the
proper time to share your concerns.

Exhorting in Love

As your relationship deepens, you may feel led to confront an area in
this person's life. Be sure to combine your exhortation with love. People need
more strokes than pokes. Often, the person already knows that the area of
sin is wrong. Exhortation without love is hard-handed judgment.
Exhortation with love is compassion.

Enthusiasm

Enthusiasm is contagious! Successful companies have enthusiastic employees because enthusiasm attracts people. No one wants to listen to dull, uninteresting people. Effective disciplers have enthusiasm as well. Allow God's light to shine through you. Use expression when you speak about Jesus. Let the person see that Christianity is not just a religion, but a relationship.

Friendliness

Eighty percent of people who come to Christ are influenced through friends, neighbors, relatives, or co-workers. If a relationship does not already exist, your goal should be to build a relationship with your new convert as quickly as possible. Don't disciple out of obligation.

MAKING DISCIPLES AS JESUS TODAY

Matthew 28:19-20: *"Therefore, go and make disciples . . . Teach these new disciples to obey all the commands I have given you."*

When Jesus told the disciples to go and make disciples of all nations, they knew what He meant. He came to seek and save the lost, and He chose to use us to accomplish this task.

Your involvement in the process of discipleship will deliver people from the chains of hell, pull them from their bondage of sin, train them in the ways of the Lord, and deploy them to do the same. Your personal involvement in the process is the only way your loved ones will ever receive the proper care and instruction needed to also become "Jesus Today." Making disciples is the only way to develop healthy Christians who will reproduce themselves, eventually reaching the world.

Will you play a part in the greatest building project of all time? Will you ask the Lord to put someone in your path to disciple? Will you make the commitment to follow through and assist in building active, healthy, reproducing disciples in your church?

Together we can win the world, one person at a time. My prayer is that each of us will rise to the challenge and take personal responsibility for the call of discipleship. The world is waiting for "Jesus Today."

MY JESUS TODAY PRAYER

Dear Jesus,
Make me one of Your disciples,
Living my life according to Your Word.
I want the foundation of my Christian walk
To be strong enough to withstand the challenges of life.
Once You have worked these truths in me,
Let me be one who works them in the lives of others.
I want to be known as a Christian
Who produces disciples, not just decisions.
Today, I count the cost
And confess it is a price worth paying.
Help me to remain obedient,
Regardless of any disappointment or setback.
Change my mindset regarding the process of discipleship.
Help me to love those You bring my way.
Help me to see them as long-lasting friends
And to remain faithful until they become mature.
In the end, I want to hear You say,
"Well done, my good and faithful servant."
Let my reward be the inheritance of many
That I have helped to become "Jesus Today."
Amen

CHAPTER TWELVE

HIS
VISION:

ENLISTING

IN THE

GREAT

COMMISSION

MARK 16:15-20

P astor Ed, this is Dave." His voice began to break up.

"You sound nervous. What's up?" Pastor Ed's question was met with a moment of silence.

Dave cautiously responded, "Can we get together for lunch today? We need to talk."

"Sure, but can you tell me what it's about?" Pastor Ed waited for his response.

"You're not going to believe this, but I think God wants me to plant a church . . . back in my hometown of Newcastle." Dave exhaled in relief, having unloaded his burden in a rush.

"You think God wants you to do what?"

The sanctuary was filled to capacity. People lined the back walls and filled the doorway that led to the foyer. As Dave stood up in the pulpit and looked out on the sea of people, it reminded him of the time Pastor Ed had called the "church-wide town meeting" to discuss the "Finley miracles." Same room, many of the same people, but definitely a different atmosphere! The last time, everyone wanted to run them out of town for bringing such confusion and division. This time, they were sending them out for bringing such unity and truth.

Dave set his Bible down on the pulpit, and the entire crowd rose to its feet and began clapping and cheering.

"We believe in you, Dave! You're gonna do it!" the mayor shouted.

"We're proud of you. We'll miss you." Mrs. Maple said from the front row.

As people began to sit down, Dave took a deep breath before speaking. "When I came to this town, I knew that something big was going to happen. But I never dreamed it would turn out like this. He does more than we could ever think or ask."

Dave picked up his Bible, opened to Mark 16, and with fire in his eyes, changed the tone of the meeting. "This book is a book that changes lives. It has changed the worst of sinners, murderers, adulterers, liars, and robbers into the greatest of people. I know it has changed many of your lives, and it has definitely changed mine!"

He continued on, "With every letter comes a responsibility to obey and an opportunity to respond to the voice of the Almighty. This book contains the plan for mankind and the plan for my life."

Dave put his finger down on Mark 16:15-20, "This particular group of verses contains the final instructions from Jesus to His disciples. These last words have become known as the Great Commission. We all know this challenging statement wasn't just for a group of men two thousand years ago, but it applies to each of us today. We are *all* called to go into the entire world and preach the Gospel. This is the vision of Christ, the very plan of God for mankind because He doesn't want anyone to perish."

Dave looked down at Pastor Ed and paused. "My pastor and friend, thanks for believing in me when no one else did. Thanks for always being there for me, thanks for allowing me the opportunity to fulfill God's call on my life." Pastor Ed was sitting in the front pew and nodding his head with great approval.

"I would like to have all of those who will be a part of my new church team to come forward." Dave waited while everyone made their way to the platform.

It was obvious that Phil would be going since it all began with him being raised from the dead. Ever since that miraculous day, the two had become like Siamese twins, literally inseparable.

Jim set his Bible down and also walked forward. His years of Bible College would now pay off.

Herb stood up, sporting a nice looking three-piece suit. It was obvious that there was a God who healed as *both* hands swung at his side, while he made his way forward.

To everyone's surprise, Mr. and Mrs. Dawson arose and made their way forward. All of the years in the funeral business had been very good to them, and they too were ready for a new chapter in their lives.

As the group gathered on the platform, Dave looked over at his new church leadership team. "Before I have Pastor Ed come and pray over us, I want to charge you with the words of our Master.

"God has given us a vision to touch the uttermost parts of the earth.

The Gospel must be preached to the entire world. *We* must be the ones. I charge you, as my team, to commit yourselves this very day to this vision God has given us. We are to be a 'great commission' church. We are to be a 'great commission' people. We are to bring a 'great commission' message."

Dave turned his head from his team and focused on the crowd. "Jesus said, *'Go into all the world and preach the Good News to everyone, everywhere. Anyone who believes and is baptized will be saved. But anyone who refuses to believe will be condemned. These signs will accompany those who believe: They will cast out demons in my name, and they will speak new languages. They will be able to handle snakes with safety, and if they drink anything poisonous, it won't hurt them. They will be able to place their hands on the sick and heal them.'*

"We take this charge seriously, and it is our intention to follow the disciples' example by going out and preaching the Gospel everywhere. The Lord will be with us, He will use us, He will bless us, and He will continue to *'confirm what they said by many miraculous signs.'* "

Pastor Ed rose to his feet and motioned to the entire church family to come forward and gather around them for a prayer of dedication. One by one, they gathered around the group that had been involved in changing their lives and their town. Although the church could not accept them at first, they now wished Dave and Phil would never leave. But they all knew this was right. It was time for them to go, and God would use them in a greater way.

———————————————————

News of Dave's return to Newcastle spread like wildfire. For the first time in Dave's life, his dad was his chief supporter.

His mother was ecstatic and could hardly keep herself under control. Ever since Cindy and Michael had given their lives to Christ, they had prayed as a family that God would restore to them all of the years that were robbed by the Evil One. Their prayers, too, were about to be answered. They would be one family in one church, serving one God.

And then there was Amy Jefferson. The very thought of having the person who led her to the Lord become her pastor brought a new level of expectation for her future. Her pastor was excited to release her to be a part of this new church plant. After all, he thought it was about time that she got out from behind the computer and used her gifts to touch lives. He knew that she had much to offer.

Even Mr. Browski heard the news. After retiring from the law firm, he had settled down out in the country. However, he still had not realized that he was in desperate need of a Savior. He thought it worth his time to see what all the commotion was about.

———————————————————————————

Each folding chair was set up in the high school gym with great anticipation. Mr. and Mrs. Dawson spent a minute at each chair, praying that God would fill it with someone who needed Jesus.

Phil and Jim began to work on the sound system. Microphone cords were plugged in, speakers were set up, and the card table holding their new mixer board was set in place.

Amy Jefferson, with her experience at the front desk of law firms and churches, set up the hallway with brochures and church bulletins. Nametags and pens were set out on a converted lunchroom table, and silk flowers were stacked in front of the high school's trophy case. Every attempt was made to make the gym feel like a church. Michael, the main usher, took his place at the door to receive the people as they came in.

Dave's sister Cindy scanned down the song list one more time, while others tuned up their guitars. Their beautiful voices would be the beginning of a powerful worship team.

Herb and Norman, Dave's friend from his college days, put the big banner up behind the instruments to broadcast the name and mission of their new church. As the final corner was hung, Herb looked up and grinned at Norman as he read the banner, "The Master's House: Exalting the Lord, Equipping the Saints, Extending the Kingdom."

As for Dave's dad and mom, they really weren't any use at all. They were so excited about this day and proud of their son that they could hardly stand it. For the most part, they just got in everyone's way.

And then there was Dave. Pastor Dave, that is. With all the details that needed attention, and tasks that needed to be done, no one noticed him sitting far off in the corner with his head down praying. No one but Jesus.

The arrival of this day brought some anxiety and a sense of expectation. As he leaned forward and put his head in his hands, he began to pray, "Dear Jesus, I want to thank you for this day and for this opportunity. Lord, I look back at my life and can now see all the stepping stones you placed perfectly in my life."

The presence of the Lord fell on him as he slipped further into a time of reflection.

"I can remember so clearly how You directed me that night to the hill outside the Activity Center. Thanks for sending Sean to share Your plan for my life.

"Thanks for that night outside Charlie's Pizza where I learned to see like You do. It was a night I will never forget. As I watched Sean lead my fraternity buddies to Christ on the sidewalk, I realized I needed Your eyes.

"And, Lord, thanks for bringing Norman up here to start this great work with us. If it weren't for You teaching me to hear Your voice, I would never have had the opportunity to lead him to Christ in that grocery store.

"I thought I would never thank You for that fateful day in The City. Lord, I thought You had left me for dead. But through it all I learned what compassion was all about. Thanks for giving me Your heart."

Dave lifted his head and looked through the gym doors at the beautiful young lady in the hallway. He closed his eyes again, "Wow, Amy sure has become a wonderful woman of God. Lord, thanks for teaching me to love the unlovely and for showing me Your never-ending grace." The thought of Amy becoming his wife one day slipped through his mind.

He looked over at Phil. "Jesus, I don't even know how to thank You for giving me this opportunity to start a church with my brother. If it weren't for You, he wouldn't be here, and I wouldn't have learned to have faith for the impossible."

Herb was adjusting the banner, giving it some final touches. Dave smiled and continued to pray, "And Lord, thanks for Herb. Thanks for giving me Your gifts for greater fruit. He is a testimony of Your desire to give great gifts to men. He is a great gift to me."

As an overwhelming sense of responsibility for his new position of Senior Pastor flooded him, he prayed, "I ask you to help me to never forget the authority You have given me. I *can* do *all* things. Just as You are, so am I in the world.

"Thank You for always allowing me access to You. I love to pray. You have taught me that nothing happens but through prayer. Lord, I pray that You would give us this day the power necessary for breakthrough.

"And God, I am empty! I am dependent on You. I will never forget my time with You at Silver Lake. Thank You for emptying all of me and filling me with all of You."

He once again scanned the room filled with his disciples, "And, Lord, I thank You for teaching me that what matters most is making disciples, not just decisions. Without them, this would have been impossible."

It was now nine-thirty, new people were entering the room, and a sense of great anticipation filled his heart. He was about to begin his first service. He concluded, "And now, Lord, let this first service bring glory to You. You draw the people here. You build Your church. And let us take Your message into all the world, to tell everyone about Your goodness."

Dave stood up, straightened his tie, cleared his throat, and made his first of many journeys down the middle aisle of the High School gym. As he looked around, many familiar faces filled the room. Some high school buddies, family members, old friends from work, and even Pastor Ed were all there for the opening service. Their months of prayer, preparation, and promotion had paid off. The room was also filled with new people, including Mr. Browski.

Amy was sitting in the front row right next to Phil. As Dave passed by, she pointed to him, leaned over and whispered, "You know, he lives life just like Jesus would."

Pastor Dave walked up the stairs onto the stage, set his Bible on the acrylic podium, and said, "I want to welcome each of you here today to 'The Master's House.' We are so glad you came. I wanted to begin today by saying . . ."

HIS VISION

MARK 16:15-20

And then he told them, "Go into all the world and preach the Good News to everyone, everywhere. Anyone who believes and is baptized will be saved. But anyone who refuses to believe will be condemned. These signs will accompany those who believe: They will cast out demons in my name, and they will speak new languages. They will be able to handle snakes with safety, and if they drink anything poisonous, it won't hurt them. They will be able to place their hands on the sick and heal them."

When the Lord Jesus had finished talking with them, he was taken up into heaven and sat down in the place of honor at God's right hand. And the disciples went everywhere and preached, and the Lord worked with them, confirming what they said by many miraculous signs.

THE NEED FOR VISION

While re-reading Dave Finley's final victories before writing my closing thoughts, I was surprised, as the author, at just how touched I was by his story. I felt like I was in the High School gym with them, preparing for my first service too! What an incredible joy it would have been to experience that moment. To see all of the people who had been touched by Dave's life—together in one place, with one purpose—would have been something quite exhilarating. I was inspired and challenged by Dave's success, as I compared his life to my own. I found myself pausing to analyze my own life and the fruit of my labors and to ask myself some hard questions: "What fruit do I have after my twenty years of Christianity? If someone were to write a book about my life, would it produce the same inspiration in the hearts of its readers? If I were to die today, would I feel as though I had accomplished the purpose for which I was born?" Even as the author of this book and the creator of Dave Finley's character, I realized that there was room for some improvement.

Let me ask you a few similar questions. Be painfully honest with yourself while pondering your answers. If today was the last day of your life and you were to give an account for all you have accomplished up until this point, would you feel encouraged or condemned? What would people say about you, and what would be your greatest accomplishments? Would there be any fruit to show from your life as a Christian, and if so, how much?

Unless you are an incredibly rare individual, your conclusion is probably the same as mine. There is room for improvement.

To take it one step further, I wonder what the response would be if we polled all the Christians across the nation and asked them the same questions. Do you think we would find different results? Would the readers of this book be farther behind on the victory curve than the rest of our Christian brothers and sisters? I hardly think so. I am convinced that with each survey taken, there would be more evidence to conclude that the body of Christ is in desperate need of possessing a "Jesus Today" vision.

There is still time for each of us to make changes in order to see the harvest we desire to reap and thus fulfill the vision of God for our lives. However, this will only occur as we first see our own need for change, ask God for fresh vision regarding our call as "Jesus Today," and then accept the responsibility to bring the message of Christ to a world in desperate need of a Savior. Change in our cities begins with change in us! It is imperative that we accept this vision as the reason for our existence and use it as the guiding compass for our daily lives.

The Bible assists in validating this crucial point by showing us what occurs when God's people participate in His vision. Biblical vision is a key instrument for breakthrough. Every time God's people acquired His vision as a divine instrument of communication and guidance, there was an atmosphere of revival birthed (see Ezekiel 12:21-25; Joel 2:28; compare Acts 2:17). On the other hand, the absence of vision in God's people resulted in spiritual decline (see Isaiah 29:11-12; Lamentations 2:9; Ezekiel 7:26; Micah 3:6). It is time to embrace the vision of God for our lives, our churches, and our cities and become a part of the greatest awakening in the history of Christianity, as we become "Jesus Today."

RECEIVING A JESUS TODAY VISION

It has been said that the last words spoken by someone usually have the greatest impact on the minds of those left behind. In Mark 16:15-20, Jesus spent His final moments on earth with those who would carry on the vision to the world. Right before His final ascension, He chose to use those parting minutes as a vision-casting meeting. Jesus imparted to His followers a vision to spread the message of Christianity worldwide.

The disciples, in turn, took this message and began preaching everywhere, resulting in the birth of the first century church. The early church preached the Gospel in Jerusalem, Judea, Samaria, and to the ends of the earth (see Acts 1:8). The spread of Christianity throughout the ages ensued, even to the present day, when the Gospel message was brought to you and to me. We now hold the same responsibility the disciples held, when Jesus stated in Matthew 24:14, *"And the Good News about the Kingdom will be preached throughout the whole world, so that all nations will hear it; and then, finally, the end will come."*

In these final words of Jesus lie the keys that unlock our destiny in Christ. These truths will help us implement the vision to our lives. However, the means to fulfilling the vision is found in the application, not just in the revelation. It is one thing to understand the vision; it is an entirely different thing to then apply it to our lives.

Here are the seven keys to finding fulfillment with a "Jesus Today" vision.

Make Sure Your "Jesus Today" Vision is a Priority

Mark 16:15: *"And then he told them, 'Go . . .'"*

Jesus lived what He preached. For over three years He modeled the urgency of spreading the Gospel to his disciples. In these last words, He seals His life with the word, *"Go."* "Go," in the Greek, literally means "to depart on a journey, to go for a walk."

That is exactly what He commanded us to do! We must depart from the comforts and cares of this world that so easily ensnare us and join Jesus on a journey of reaching all those who need Christ. And we must do it today! It is time to get up out of the pews and go where lost people are. A "Jesus Today" vision will help to strip away all our excess baggage and inspire us to reach out to the ends of our streets, to the ends of our families, to the ends of our workplaces, and ultimately to the ends of the earth.

Each night when I lay my head on my pillow, I ask myself this question, "Did I accomplish things of eternal significance today?" Not yesterday, not last week, not one time last year, but *today*! Vision takes place *today*. Revival starts *today*! Change starts *today*! We can no longer live our lives on the basis of yesterday's memories or tomorrow's dreams, but we must have our vision in sight *today*. It is tragic that many have not made this vision a priority for their lives, but are blinded to it.

Helen Keller was once asked, "What would be worse than being born blind?" She smiled and responded, "To have sight without vision."

Before reading any further, stop and ask the Lord to make His vision your vision, that it might become a priority in your life. Don't let another day pass! From this day forward, ask yourself every night if you made His vision a priority for that day.

Make Sure Your "Jesus Today" Vision Is Big

Mark 16:15: "... *into all the world* ..."

Jesus made sure to communicate the importance of the size of His vision, not just the urgency of it. He said, "*All the world*," meaning every human being on the face of the planet!

Imagine the disciples as they heard these parting words. Imagine their emotions as they remembered following the traumatic events of recent weeks—the persecution, the trial, the imprisonment, the crucifixion—and now they were being asked to go back into the city and start all over again! How many would have signed up on that clipboard? As Ed Silvoso said, "The assignment to begin the great commission in Jerusalem, therefore, was as appealing and pathetic as being asked to go to Waco, Texas, to relaunch the Branch Davidian Church the week after David Koresh and his followers went up in flames." [73]

It would have been one thing for Jesus to say, "Hey guys, why don't you just head off to another country, take a vacation, and give it another go next year. Lead a few people to Christ behind the scenes. After all, there are only a few of you, and you are probably tired." But His vision was bigger. It was for all of humanity, including Jerusalem. He loved the whole world, not just a few (see John 3:16). He knew that the only way His disciples would ever become what they were to become was by making them do what they didn't want to do—and that meant having a big vision.

John Maxwell says, "You must daily ask yourself, 'Survival, success, or significance? Are you striving to simply survive, are you dreaming about success, or are you really out to make a truly significant difference?'" [74]

Great leaders are not built in a day, but they are built daily! What of significance are you going to do once you put this book down? Make a plan every day to dream big for that day.

But remember that our significance will never be found in who we are but in who He is in us. The Bible says, *"I can do everything with the help of Christ"* (Philippians 4:13). The word "all" literally means "all," but there is a condition: it must be through Him.

Moshie Roisen has developed a simple, but thought-provoking, test for challenging the size of your vision. Read the following statement and fill in the blanks:

> "If I had _____,
> then I would _____." 75

Whatever your answer was for the first blank, it was too small! Go back and make the vision larger. Read it again. Most likely, it is still too small. Change it again. Remember what we learned in chapter 6 about having faith for the impossible? God's vision for your life is much bigger than your own vision for your life. Begin to dream impossible dreams! Begin to believe for the unbelievable! Begin to think of the unthinkable!

George Barna, in his book, *The Power of Vision*, states,

> How suffocating it can be to live within the boundaries of human ability. When we confine our thinking to the limitations of what is known, what we have experienced or what we are able to imagine, the mental playing field is relatively small. When you have captured God's vision, . . . one of your first reactions will be, "But that is ridiculous; we could never do that." If you persist, though, and conclude that this is what He is calling you to do, often you will recognize that His dreams are bigger than yours and that they call for you to expand the size of your mental playing field to accommodate His vision. Great power can result from dreaming big. [76]

Make Sure Your "Jesus Today" Vision is Contagious

Mark 16:15: *" . . . and preach . . . "*

The word, "preach," is the Greek word *kerusso*, which is translated, "to herald (as a public crier), especially divine truth (the Gospel)." [77] Jesus didn't want the vision to remain internalized; He wanted it to be heralded with great passion and anointing. Jesus' desire was that His disciples would passionately herald the message and that all would hear and also believe! But if all were to believe, it would require many more laborers than the original twelve disciples. Their passionate vision would have to become contagious and spread throughout the hearts of humanity. His vision was a contagious vision!

What was it that attracted you to Christianity? Can you remember the person who was influential in bringing you to Christ? What contagious character qualities did he or she possess? Now, turn the focus toward yourself since you have become a Christian. Does your life attract people to, or repel people from, Christ? Are there many in church today imitating your contagious lifestyle? Which of your character qualities have become contagious in the lives of others?

Many years ago, I was involved in coaching my daughter's Bobby Sox softball team. Before and after each game we would have the girls kneel down in the middle of the field and read the Bobby Sox's prayer. I would give each one of them the opportunity to lead in prayer. We thought it would be a great way to get many of the little girls (who would normally never pray) to pray to God. One mother in particular paid close attention to our prayer time and the way we treated the girls with respect. She closely observed the way we spoke greatness into their lives and encouraged them every step of the way.

One day, a few hours after a Saturday game, she called me on the phone, screaming hysterically, "Coach Marc, my son, he's gone! He's gone! Please pray to your God and ask Him to find my son." Evidently, her three-year-old son had wandered from the school playground when she thought that her daughter had taken him with her. It wasn't until hours later, when her daughter came home alone, that she realized his disappearance. I told her we would pray that God would bring him back immediately, and then offered to assist in any way. We prayed, and God answered without delay! She called me back within three minutes. She was crying and laughing at the same time and thanked me, "You know, I knew that God would answer your prayers. I have seen you on the field with the girls and have watched the way you treat them. I really want what you have. . . ." This is a simple example of being contagious.

Enthusiasm is contagious, but vision is more contagious. Take the vision of God for the lives of everyone you know and begin spreading the Good News about their future. Tell them of the peace, the goodness, the love, the joy, the blessing, the protection—it is all there, just waiting for them today. Become a contagious Christian.

Make Sure Your "Jesus Today" Vision is from God

Mark 16:15: *". . . the Good News . . ."*

Jesus didn't want His disciples preaching just anything; He wanted them preaching eternal life. He knew what was most important for those He had created, and He gave specific instructions to His disciples to impart the vision of God to others.

As Christians, we must see our vision as a reflection of what God wants to accomplish through us, and not what we can accomplish through God. Our vision needs to be directly from Him. The future of the Church is too important for Him to allow any of us to lean on our own human dreams, trendy fads, or creative imaginations. I often tell my staff, "I don't want any good ideas, only God-ideas!"

A vision from God is worth pursuing for a lifetime. If what you are currently doing right now is not producing eternal fruit and is not worth reproducing, maybe it is time to ask yourself whether you should continue. The goal of every Christian's existence should be to reach lost people. It doesn't matter if you are a homemaker, a business executive, a hamburger flipper at McDonald's, or a full-time student. The goal is lost people. God's vision must become our vision.

We must turn our nurturing times into equipping opportunities for fulfilling the greater purpose. If you are a parent, your goal is not just to raise godly children. Your goal should be to raise godly children who will reach ungodly children with the Gospel, so that they, in turn, might also become godly. Although there are some aspects of our Christian walk that do not focus primarily on the harvest (i.e., worship, devotion, parenting, study, etc.), according to Jesus, a harvesting philosophy must be at the foundation of almost anything we do for Him.

Make Sure Your "Jesus Today" Vision is Clear

Mark 16:16-18: *"Anyone who believes and is baptized will be saved. But anyone who refuses to believe will be condemned.*

*These signs will accompany those who believe: They will cast
out demons in my name, and they will speak new languages.
They will be able to handle snakes with safety, and if they
drink anything poisonous, it won't hurt them. They will be
able to place their hands on the sick and heal them."*

Once Jesus had communicated this huge God-vision as a priority, He
then began to describe in exact detail what the disciples were supposed to
accomplish. For more than three years, much of His vision was modeled
through His own ministry. He gave them the blueprint to follow and left no
question as to the procedures for fulfilling the vision. The message was plain,
and the vision was clear.

"Vision" has been defined as "a *clear* mental image of a preferable
future imparted by God to His chosen servants and is based upon an accurate understanding of God, self and circumstances."[78] If your vision of
becoming "Jesus Today" is not crystal clear in your mind, it will be almost
impossible to fulfill. On the other hand, if you have a picture in mind of the
things that should be done in the days ahead, it will allow you to accomplish
just about anything!

For example, when Disney World had just opened in Orlando, Florida,
Mrs. Disney was asked to speak at the grand opening because Walt had
passed away. The man introducing her said, "Mrs. Disney, I just wish that
Walt could have seen this." She stood up and said, "He did!" and sat down.
He did see it . . . in his mind! The reason Disney World existed was because
the vision was clear, first in his mind, and only then was the vision birthed
into existence.

Do you have a concrete plan of how you are going to become "Jesus
Today" to your friends and neighbors? What decisions and changes have
you made in your life in response to the previous chapters? Have those
changes been implemented, and are they working? Furthermore, have you
taken the time to write down any goals for reaching lost people? What are
the names of those you are trying to reach? Will you invite them over for
dinner or out to lunch?

Let's make sure the vision to become "Jesus Today" is clear so that we
might be able to fulfill it.

Make Sure Your "Jesus Today" Vision is Fulfilled

Mark 16:19: *"When the Lord Jesus had finished talking with them, he was taken up into heaven and sat down in the place of honor at God's right hand."*

In the final encounter with His disciples, Jesus knew that He had completed all that He had come to accomplish. All that remained was to leave His disciples with parting instructions and then ascend to the right hand of the Father. As He did so, His vision was fulfilled.

What is your vision? Will it be fulfilled?

One day we will all stand humbly before the Lord Jesus with no ability to go back and change the way we lived. This revelation has always brought great soberness to my life. From my first days as a Christian, I can remember the words of my pastor, "What words do you want to hear? 'Well done, good and faithful servant,' or 'Depart from me'? The choice is yours!" I want my life to count. I want not only to run in the race, but finish the race. I might get knocked down, beaten up, and torn to pieces, but I continually ask the Lord to help me finish strong and finish right! It is the reason I exist today!

Walter Payton, one of the greatest football players of our time, set the record for most yards ever rushed. Two commentators were discussing his great accomplishment, and one said, "Do you know that if you were to total all of his rushing yards, he would have rushed for over nine miles?" The other one quickly responded, "Yeah, and he got knocked down every four yards of the way!" So it is with Christianity. It isn't how many times you have been knocked down, but how you finish the race. Fulfill your destiny and dreams!

Years ago, I came across a powerful pledge by Bob Moorehead called, "Fellowship of the Unashamed." Many times this pledge has caused me to pull myself out of my discouragement and defeat, from the weariness of my well doing, or from the dryness of a desert season. These words have allowed me to hold on to the vision of fulfilling my destiny as "Jesus Today," regardless of what comes my way. Put your name in the blank and read it slowly.

I, ———————————————————— , am part of the "fellowship of the unashamed." The die has been cast. The decision has been made.

I have stepped over the line. I won't look back, let up, slow down, back away or be still.

My past is redeemed, my present makes sense and my future is secure. I'm finished and done with low living, sight walking, small planning, smooth knees, colorless dreams, tamed visions, mundane talking, cheap giving and dwarfed goals.

I no longer need preeminence, prosperity, position, promotions, plaudits or popularity. I don't have to be right, first, tops, recognized, praised, regarded, or rewarded. I now live by faith, lean on His presence, love with patience, live by prayer and labor with power.

My face is set, my gate is fast, my goal is heaven, my road is narrow, my way is rough, my companions are few, my Guide is reliable, and my mission is clear. I cannot be bought, compromised, detoured, lured away, turned back, deluded, or delayed.

I will not flinch in the face of sacrifice, hesitate in the presence of adversity, negotiate at the table of the enemy, ponder at the pool of popularity, or meander in the maze of mediocrity.

I won't give up, shut up, let up, or slow up, until I have stayed up, stored up, prayed up, paid up and spoken up for the cause of Christ. I am a disciple of Jesus. I must go until He comes, give until I drop, preach until all know and work until He stops me.

And when Jesus comes for His own, He will have no problem recognizing me. My banner is clear: "I am a part of the fellowship of the unashamed!"

Make Sure Your "Jesus Today" Vision is Reproduced

Mark 16:20: *"And the disciples went everywhere and preached, and the Lord worked with them, confirming what they said by many miraculous signs."*

It is evident that after Jesus completed His earthly ministry and ascended into heaven, His disciples picked up right where He left off. He had successfully reproduced Himself into the lives of others who would, in turn, carry the vision into the entire world. The vision was never intended to stay with Jesus, or for that matter, with His disciples. The vision of each disciple, becoming Jesus to the world, was to be passed on throughout the generations and has now been given to you!

Robert Coleman wrote, "One must decide where he wants his ministry to count; in the momentary applause of popular recognition or in the reproduction of his life in a few chosen people who will carry on the work after they are gone. Really it is a question of which generation we are living for." [79] As we proceed in this critical hour, we too must decide if our lives are worth reproducing, and if we are willing to commit ourselves to that cause.

Many would remember the 1996 Summer Olympics when the United States men's 400 meter relay team was favored to win the gold medal. Much to their surprise and disappointment, poor baton passes involving the second runner resulted in the loss of the race. It was the only loss in Olympic-medal race history for the U.S. men's 400 meter relay team (the team was disqualified three previous Olympics and boycotted a fourth). What a tragedy it must have been to spend years preparing for their moment of glory, only to lose it because of baton-passing mistakes—instead of being slower runners.

The same would apply to us. We have been given the privilege to run in the most important race in the history of mankind. It is our glorious moment in the annals of Christian history. We have spent years preparing, and we too are favored to win the race. We are now on the track. The "cloud of witnesses" (see Hebrews 12:1) is cheering us on. Will we be successful in fulfilling our part of the race and handing off the baton to others without error? Only the future will tell.

WHERE DO WE GO FROM HERE?

Hopefully, this book has inspired you to consider making some changes in your life. The story of Dave Finley has been meant to encourage you that, despite setbacks, God can still use those who will learn from their mistakes and move forward in fulfilling their purpose in life.

Dave's story ends with a question mark. At this point, your life has a question mark attached. Your book is still being written. There are many more chapters to be penned, stories to be told, and victories to be won. You have the privilege of being the author of your own version of "Jesus Today." However, your book is for real!

It's not too late to determine your future! God believes in you. He is waiting right now. Take your life and put it into the hands of the Author of your life and begin writing the next chapter in the story of the greatest Christian who ever walked the planet. . . . That would be you—"Jesus Today!"

MY JESUS TODAY PRAYER

Dear Jesus,
Lord, let this final prayer
Become the beginning of my new life in You.
No more excuses, no more putting You off,
I accept, today, the vision of God for my life.
The parting words to Your disciples,
I must admit, are a challenge, but very clear to me.
Help me in accepting my place on Your team
And give me the strength to take Your vision to the ends of the earth.
I have aligned my life with a new mission
And can now see as You see.
I have learned how to respond to Your voice
And have a new compassion for the lost.
Your grace has helped me to love the unlovely
And Your faith is the only way I can believe in the impossible.
I trust You for a greater release of the gifts in my life
As I exercise my authority in a world filled with darkness.
Unleashing the power of prayer in my life has also helped me
To see the need to adjust my priorities for greater usefulness.
I am believing that it will result in greater fruit
As I partner with You in making disciples.
I am "Jesus Today," right here and right now,
And I will make an impact in the days ahead.
I commit to You to finish the closing chapters
Of my book with a glorious ending that will make You proud.
And on the day when I meet you face to face,
I pray that my life will have counted for something.
And finally, Lord, I long to hear You say to me,
"Well done, good and faithful servant. . . . You became Jesus Today."
Amen

NOTES

1   Gary Beasley and Francis Anfuso, *Complete Evangelism* (South Lake Tahoe, Calif.: Christian Equippers International, 1990), 443.

2   Taken from *Biblesoft's Jamieson, Fausset and Brown Commentary,* as found on PC Study Bible 3.0 (Biblesoft, 1997).

3   George Barna, *Evangelism that Works* (Ventura, Calif.: Regal Books, 1995), 22.

4   Ibid., 35-37.

5   Ibid., 77.

6   W.E. Vine, Merrill F. Unger and William White, *Vines Expository Complete Expository Dictionary of Old and New Testament Words* (Nashville, Tenn.: Thomas Nelson Publishers, 1985), 219.

7   Joseph H. Thayer, *Thayer's Greek-English Lexicon of the New Testament* (Peabody, Mass.: Hendrickson Publishers, 1996), 470.

8   Vine, *Expository Dictionary*, 60.

9   Taken from *Matthew Henry's Commentary on the Whole Bible: New Modern Edition*, as found on PC Study Bible 3.0 (Biblesoft, 1996).

10 Vine, *Expository Dictionary,* 189.

11 Taken from *International Standard Bible Encyclopedia*, as found on PC Study Bible 3.0 (Biblesoft, 1996).

12 Max Lucado, *Just Like Jesus* (Nashville, Tenn.: Word Publishing, 1998), 41-42.

13 As heard in sermon by Wendell Smith (Kirkland, Wash.: The City Church).

14 Bill Bright, *The Four Spiritual Laws* (Orlando, Flor.: New Live Publications, 1965).

15 Francis Anfuso, *Two Question Test* (South Lake Tahoe, Calif.: Christian Equippers International, 1981).

16 Marc Estes, *Eternity, The Ultimate Choice* (Portland, Oreg.: City Bible Publishing, 1997).

17 Vine, *Expository Dictionary*, 296.

18 Taken from *International Standard Bible Encyclopedia*, as found on PC Study Bible 3.0 (Biblesoft, 1996).

19 Diogenes Allen, *Christian Belief in a Postmodern World* (Philadelphia, Penn.: Westminster Press, 1989), 2.

20 Leith Anderson, *A Church for the 21st Century* (Minneapolis, Minn.: Bethany House, 1992), 17.

21 Gene Edward Veith Jr., *Post Modern Times: A Christian Guide to Contemporary Thought and Culture* (Wheaton, Ill.: Crossway Books, 1994), 19.

22 Ibid., 47.

23 Donald Posterski, *Reinventing Evangelism* (Downers Grove, Ill.: InterVarsity Press, 1989), 146.

24 Vine, *Expository Dictionary,* 116.

25 Jack Canfield, Mark Victor Hansen, Hanoch McCarty and Meladee McCarty, *Fourth Course of Chicken Soup for the Soul* (Deerfield Beach, Flor.: Health Communications, Inc. 1997), 60.

26 Posterski, *Reinventing Evangelism*, 158.

27 Jim Petersen, *Living Proof* (Colorado Springs, Col.: Navpress, 1989), 108.

28 Frank S. Mead, *12,000 Religious Quotations* (Grand Rapids, Mich.: Baker Book House, 1965), 201.

29 Petersen, *Living Proof*, 108.

30 Phillip Yancey, *The Jesus I Never Knew* (Grand Rapids, Mich.: Zondervan Publishing House, 1995), 156.

31 Frank Damazio, *Seasons of Revival* (Portland, Oreg.: City Bible Publishing, 1996), 251.

32 Yancey, *The Jesus I Never Knew,* 153.

33 Ibid., 155.

34 Taken from internet site www.positiveprofiles.com/stories/bald.

35 Donald L. Milam Jr., *The Lost Passions of Jesus* (Shippensburg, Penn.: Destiny Image Publishers, 1999), 62-63.

36 Smith Wigglesworth, *Smith Wigglesworth On Faith* (Altamonte, Flor.: Creation House, 1996), 47.

37 Frank S. Mead, *12,000 Religious Quotations* (Grand Rapids, Mich.: Baker, 1965), 135.

38 Ibid., 134.

39 Ibid., 130.

40 Ibid., 131.

41 Ibid., 135.

42 Milam, Jr., *The Lost Passions of Jesus*, 60.

43 Paul Lee Tan, *Encyclopedia 7,700 Illustrations* (Rockville, Mar.: Assurance Publishers, 1979), 403-404 .

44 Joy Dawson, *Intercession: Thrilling and Fulfilling* (Seattle Wash.: YWAM Publishing, 1997), 49-50.

45 Jack Deere, *Surprised by the Power of the Spirit* (Grand Rapids, Mich.: Zondervan, 1993), 225.

46 Ibid., 223.

47 Edward Gross, *Miracles, Demons and Spiritual Warfare* (Grand Rapids, Mich.: Baker, 1990), 69.

48 Dean Sherman, *Spiritual Warfare for Every Christian* (Seattle, Wash.: YWAM Publishing, 1990), 110.

49 Taken from *Nelson's Illustrated Bible Dictionary*, as found on PC Study Bible 3.0 (Biblesoft, 1996).

50 Merrill F. Unger, *The New Unger's Bible Dictionary* (Chicago, Ill.: Moody Press, 1988).

51 C. Peter Wagner, *Confronting the Powers* (Ventura, Calif.: Regal Books, 1996), 125.

52 Sherman, *Spiritual Warfare for Every Christian*, 119.

53 Neil Anderson, *Victory Over the Darkness* (Ventura, Calif.: Regal Books, 1990), 41-42.

54 C. Peter Wagner, *Churches that Pray* (Ventura, Calif.: Regal Books), 17-18.

55 Arthur Wallis, *In the Day of thy Power* (City Hill Publishing, 1956), 151.

56 As heard in sermon by Dr. Gary Kellner, at the "Institute of Leadership Development" (Portland, Oreg., City Bible Church, May 28, 1997), AM General Session.

57 Taken from *The New Strong's Exhaustive Concordance of the Bible* as found on PC Study Bible 3.0 (Biblesoft, 1996).

58   Frank Damazio, *Seasons of Intercession* (Portland, Oreg.: City Bible Publishing, 1998), 130.

59   Barna, *Evangelism that Works*, 149.

60   Taken from *Matthew Henry's Commentary on the Whole Bible: New Modern Edition*, as found on PC Study Bible 3.0 (Biblesoft, 1996), Vol. 5.

61   As heard in sermon by Pastor Ken Burkey, (Placerville, Calif.: Greenvalley Community Church, April 10, 1994), AM Sunday Service.

62   Tan, *Encyclopedia of 7,700 Illustrations*, 1040.

63   E. Stanley Jones, *The Unshakable Kingdom* (Nashville, Tenn.: Abingdon Publishing, 1972), 54.

64   Tan, *Encyclopedia of 7,700 Illustrations*, 1480.

65   As heard in sermon by Pastor Gary M. Beasley (South Lake Tahoe, Calif.: Glad Tidings, 1980's).

66   Bill Hull, *The Disciple Making Church* (Grand Rapids, Mich. : Fleming H. Revel/Baker Book House, 1990), 9.

67   Unger, *The New Unger's Bible Dictionary*.

68   Taken from *International Standard Bible Encyclopedia*, as found on PC Study Bible 3.0 (Biblesoft, 1996).

69   Frank Damazio, *Vision Management Manual*, unpublished.

70   Vieth Jr., *Post Modern Times*, 18.

71   George Barna, *The Invisible Generations* (Glendale, Calif.: Barna Research Group, 1992), 139.

72   Beasley, Anfuso, and Estes, *Complete Evangelism*, 26-27.

73   Ed Silvoso, *That None Should Perish* (Ventura, Calif.: Regal Books, 1994), 59.

74   John Maxwell, *Developing the Leader Within You* (Nashville, Tenn.: Thomas Nelson Publishers, 1993), 143-144.

75   Ibid., 481.

76   George Barna, *The Power of Vision* (Ventura, Calif.: Regal Books, 1992), 107.

77   Vine, *Expository Dictionary*.

78   Barna, *The Power of Vision*, 23.

79   Marc Estes, *Christians in Pursuit of Changing their World for Christ* (South Lake Tahoe, Calif.: Christian Equippers International, 1993), 21.